DEVELOPING EFFECTIVE PART-TIME TEACHERS IN HIGHER EDUCATION

D1569481

Part-time teachers have become an increasing part of the workforce in universities throughout the world. They work in a sector undergoing enormous change and debate about the purposes of the university for individuals, societies and economies. As part-time employees, however, they are not necessarily offered the same level of support or recognition as full-time lecturers. This book, drawing on the voices of part-time teachers and the expertise of those who support them, considers whole-institution strategies to promote individual and collective professional development.

Utilising real action research undertaken by expert practitioners from Australia, New Zealand and the UK, this book explains:

- what motivates part-time teachers;
- the development of effective policy and practice to support part-time teachers;
- what part-time teachers' voices tell us about the content and delivery of induction programmes and ongoing support;
- the implications of change and future directions of Higher Education and part-time educators;
- how to build sustainable frameworks for the professional development of part-time staff.

Developing Effective Part-time Teachers in Higher Education explores the extent to which part-time staff are utilised, the effectiveness of their teaching, their integration into the broader teaching environment, and their training and development. This international text will prove an invaluable source for anyone involved in academic and educational staff development in Higher or Further Education, and is essential reading for Human Resources directors and managers, senior academics and all part-time teachers.

Fran Beaton is a Senior Lecturer in Higher Education and Academic Practice at the University of Kent, UK.

Amanda Gilbert is a Lecturer in Academic Development at Victoria University of Wellington, New Zealand.

The Staff and Educational Development Series

Series Editor: James Wisdom

SEDA is the professional association for staff and educational developers in the UK, promoting innovation and good practice in higher education. SEDA offers services to its institutional and individual members through its Fellowship scheme, its Professional Development Framework and its conferences, events, publications and projects. SEDA is a member of the International Consortium for Educational Development.

SEDA
Woburn House
20–24 Tavistock Square
London
WC1H 9HF
Tel: 020 7380 6767
www.seda.ac.uk

DEVELOPING EFFECTIVE PART-TIME TEACHERS IN HIGHER EDUCATION

New approaches to professional development

**Edited by Fran Beaton
and Amanda Gilbert**

LONDON AND NEW YORK

First published 2013
by Routledge
2 Park Square, Milton Park, Abingdon, Oxon OX14 4RN

Simultaneously published in the USA and Canada
by Routledge
711 Third Avenue, New York, NY 10017

Routledge is an imprint of the Taylor & Francis Group, an informa business

British Library Cataloguing in Publication Data
A catalogue record for this book is available from the British Library

Library of Congress Cataloging-in-Publication Data
Developing effective part-time teachers in higher education : new approaches to professional development / Edited by Fran Beaton and Amanda Gilbert.
pages cm
Includes index.
1. College teachers, Part-time. I. Beaton, Fran, editor of compilation. II. Gilbert, Amanda, editor of compilation.
LB2331.7.D48 2013
378.1'2–dc23
2012015703

ISBN: 978–0–415–51708–9 (hbk)
ISBN: 978–0–415–51707–2 (pbk)
ISBN: 978–0–203–08495–3 (ebk)

Typeset in Garamond
by Keystroke, Station Road, Codsall, Wolverhampton

Printed and bound in Great Britain by
CPI Group (UK) Ltd, Croydon, CR0 4YY

Contents

Figures

Tables

Notes on contributors

Fran Beaton is a Senior Lecturer in Higher Education and Academic Practice at the University of Kent, which she joined in 2004. Prior to that she was Programme Co-ordinator for Modern Languages courses for part-time students at Goldsmiths, University of London, where her work included professional development for the part-time staff teaching these programmes. She has worked as a teacher educator since the early 1990s, initially in Modern Foreign Languages and ESOL and subsequently in the broader field of HE and FE teacher development. Her current research focuses on the impact of different kinds of interventions and experiences on early career academics' conception of their identity.

Bronwyn Bevan-Smith is a PhD student, and tutor in the School of Biomedical Sciences at the University of Queensland. She began tutoring in 2007, and quickly realised she had a strong interest in the effect that tutors have on student learning gains, and the professional development provided to casual academics. She has been investigating the professional development needs of casual academics throughout the University of Queensland, with a focus on the Faculty of Science. Currently, she is exploring the teaching approaches and practices used by tutors in undergraduate science classes, to educate students to develop critical thinking skills.

Bruce D'Arcy is a Senior Lecturer in Food Chemistry at the University of Queensland, holding a full-time academic appointment since 1991 and a Teaching Focussed position since 2007. While he has a strong commitment and passion for teaching, his research interests lie in food chemistry/nutrition related to *in vitro* digestion of food phytochemicals, and in teaching and learning related to the roles of tutors in first-year chemistry courses, particularly involving online learning. Dr D'Arcy's passion for teaching extends to postgraduate research supervision, having supervised 20 PhD, six Master's and 15 Honours (1st Class) students to completion (1996–2012).

Muyessur Durur was Executive Director People and Culture at La Trobe University, Melbourne from 2008 to 2011. She is the inaugural Campus Director of Charles Sturt University at Port Macquarie. She holds a PhD and a Master of Business Administration (HRM) from University of New England,

Australia. She is a Fellow of the Australian Human Resources Institute and of LH Martin Institute Centre for Higher Education Leadership and Management. She has a background of over 20 years in Human Resources and Change Management in Higher Education and Public Sector. Dr Durur's professional interests are strategy, organisational change and development of sustainable organisational capability.

Anne Gaskell is a Senior Project Manager in Teaching and Learner Support, The Open University, UK. She was Assistant Director, Associate Lecturer support and Professional Development from 2004 to 2010 after many years working in the OU's Cambridge Regional Centre. She was Editor of *Open Learning*, a leading international journal of distance education from 2004 to 2012, and Co-Director of the Cambridge International Conference on Open, Distance and e-Learning from 2003 to 2011. She is a Fellow of the European Distance and e-Learning network (EDEN). Her interests include the professional development and management of part-time tutors, institutional strategy and policy issues, models of learner support and developments in blended learning.

Amanda Gilbert is a Lecturer in Academic Development at Victoria University of Wellington, New Zealand. Her academic career began in Psychology in the UK where she taught in both full-time and part-time positions. She began teaching having been given no training but has since completed a PG Certificate in Tertiary Teaching. Since moving into higher education, she has worked in universities in both New Zealand and the UK. Her current research interests focus on active learning in science and the development and support of part-time teachers in higher education.

Jennifer Gilmore was the Director of Human Resources at the University of Technology, Sydney from 2003 to 2011. She has a BA Hons from the University of Sydney and a Master's of Commerce (Employment Relations) from the University of Western Sydney. She has a background of over 20 years working in human resources, spanning a range of roles in the telecommunications and higher education sectors in Australia and Europe. Her professional interests are workforce planning, organisational change and development, and the enhancement of organisational performance through people.

Meegan Hall is a Lecturer in Academic Development at the Centre for Academic Development, Victoria University of Wellington. For many years she developed and delivered the university-wide tutor training programme. She also teaches on the Postgraduate Certificate in Higher Education Learning and Teaching programme and on courses in the School of Māori Studies. Her current research focus is Māori academic development; however, she remains involved in tutor-related training and research, particularly in regard to culturally responsive teaching and learning practices for Māori students and tutors.

Patricia Kelly works as a consultant in academic development at a number of Australian universities. Her background includes secondary teaching, TESOL, media studies, transnational education and Futures Studies, which has informed her work since the 1990s. This includes research into transformative education with first-year engineering students, published as *Towards Globo Sapiens: Transforming Learners in Higher Education* (Rotterdam, Sense Publishers, 2008). At the University of Canberra, she led a two-year sessional staff development project which informs her contribution to this book. Her current work includes mentoring and capacity building through institutional and national teaching awards, a quality assurance curriculum project with RMIT University in Melbourne and embedding teamwork skills in engineering education at the University of South Australia. Dr Kelly is a Senior Fellow of the United Kingdom Staff and Educational Development Association.

Jayne Keogh is a Lecturer in the School of Education and Professional Studies at Griffith University, where she convenes a number of courses in the teacher education programmes. She worked for many years as a teacher in both British and Australian schools. She also has extensive experience working as a sessional tutor in a range of university faculties at three universities in Australia. During her time as a tutor she became interested in the role and position of casual academics in academia. She is a qualitative researcher with an interest in institutional arrangements, roles and relationships, and social justice issues.

Anne Lee works independently for universities across northern Europe. She has given workshops and led seminars at Oxford and Cambridge as well as many other universities in the UK, Eire, Scandinavia and Estonia. Her best-known work is *Successful Research Supervision* (Routledge, 2011) and it is this research that led her to uncover the holistic framework that she now uses to critique pedagogical developments. Formerly she was Senior Academic Development Advisor at the University of Surrey. Dr Lee's experiences working in the public and private sector outside education enable her to understand the different worlds that many part-time lecturers are coming from.

Coralie McCormack is Associate Professor in the Teaching and Learning Centre at the University of Canberra. She specialises in capacity building for leadership in learning and teaching through institutional and national teaching awards, programmes for early career academics and sessional staff, and teaching and learning communities of practice. She is a partner in the Australian

Learning and Teaching Council-funded project Benchmarking Leadership and Advancement of Standards in Sessional Teaching (BLASST) that is establishing national standards to support and enhance quality teaching by sessional staff in higher education. She convenes the Graduate Certificate in Tertiary Education, a shared vision of the three participating universities (University of New England, University of Central Queensland and University of Canberra) to provide a high-quality qualification in tertiary teaching and learning. Dr McCormack is a member of the Higher Education Research and Development Society of Australasia (HERDSA) Executive and an active member of the HERDSA Fellowships group and the New Scholars of Learning and Teaching group.

Pam Parker is the Associate Director of the Learning Development Centre and a Reader in Educational Development, City University London. She is the Programme Director for the MA Academic Practice programme and the MPhil/PhD in Professional Education. Her interests are in the practice and research around curriculum, reward and recognition of teaching excellence, disseminating good practice, educational development and staff development. Dr Parker is also an active member of the Staff and Educational Development Association (SEDA) as the current co-chair of the conference committee and a member of the SEDA executive.

Karen Starr, PhD, is the Foundation Chair, School Leadership and Development in the Faculty of Arts and Education at Deakin University, Australia. Prior to this Professor Starr was a school principal for 15 years, as well as being the Chief Writer of South Australia's Curriculum, Standards and Accountability Framework. In 2004 she won the Australian Telstra Business Women's Award for the not-for-profit sector. She is a Fellow of the Australian Institute of Company Directors, the Australian Council for Educational Leaders and the Australian College of Educators. Her research interests lie in educational leadership, change, professional learning, governance, educational policy, gender and equity.

Neal Sumner is a Senior Lecturer in Educational Development in the Learning Development Centre, City University London. He is the Module Leader for Technology Enabled Academic Practice, and Information and Communication Technologies in Higher Education on the MA in Academic Practice programme at City University London. He provides support for a range of staff in using technology to support and enhance learning and teaching. His areas of interest include blended learning, the digital researcher, impact of technology on academic roles and identities, e-portfolios, educational research, online communities.

Kathryn Sutherland is Associate Dean in the Faculty of Humanities and Social Sciences, Victoria University of Wellington. She is an award-winning teacher and researcher whose primary area of interest is the experiences of early career academics. She won the university's Sustained Excellence in Teaching Award in 2007, in part for her role in the development of the university's tutor-training programme. Dr Sutherland's research on tutors has won international awards and she serves on several international advisory groups for projects on the experiences of tutors, sessionals and part-time teaching staff.

Bland Tomkinson is Visiting Lecturer at the University of Manchester, having 'retired' as University Adviser for Pedagogic Development. He is a Visiting Fellow at the International Research Institute in Sustainability at the University of Gloucestershire. He has been engaged on studies looking at the embedding in the curriculum of education for sustainable development and also smaller studies on assessment and on the use of portfolios for academic and personnel decision-making. He currently teaches on a master's course in the management of projects, in particular a course unit on managing humanitarian aid projects, as well as supervising a number of dissertations.

Shân Wareing is Dean of Learning & Teaching Development at the University of the Arts London, where she has responsibility for the Centre for Learning and Teaching in Art and Design (CLTAD), which provides HEA-accredited courses and supports e-learning, and the Student Enterprise and Employability Service (SEE). Professor Wareing also leads institutional-change projects in assessment, student representation and digital literacies. Her academic background is in English Language and Literature, and Education. She has worked in pre-92 and post-92 universities in England and Wales and also worked as a Visiting Professor in Linguistics at Michigan State University, USA, and taught English for Academic Purposes in Kobe, Japan. She is the Fellowships Co-ordinator for the Staff and Educational Development Association and a National Teaching Fellow.

Louise Wilson leads, and teaches on, the Postgraduate Certificate in HE Professional Practice, Coventry University, and provides training to support academic development across the university. She became an educator in 2002 having gained teaching experience in further, higher and adult education. Prior to this, she acquired over 20 years of applied management practice within the private sector, leading departments and projects at different levels. In 2005, she joined Coventry University, teaching and leading dual-accredited management development programmes. By 2007, she had begun to establish herself as an educational developer within the Centre for the Study of Higher Education.

As an educational researcher, her interests focus on the early careers of new teachers, academics and academic leaders who join the community from different pathways. This work sees her investigating the transition process, identity and transformative learning for the academic workplace.

Foreword

THE LOST TRIBE

Tony Brand

I have frequently described part-time teachers in higher education as the lost (or invisible) tribe.

Lost in the sense of complex national and international terminology describing such posts and an associated complexity of status linked with employment contracts. This is evidenced in the US where they are described as 'adjunct faculty' or 'para-academics'; in Australasia, as 'sessional' or 'casual academic' staff; in the UK, as 'sessional' or 'visiting lecturers/tutors' or most frequently simply as 'part time'. In regard to employment status, tenure or permanence is generally not provided, though to add confusion and complexity some teachers in the UK who are on permanent fractional posts are grouped in with the designation of being part-time.

Invisible in the sense that they are not seen as being part of the core team which develops and delivers the course or programme of study. They are rarely included in structural changes or developments and frequently work in the shadows with minimal support or recognition. Yet in some disciplines delivery could not be achieved without input from the part-time or adjunct faculty. In the UK the Higher Education Statistics Agency (www.hesa.ac.uk), in providing data for academic staff in 2009/10, show that some 35 per cent were categorised as part-time. Indeed one institution in the UK – The Open University (OU) – would be unable to function if it were not for the bank of Associate Lecturers (ALs) who are responsible for delivery; all are employed on a semi-permanent, part-time basis. With a context such as this, provision for induction, developing and supporting ALs has to be made in the OU and these are explored later in this book. While this may be seen as an extreme situation, increasing numbers of courses require highly specialist input from experts whose main occupation is elsewhere in public or private practice. Sometimes their input is seemingly provided on a pro bono basis when comparing academic pay with professional fees.

Taken all together, such individuals are often employed without any systematic access to training or development and may be under-supported in their teaching role. This, then, is the territory which this book attempts to explore, drawing upon a range of international experiences and associated case studies.

Defining the intangible

It would seem that the spectrum of deployment of part-time staff can range from a single master class to an annual sessional contract and permanent fractional posts. Associated with this are professional and contractual issues sometimes constrained and informed by national policies and the status of the institution. The seamless web of education in the UK does not appear to extend across institutions of further education and the university sector. For those employed in UK universities there is a growing expectation that teaching staff are Associate Fellows or Fellows of the Higher Education Academy: 'Our recognition scheme contributes towards the professionalisation of teaching by conferring the status of Associate, Fellow or Senior Fellow of the Higher Education Academy. The scheme is closely referenced to the UK Professional Standards Framework' (www. heacademy.ac.uk). Those teaching higher education awards but employed by the Further Education College will be subject to a nationally imposed requirement to hold qualified teacher status for lifelong learning and comply with annual CPD requirements set by the Institute for Learning (IfL). The remit of the IfL includes:

- *registering teachers* and trainers in FE and skills;
- keeping an overview of teachers' *continuing professional development (CPD)*;
- conferring the professional status of Qualified Teacher Learning and Skills (QTLS) and Associate Teacher Learning and Skills (ATLS) through the *Professional Formation process* (www.ifl.ac.uk).

Dislocations such as these can be seen in the structure of higher-education provision around the world. Dare one even raise the issue of the internationalisation of higher education with many First World institutions validating or providing awards in places such as South East Asia? Might staff employed in these local colleges be seen in some way as part-time in relation to the validating institution? Issues such as these were explored in Brand (2007).

Around 2006/07 the Higher Education Academy provided some modest funds and support to establish a Part-Time Teachers' Support Network. Like earlier, similar initiatives this proved hard to sustain in a fast-moving sector which was increasingly constrained and directed by funding and other factors. Sadly, the outcomes of the Network have evanesced on the HEA website, which in the resource area has a limited and dated selection of papers – one indeed from 2001 presenting information about the training of part-time staff in the USA.

Signs of life

If the tone up to this point has established a bleak picture of support for part-time staff, there have also been many bright spots. With such a significant dependence upon part-time tutors, the OU, from inception, needed to have in place support structures. At first these may be considered modest as the initial cohorts of Associate Lecturers were predominantly drawn from teachers employed elsewhere in the sector. However, inevitably, as the years passed by the overall demographic changed. By 2003 the OU's Associate Lecturer Development and Accreditation Pathway (ALDAP) was established and recognised through the Staff and Educational Development Association's (SEDA) Professional Development Framework (PDF). The approach adopted within ALDAP included a range of Workshops and concluded with a 'professional conversation' – leading to the award of the SEDA PDF Certificate in Supporting Learning. During 2003, 243 OU Associate Lecturers had signed up for ALDAP workshops.

SEDA–PDF was established in 2002 and through a range of recognition awards provided opportunities for developing a wide range of staff, working in various capacities, who supported student learning to gain certification. While at the University of Hertfordshire (UH) I was able to use this Framework in a number of creative ways. First, and directly in relation to part-time hourly paid staff at the University, Faculty Deans enabled participation in a three-day introductory workshop which was recognised through SEDA's Supporting Learning PDF named award. It was enabled through the mechanism of providing the part-time staff members with a modest but meaningful payment for attendance. Over a number of years this continued to be the main mechanism for developing part-time staff and proved highly popular. The University of Hertfordshire, like many others, has validation links with overseas institutions. Since working on delivering the (UH) degree awards formed only a portion of staff time these lecturers too might be regarded as being categorised as part-time. The same three-day workshop with the associated SEDA recognition through PDF was provided to associate institutions in Malaysia and Greece. Through this route several hundred staff in overseas institutions gained development and recognition through the SEDA–PDF-recognised workshop.

Various national funding routes have also provided developmental work to support part-time staff. One in particular established through the Fund for the Development of Teaching and Learning (FDTL) enabled, in 2007, the release of Art and Design – Enabling Part Time Tutors (ADEPTT) (www.adeptt.ac.uk). The outcome was an impressive and comprehensive resource pack available as an open-source download. While seemingly aimed at those teaching in the areas of art and design, the materials are appropriate across the range of discipline areas found in modern universities. The ADEPTT project further highlighted the importance of what to others may appear to be insignificant aspects of employment. For those working part-time and not infrequently during twilight hours, access to photocopiers becomes an issue; who is responsible for dealing with monthly claims and much more? This highlighted the importance of the role of the person who may be called or described as the course or programme leader.

Quo vadis?

What follows here is an attempt to provide a more current picture of the support and development opportunities available to those who are increasingly becoming recognised as key members of the academic community. Rightly, the editors have selected a rich range of case studies drawn from a number of national and international perspectives.

Reference

Brand, Anthony (2007) 'The long and winding road: professional development in further and higher education', *Journal of Further and Higher Education*, 31(1): 7–16.

Acknowledgements

We are indebted to many colleagues without whose support this book would not have been possible. We thank first all our contributing authors who have been willing to share their expertise and experience and helped our work as editors immeasurably by responding constructively to comments and keeping to deadlines.

We would also like to thank James Wisdom at SEDA for his moral and practical support in framing the book proposal for Routledge, Philip Mudd at Routledge both for steering the proposal through and providing us with useful feedback on the final manuscript and Routledge's Vicky Parting for her patience and good humour in the final stages of the book's production. We are grateful for support given by Ako Aotearoa, New Zealand's National Centre for Tertiary Teaching Excellence (http://akoaotearoa.ac.nz/) for the literature review that informed the development of this book. Finally, thanks to our colleagues at the University of Kent and Victoria University of Wellington for their continuing encouragement throughout the writing of this book.

Fran Beaton and Amanda Gilbert

Series editor's preface

I hope this will become one of the most significant books published in the SEDA Series. Over the last twenty years SEDA's members – the professional educational developers of the UK – have been creating and improving the programmes through which their colleagues in their institutions can become as professional as educators as they are in their research and other roles. Part-time teaching has been one of the familiar routes of induction into the established academic community.

What a comfortably stable image that paragraph represents. It has not been like that at all. When the focus of the vision moves from the preparation and induction of the traditional teacher to the reality of how students are learning and experiencing their valuable years of study, it is hardly surprising that members of SEDA and of HERDSA in Australasia are amongst the first to report the inadequacy of existing models for recruiting and supporting all those who teach. Customary practice which evolved to suit one set of circumstances can quickly become inequitable when contexts change.

The authors whom Fran Beaton and Amanda Gilbert have brought together are reporting the modern realities of academic life in a rapidly changing world. They show us the rich variety of people who choose to teach in higher education, their different backgrounds, motives, hopes and needs. They also show us how some of the traditional assumptions about part-time teaching must quickly be replaced by better and more modern institutional policies and practice.

Teaching is one of the great human activities, a relationship which calls us all in different ways throughout our lives. The significance of this volume is that it is not just the students of higher education who are changing – it is their teachers as well. As our institutions negotiate their various futures, we must reconsider some of our practices and expectations. If we do this well, our students will reap the rewards and all our professional lives will be enriched.

James Wisdom
Visiting Professor in Educational Development, Middlesex University

1
INTRODUCTION
THE EXPANSION OF PART-TIME TEACHING IN HIGHER EDUCATION AND ITS CONSEQUENCES
Amanda Gilbert

Introduction

Across the world the employment patterns in higher education (HE) are changing. Retiring academics will be leaving a profession very different from the one they joined 40 years ago. One of the main differences is the increased proportion of academic and teaching staff working on non-standard contracts in universities. It is now estimated that more than 40 per cent of university teaching staff are not in permanent full-time positions (Percy *et al.*, 2008) and the percentage is increasing by the year.

The reasons for this change are many and varied as are its implications. One major implication, the challenge of preparing these teachers to assume the many and variously interpreted functions in changing academic communities, is the subject of this book. Each chapter will focus on a different aspect of this issue and provide insights and ideas to help ensure that students continue to receive the best quality learning experiences. To begin with we will discuss the teachers who are the subject of this book and try to answer the question . . .

How did we get here?

If you ask how universities have come to rely so greatly on teachers in non-standard contracts, the answer may well be different depending on whom you are asking. As we will consider later in this chapter and in this book, part of the answer lies in the changing curricula which universities have developed in response to changing employment expectations. One example of this is the development of nursing as a graduate profession, resulting in students being taught both by academics and experienced health-care practitioners. Broadly, however, the discussion is most likely to be a financial one. Part-time and temporary teachers are cheaper to employ than permanent or tenured staff. Although there has always been some truth in this statement, higher education in the twenty-first century has become more aware of it for a number of reasons.

More students, fewer teachers

Numbers of students worldwide have increased hugely in the past 40 years and are set to rise further as long as governments strive to send higher percentages of young people to university. Coates *et al.* (2009) report that between 1989 and 2007 there was a 107 per cent increase in student numbers in Australia. The same trend has also been observed in the UK. Between 1995 and 2011 UK higher education has seen a 60 per cent increase in student numbers (Higher Education Statistics Agency, www.hesa.ac.uk) though there is mounting evidence that increases in fees are beginning to halt this rise (Grove, 2012), even if this may not be uniformly even across subject areas. In New Zealand changes in legislation led in 2011 to the introduction of capped enrolments for universities (Tertiary Education Commission, 2010) which in turn has led to a levelling of numbers of students entering higher education. In the UK, too, the numbers of under-graduate UK students are controlled by broader policy and legislative frameworks and perceived imperatives.

The increase in student numbers has not, however, been matched by the number of full-time academics; Coates *et al.* found that during the same period (1989–2007) the increase in full-time equivalent staff was only 37 per cent as a whole. As a result, staff/student ratios in Australia which were around 1:14 in 1989 rose to 1:22 in 2007 and are still rising. The relative decrease in teaching staff in comparison with student numbers is not in itself a driver for casualisation of the academic workforce. The limited amount of resources allocated to teaching, however, does mean that part-time and temporary teaching staff may be perceived as a more cost-effective means of maintaining staffing ratios.

Flexibility

Institutions, particularly those which offer a more modularised programme of study, often need to vary their staffing depending on each intake of students. Although universities may provide, or be issued with, guidelines for the numbers of students they can accept on particular courses, in reality numbers can vary significantly. This is particularly the case in HE systems which feature large, first-year courses without prerequisites. Again, part-time and temporary teaching staff can facilitate the teaching of larger numbers – teaching more groups of students without increasing group sizes – with relatively little forward planning or long-term investment in staff.

Although flexibility of employment can be seen to be driven by the needs of the institution, there can also be advantages for the teaching staff. There are some who prefer a part-time working week because it allows them to focus on other aspects of life, for example childcare. It is for this reason that casualisation of university teaching has sometimes been discussed from the perspective of gender (Keogh and Garrick, 2005). We will return to this later in the chapter and Karen Starr provides more detailed insights in Chapter 10.

Changing needs, changing provision

With widening participation in university education comes changing educational needs. Students enter higher education today with vastly different experiences and levels of preparedness for tertiary study. It is unlikely that the different needs of students can all be met by the same individual. Over time, therefore, the teaching role has come to be the responsibility of more people than an individual lecturer on a particular course. So, as the teaching role changes, the breadth of skill required also changes and for many, teaching becomes a sub-section of a job rather than the defining characteristic. Students can increasingly expect to meet and be taught by librarians, IT specialists, subject tutors, study skills teachers and technicians in addition to the course lecturers. Each one of these can be said to be in a non-standard teaching role, often designated as a learning support role, whether they have dedicated teaching contracts or not.

As mentioned earlier in this chapter, many disciplines also benefit from teaching by individuals who are employed in other professions but who bring their professional expertise to the classroom or who supervise students in the workplace. Many lecturers in medicine, architecture, law and other professions take on teaching in a part-time capacity. This arguably provides students with a more current and professionally oriented learning experience as their lecturers provide examples of day-to-day practice and relevant cases which can illustrate theory and increase relevance. This freshness of approach for the student can be equally professionally satisfying for the practitioner provided that systematic and thoughtful support is provided at the right time. Louise Wilson (Chapter 8) considers the nature of the 'just-in-time' approach for such staff.

Choice

The question of whether or not working in non-standard academic contracts is a matter of choice or requirement becomes important as we begin to consider the needs of these teachers. As we will see in Chapter 2, different teachers have differing motivations as well as a variety of needs and the degree to which support or regulation can be administered may well be dependent on these. Some teachers on non-standard contracts see themselves as being exploited by the institutions for which they work and are resentful of any further expectations placed on them. Others may be keen for support and development but simply be unable to take advantage of it. Finally, the observation that some teachers work in more than one (and sometimes as many as five) part-time teaching positions does not support the idea of choice (Gottschalk and McEachern, 2010). By working on numerous different contracts, teachers are forced to abandon the notion of flexibility in order to earn sufficient money on which to live (Burgess *et al.*, 2008).

In a survey of academic staff in Australia, Junor (2004) asked whether staff were content with the contract under which they currently worked and what preferences they might have. Her findings indicated that it was not the part-time nature of work to which staff responded negatively, but the lack of security associated with it. Only 28 per cent of casual staff preferred this type of work while 56% would have opted for a continuing contract of some type. Other authors have commented on the degree to which academics on non-standard contracts aspire to traditional academic careers. The findings of Junor (2004) and Edwards *et al.* (2011) suggest that many would prefer this but others, such as Coates *et al.* (2009), comment that an academic career is becoming less attractive in comparison with more lucrative and stable options. It seems, then, that the desirability of an academic career is relative and may well depend on the type of non-standard contract as well as on motivation.

Is gender an issue?

When one of the editors discussed this book with some colleagues at a women's writing retreat, the first question that they asked was about the prevalence of women within the casual academic workforce. They felt that part-time work was necessarily gendered in western society and believed that women would out-number men in this context. A quick look at recent data does support this perception. HESA (2012) report that in the UK during 2010/11, 39 per cent of full-time academic staff were female compared with 55 per cent of part-time staff.

Some authors have argued that there is a trend away from the traditional gendered idea of part-time work where women with other responsibilities (e.g. family) undertake some work around these (e.g. Gottschalk and McEachern, 2010). Indeed, there are some areas in which women are not in the majority and the example of individuals taking between two and five part-time positions suggests that motivations for such work have moved away from working around other responsibilities towards financial necessity. Others feel that there are still gender issues to discuss. Donovan *et al.* (2005) reported that the Open University in the UK has been able to appoint a larger proportion of women to associate lecturer (AL – part-time distance teaching) posts because of the flexibility that these appointments offer. Women see the role as being a way to take a career break or as a means to re-enter conventional academic careers. However, many of the women interviewed in their study felt that they were over-qualified for the role of AL but were prohibited from working in full-time continuing posts because of their need for flexibility.

Given that women are generally in the majority (though this may vary for different types of part-time position), there is definitely a need to discuss the needs of women in non-standard academic posts. The under representation of women in senior academic positions (Armstrong, 2011) supports the contention that non-standard posts (particularly those that include large teaching loads) may be disadvantageous (Keogh and Garrick, 2005). Karen Starr (Chapter 10) provides rich insights in relation to women's experiences and needs.

Definitional difficulties

As this chapter continues, it is becoming increasingly obvious that there are many different types of people who might be classified as having a non-standard academic post. It has now become important to consider the ways in which we might identify this elusive group. Researching this chapter has revealed that, though the literature is broad and interesting, every study refers to a different group of people and every definition is different. This book will refer to a variety of people who occupy non-standard academic positions. Different authors have elected to use different terminology for the teachers they are writing about and their definitions will be made clear in each case. In general, however, the ideas and advice presented here will have applications for other groups and different types of part-time staff; readers should aim to utilise what they find most useful in their particular context and to adapt ideas to suit their specific needs.

What is standard?

The issues discussed in this book may have relevance to anyone who is engaged in teaching in higher education and who is not employed in a full-time (or mostly full-time) continuing academic position. In this case, 'continuing' refers to tenured, permanent or extended fixed-term positions. Rather than set out criteria for non-standard contracts, Box 1.1 below describes some of the people whose experiences might inform our writing and who might benefit from the ideas discussed in this book.

What's in a name?

The RED report (Percy *et al.*, 2008), produced by the Council of Australian Directors of Academic Development in 2008, discussed the (R)ecognition,

Box 1.1 Who are our part-time teachers?

The professional

Anne is a consultant in a large teaching hospital and part-time senior lecturer in Paediatrics. She is employed on a 0.4 contract to lecture to medical students and to supervise students on paediatric rotational placements. She has been employed by the university which oversees the medical school for the past six years but has very little involvement with the university and its 'administrivia' as she is based mostly in the hospital and uses her shared office only for meetings with students. She attends weekly staff meetings at the university but conducts her research on the wards.

The career part-timer

David is a part-time lecturer in Film Studies. He has been lecturing the same course for several years and has a contract for one day per week spread over the whole year although his workload varies in and out of term times. He is an aspiring script writer and prefers to write at home so he comes into work specifically for his lectures and office hours. He also works in his local bar three evenings a week.

The aspiring academic

Jeanette is a full-time sessional teacher in Psychology. She was appointed at the beginning of the academic year at quite short notice and relatively informally as she had completed her Master's degree in the same department some years previously. Part of her role is to oversee the large number of first-year students who have been accepted to study Psychology. She is responsible for lecturing on the first-year courses, co-ordinating postgraduate tutors and managing the weekly laboratory sessions as well as undertaking marking and providing feedback. At the end of the year she will mark exams and compile assessment data before attending the department's exam board meeting. Her contract will end with the end of the academic year. Jeanette is hoping to gain a permanent academic post within the department but does not currently have a research component within her contract.

The tutor

Nikolas is a postgraduate student in Linguistics. He intends to move into diplomatic work and has decided to take some work as a tutor in order to support himself during his study. He has never tutored before but now sees three groups of 20 students once a week for a semester. The course lecturer provides tutorial materials and he has attended a short introductory course on tutoring. He receives an hourly rate for tutoring based on the university's formula which includes extra hours for preparation and marking. Next week he will receive 60 x 1500 word essays which he will need to read, mark and provide feedback on in the following fortnight.

The online teacher

Deeta is an online tutor for a distance-based course in International Relations. She has been sent the course readings and has contact with her students through the university's learning management system. She enjoys the work as it is very flexible and gives her time to care for her young daughter but she misses working in a busy department and hopes that this experience will serve her well when she applies for a full-time position next year.

The retiree

Tony is an Emeritus Professor in the School of Biological Sciences. He has retired from his academic post but, as an expert in invertebrate physiology, he returns to teach part of the first-year introductory course and a final-year special topic. He enjoys the links he maintains with the students and the department but is grateful not to have to worry about committee work and university politics.

(E)nhancement and (D)evelopment of sessional staff at a sample of universities in Australia. This report has been very influential and will be discussed later in this chapter as well as informing many of the institutional examples Muyessur Durur and Jennifer Gilmore offer in Chapter 11. The work was based on the following group: 'sessional teachers including any higher education instructors not in tenured or permanent positions, and employed on an hourly or honorary basis' (Percy *et al.*, 2008: 4). Some, though not all of the part-time teachers we described in Box 1.1, were therefore included in this particular report. Other reports on part-time or casual staff tend to leave out other significant groups from the list as we shall see later. For example, the UK's statistics on part-time teachers in higher education explicitly exclude those who are employed in short-term, hourly positions from their main calculations (HESA, 2012).

In Chapter 2 we will consider the different types of part-timer in more depth. The following is a list of terms that are commonly used in the literature, although the terminology used in individual universities may not be used consistently in the same way:

Sessional: a term used in Australian universities to denote short-term, usually hourly paid contracts.

Casual: similar to sessional, but a term more common in the UK and New Zealand.

Part-time: usually used to describe those who work in longer-term positions but for a limited number of days/hours per week. This term is sometimes used interchangeably with sessional and casual but this can be misleading as 'part-time' generally implies a greater degree of permanence than these.

Graduate (teaching) assistant: a term used in the US university system and in some UK universities to describe postgraduate students who teach.

Tutor: can be understood in different ways. The role can be academic, pastoral or a combination of the two. In British universities tutors can be tenured academics who meet with small groups of students or (also in Australian and New Zealand universities) part-time teachers, often postgraduate students, who run sessions aimed at supporting students' learning. As student numbers have increased, the student–tutor ratio has also increased and, in some courses, tutors may have responsibility for 20–25 students at a time.

Measuring numbers

With so many different types of non-standard teaching positions, the numbers of teachers concerned are difficult to calculate and comparisons are virtually impossible. Bland Tomkinson explores this further in Chapter 2. There is no guarantee that estimations across different countries are based on similar data collection techniques or even on the same understandings of terms. A further problem, and one which we will explore later, is that the numbers of part-time and casual teaching staff may be relatively unknown even within their own institutions. Casual teaching staff have reported being classified differently in different institutions or being listed several times due to being on different contracts or having been recruited 'locally' (by individual departments to whom they are already known) rather than centrally as full-time academic staff would be.

Worldwide data

The OECD collects and reports on data from around the world in relation to all sorts of measures. Universities and other organisations can subscribe to their databases and use their data to compare different countries. Figure 1.1 shows a comparison of the percentages of part-time teachers working in higher education institutions in a number of countries, based on full-time equivalents. The OECD data are collected according to a set of clear guidelines which specify exactly how the numbers should be calculated. In relation to the collection of data on part-time and full-time lecturing staff the key statistical concept is described as follows:

> Full-time educational personnel refers to staff employed for at least 90% of the normal or statutory number of hours of work for a full-time employee over a complete [academic] year. Part-time educational personnel refers to staff employed for less than 90% of the normal or statutory number of hours of work for a full-time employee over a complete [academic] year. Full-time equivalent sum both full-time personnel and part-time personnel converted to full-time equivalent (for example, personnel employed for 50% of the normal number of hours of work is considered as 0.5 full-time equivalent).
>
> (OECD, 2012)

Figure 1.1 shows that percentages of part-time teachers have increased slowly but steadily (apart from in France) between 2004 and 2009, based on the measures used.

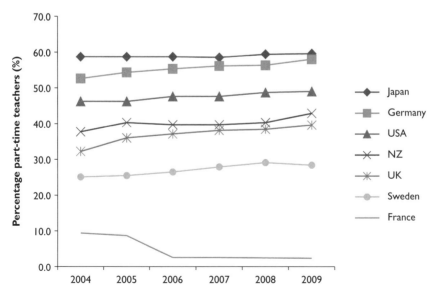

Figure 1.1 Percentages of part-time faculty in tertiary institutions in selected different countries between 2004 and 2009 (OECD 2012)

These data do provide some evidence of an increase in the number of part-time teachers but we need to be careful when we quote them. Coates *et al.* (2009) note that the use of full-time equivalent data disguises the real numbers of teachers with whom we are dealing; five teachers working on 0.2 contracts may consume more development resources than an individual full-time teacher. Many organisations have therefore decided to use headcount when reporting teacher numbers. Coates *et al.* (2009) use the full-time equivalent (FTE) measure when documenting changes in staff–student ratios because it controls for the differences between part-time teachers but report headcounts when comparing proportions of part time to full-time staff.

United Kingdom

The Higher Education Statistics Agency (HESA) in the UK provides yearly data on staff in UK higher education institutions, sliced in a variety of ways. For 2011 they reported that, of a total of 181,185 'academic professionals' in higher education in the UK, 35 per cent worked part time. This percentage is lower than might be expected based on the increasing trend shown in the OECD data (which would predict a figure closer to 41 per cent). However, the HESA data includes another category alongside 'part time' and 'full time': 'atypical'. The HESA website defines atypical staff as 'those members of staff whose contracts involve working arrangements that are not permanent, involve complex employment relationships and/or involve work away from the supervision of the normal work provider' (www.hesa.ac.uk). Authors in this book might well argue that, based on this definition, the part-time staff with whom they deal would not be counted within the 'part-time' category. Student tutors or demonstrators, professional visiting lecturers and some online tutors could easily be excluded from this count. If you were to include teachers on atypical contracts in the calculations then 54 per cent of academic-related contracts might be said to be *not* full-time, continuing posts. HESA's total headcount of 'academic professionals' also includes, of course, academics on research-only contracts but that is another story beyond the scope of this book.

Australia

Data relating to the teachers in Australian higher education are problematic in an entirely different way. The Department of Education, Employment and Workplace Relations (DEEWR, www.deewr.gov.au) report statistics about staff employed in all HE institutions across Australia in a variety of combinations. It is possible to compare the numbers of staff in different institutions by gender, type of contract and function[1] but not together. In 2011 DEEWR reported that of the 109,524 staff (both academic and non-academic) working in Australian HE institutions, 24 per cent were part time and 32 per cent were on either teaching or teaching and research contracts. It is not clear, however, what percentage of teachers within these contract groups were also part time.

This discussion has demonstrated the real challenges associated with reaching teachers on non-standard contracts. Not only is it difficult to be sure that the names given to those contracts mean the same thing, but also there are real difficulties in describing prevalence accurately and, therefore, comparing the experiences of the people they represent. These are not the only challenges that HE has to face. In the following section we will consider how changing demographics amongst teaching staff in the tertiary sector have affected those who have roles to play within it.

Challenges

Increases in part-time and casual teaching staff across the tertiary sector have given rise to a variety of challenges for all who exist within it. In the following sections we discuss how different stakeholders may be affected.

Challenges for part-time teachers

Working part time in a large organisation such as a university can be a very isolating experience. Part-time teachers may often feel excluded from the community of colleagues; they may not be invited to staff meetings, research seminars or social functions or are expected to attend these outside the bounds of their contracts. Resources for teaching, such as stationery and photocopying or office space for meeting with students, may not be easily obtainable. Tutors may also be working in a context which requires the development or maintenance of particular skills sets for their current role (Pam Parker and Neal Sumner consider this in Chapter 9) or encouragement to consider how their approach to that role may help them develop their future careers. Meegan Hall and Kathryn Sutherland examine this question in Chapter 6.

The contracts themselves may serve to isolate staff further. Part timers can be seen as an administrative hassle rather than as a valued member of staff. An individual may find themselves employed on different contracts and records may not identify the same person from one year to another. One teacher reported that, although she had worked as a part-time member of staff in the same department for the past nine years, the institution's payroll records department could find no trace of her ever having worked there (personal communication). In the course of one of the editor's temporary and part-time teaching career, the speed with which an institution removes access to computer systems and inclusion in payment schedules has been bewildering, particularly when a new contract begins the following day. This enthusiasm to close contracts is rarely matched when it comes to opening them: it may take days or even weeks to restore the staff member to full access to institutional systems. In another case, when one of the editors left a university where she had worked continuously for 19 years (11 as a part-time teacher) a farewell letter from human resources (HR) thanked her for the 'eight and a half years of service' which the full-time post had covered.

Aside from the administrative difficulties surrounding part-time teachers, job insecurity may make the life of a part-time or casual teacher very stressful. Teachers may be reliant on student numbers for employment and they may not know whether they will be working on a particular course until a few days before its beginning. In addition, if the teaching they offer occupies only a small percentage of the course time, they may find that it is cancelled with little notice if the main part of the course overruns or if another activity is suddenly included.

Challenges for their full-time colleagues

The RED report (Percy *et al.*, 2008) noted in its main findings that though a large percentage of HE teaching was being delivered by part-time teachers, this disguised a large supervisory load on permanent staff. Permanent staff generally take responsibility for convening and administering courses as well as, in some cases, managing part-time teachers. Coates *et al.* (2009) have explored the way in which this has affected permanent academics' views of the academic profession. They report that Australian academics are becoming increasingly dissatisfied with academia as a career (with the exception of the UK, they were the least job-satisfied). Coates *et al.* suggest that this view also arises from the perception that part-time teaching is now less likely to lead to a 'real' career (Coates *et al.*, 2009: 53). They argue that this view, coupled with the fact that 50 per cent of senior academics will be retiring in the next ten years, presents a real danger for the academic profession as a whole. One effect of the changing policy discourse in the UK may be that younger staff involved in teaching or supporting learning feel simultaneously a responsibility to engage and enthuse students (who themselves have higher expectations) while questioning whether university teaching remains an attractive career option.

Challenges for academic developers

The main challenge faced by academic developers is one of knowing who to develop. The part-time teachers who teach at their institution are sometimes invisible even in their own school or Faculty, let alone to the rest of the institution. Academic development units must, therefore, develop a system for finding out to whom to offer opportunities for development. These teachers, having been identified, may not actually wish to engage in professional development. There could be a number of reasons for this: the time it takes and who pays for that time; the fact that it might overlap with some other activity (paid or otherwise); or the perceived lack of need for professional development that is occasionally found amongst academics.

There are also challenges associated with determining the needs of this very disparate group. Their needs will vary with experience and also with intention. Aspiring academics may have quite clear goals in relation to developing their teaching and research skills. Others will be undertaking part-time teaching as a means to a different end and their needs will often be more oriented towards pragmatic outcomes. These teachers may be less inclined to embark on long-term training and development. They may wish to address quite definite or institution-specific needs and may be unwilling or unavailable to undertake training without remuneration. Several chapters, such as Bron Bevan-Smith, Jayne Keogh and Bruce D'Arcy's Chapter 3 and Anne Lee's Chapter 5, address these questions in more detail.

Academic development is a scarce resource in most universities and decisions about the amount of investment that should be made in developing part-time staff in comparison with meeting the university's other academic needs must also be considered. This is a question which will be discussed in more depth later in the book in particular by Anne Gaskell (Chapter 4) and Shân Wareing (Chapter 12), in which the institutional and individual benefits are considered in relation to the longer-term demands placed on those responsible for development. Coralie McCormack and Patricia Kelly (Chapter 7) pose the simple but essential question for all involved in the development of staff: 'How do we know it works?'

A question of quality

Increases in numbers of part-time teachers have led to concerns about the quality of teaching. In the US, Umbach (2008: 2) found that compared with their full-time peers, part-time teachers interacted less frequently with students, spent less time on preparation and had lower expectations of their students . In their study of marking in two Australian universities, Smith and Coombe (2006) identified a number of quality issues relating to the recruitment and development of this group. Overall, they identified a need to address quality issues for part-time staff noting that, 'although, there was no firm evidence that the sessional staff in the study were deficient as markers, there was every indication that if they were deficient, it would be hard for the universities to find out' (Smith and Coombe 2006: 65).

The RED report sets out its recommendations for the tertiary sector and institutions within it according to its key findings: Recognition, Enhancement and Development (Percy *et al.*, 2008: 6).

Recognition

Possible actions to improve the identification and recognition of sessional teachers include:

- the development of data-collection and reporting systems that accurately represent the changed employment structure;
- the development of policy and risk-management practices that recognise that structure;
- improved means of accounting for and comparing the contribution of sessional teachers;
- the articulation of clear lines of management and responsibilities for supervisors of sessional teachers;
- provision of professional development and support networks for the supervisors of sessional teachers;
- attendance to the professional needs of sessional teachers within quality enhancement frameworks;
- the development of quality-enhancement processes at local levels that recognise the diversity of roles, qualifications and experience and the complex challenge this poses for induction, management and professional development.

(p. 10)

Enhancement

The RED report (Percy *et al.*, 2008) found that, in general, management and support of sessional teachers was not adequately supported by policy at the institutional level. In addition, policies for recruitment and remuneration were rarely formalised or transparent. Induction practices were found to be variable and sometimes problematic given the complexity of the population. The report also noted the importance of appointing a sessional staff supervisor or tutor coordinator to support quality processes within universities. Finally, the importance of ongoing (preferably paid) professional development and recognition for sessional teachers was emphasised. The authors noted that the integration of sessional staff into the academic community, through curriculum and subject design, was often valued as much as or more than awards for teaching. This is a theme which Shân Wareing amplifies in Chapter 12.

Development

Answering the question 'How can sector-wide improvements be made?', the RED report identified a number of important areas for change:

- systemic and sustainable policy and practice:
  - taking a 'whole of university' approach;
  - improving communication to better address needs;
  - developing resources to address specific needs;
  - creating systemic and sustainable policy;
  - attending to the needs of sessional teachers within all quality enhancement initiatives.
- employment and administrative support:
  - reviewing recruitment and employment policies;
  - developing faculty or school procedures for employment;
  - communicating the availability of administrative support;
  - providing mechanisms for negotiation of pay and terms.
- induction and academic management:
  - improving relevance and accessibility of induction;
  - including relevant teaching and learning components in induction processes;
  - articulating responsibilities for supervisors of sessional teachers;
  - providing professional development for supervisors of sessional teachers;
  - providing better communication channels between sessional teachers, their teaching team and the school/faculty/university.
- professional and career development:
  - developing contextualised, accessible, mandatory and paid approaches to professional development;
  - including professional development in overall performance management.
- reward and recognition
  - developing improved means of rewarding and recognising sessional teachers' contributions;

– developing mechanisms for sessional teachers to provide feedback on their engagement at the faculty and university level.

(Percy *et al.*, 2008: 15–16)

The RED Resource contains more information about these different areas and includes some examples of good practice. The project website address is: www.cadad.edu.au/sessional/RED.

Consideration of these recommendations and examples of how they have been put into practice are at the heart of Muyessur Durur and Jennifer Gilmore's contribution (Chapter 11), in particular how these can be sustained longer term.

Conclusions

This chapter has helped us to identify some of the issues faced by university teachers who work in non-standard contracts and by the institutions that employ them. Casualisation of the academic workplace, estimated at around 40 per cent, is higher than in many other areas of work (Junor, 2004) and the diversity of the workforce is rarely acknowledged in the literature (Smith and Coombe, 2006). This diversity of part-time, sessional and casual teachers within HE means that identification of individuals, let alone their needs, can be extremely problematic. Measures of demographics between and within different countries and institutions are therefore unreliable and provide little grounds for comparison.

Nevertheless, the information that is available tells us that this is a large group which, once we explore it in depth, has a variety of needs and for which little provision is made. As the HE sector becomes increasingly concerned with the quality of students' learning experiences, the development of policy and practice to ensure that all teachers, regardless of their contract, are able to respond to this concern becomes essential.

The RED Report, among others, has highlighted the important role for academic developers in preparing these teachers to teach and in providing adequate professional development and ongoing support. The complexity of the casual and part-time workforce requires that universities develop creative and resourceful approaches to provision. We hope that the work presented in this book provides some useful ideas and background which will help in this enormous task.

Note

[1]   Teaching-only, research-only, research and teaching, and other.

References

Armstrong, C. (2011) 'Statistical overview of staff employed in higher education in the UK', Online. Available HTTP: www.jobs.ac.uk/careers-advice/working-in-higher-education/1826/statistical-overview-of-staff-employed-in-higher-education-in-the-uk-2009-2010/ (accessed 3 April 2012).

Burgess, J., Campbell, I. and May, R. (2008) 'Pathways from casual employment to economic security: the Australian experience', *Social Indicators Research*, 88(1): 161–178.

Coates, H., Dobson, I.R., Goedegebuure, L. and Meek, L. (2009) 'Australia's casual approach to its academic teaching workforce', *People and Place*, 17(4): 47–54.

Donovan, C., Hodgson, B., Scanlon, E. and Whitelegg, E. (2005) 'Women in higher education: issues and challenges for part-time scientists', *Women's Studies International Forum*, 28: 247–258.

Edwards, D., Bexley, E. and Richardson, S. (2011) 'Regenerating the academic workforce: the careers, intentions and motivations of higher degree research students in Australia', Report for the Department of Education, Employment and Workplace Relations, ACER–CSHE.

Gottschalk, L. and McEachern, S. (2010) 'The frustrated career: casual employment in higher education', *Australian Universities' Review*, 52: 37–50.

Grove, J. (2012) 'Applications fall 10% in England', *Times Higher Education Supplement*. Online. Available HTTP: www.timeshighereducation.co.uk/story.asp?sectioncode=26&storycode=418874 (accessed 3 April 2012).

Higher Education Statistics Agency (2012) 'Statistics – Staff employed at UK HE institutions.' Online. Available HTTP: www.hesa.ac.uk/index.php?option=com_content&task=view&id=1898&Itemid=706 (accessed 3 April 2012).

Junor, A. (2004) 'Casual university work: choice, risk, inequity and the case for regulation', *Economic and Labour Relations Review*, 14: 276–304.

Keogh, J. and Garrick, B. (2005) 'On the need to investigate the situation of casual academic work in new times', *HERDSA News*, 27(3): 15–18.

Organisation for Economic Cooperation and Development (2012): OECD Education Statistics ESDS International, University of Manchester. (Data extracted from Educational Personnel database, 31 January 2012.)

Percy, A., Scoufis, M., Parry, S., Goody, A., Hicks, M., Macdonald, I., Martinez, K., Szorenyi-Reischl, N., Ryan, Y., Wills S. and Sheridan, L. (2008) *The RED report: Recognition – Enhancement – Development: the contribution of sessional teachers to higher education*, Canberra: Australia Learning and Teaching Council (ALTC).

Smith, E. and Coombe, K. (2006) 'Quality and qualms in the marking of university assignments by sessional staff: an exploratory study', *Higher Education*, 51: 45–69.

Tertiary Education Commission (2010) Performance linked funding. Online. Available HTTP: www.tec.govt.nz/Funding/Policies-and-processes/Performance-linkedfunding/ (accessed 10 August 2011).

Umbach, P.D. (2008) 'The effects of part-time faculty appointments on instructional techniques and commitment to teaching', paper presented at the 33rd Annual Conference of the Association for the Study of Higher Education, Jacksonville, FL, November.

SECTION I

CONTEXT

AN OVERVIEW OF THE NATURE AND MOTIVATION OF PART-TIME TEACHERS

2

SUPPORTING PART-TIME AND OTHER TEACHING STAFF

WHO ARE THEY AND WHY ARE THEY IMPORTANT?

Bland Tomkinson

My initial interests in the professional development of part-time teaching staff originated, quite some time ago, in concerns that significant amounts of teaching were being undertaken by part-time staff. At that time we had provision for new full-time academic staff and occasionally this was taken up by part-timers. One event that focussed our minds in those days was that of the part-time professor who could only attend events on one of his 'university' days! I was also instrumental in designing an online package for occasional teachers which effectively demonstrated the approach but the use of which sadly declined due to lack of institutional support. Having formally retired from the university I now find myself employed, part time, as a Visiting Lecturer.

'Lies, damned lies and statistics' – that aphorism has possibly as many versions as attributions, yet it is quite apposite for this present chapter. Getting to the nub of how many part-timers teach in higher education, and what they do, is fraught with difficulties and this chapter will not produce a definitive answer – there are probably more variants of an answer than there are of that first quotation. The principal questions posed are not just 'How many are there?' but, first, 'Who are they?' A simplistic view might assume that the first is predicated on the second and this is true, but only to some extent. The importance of this group of people lies partly in the answers to those questions but also in the extent to which those individuals are prepared for the task of teaching. When there is a focus on development and training of those new to teaching, concern must be expressed about the training of a considerable number of people who might have a significant role in teaching yet do not feature as 'lecturers' or 'professors'. In the US there has been disquiet for some time that students are taught by graduate assistants and not by the professorial heads of department (e.g. Schmidt, 2010); this is becoming a more widespread concern, particularly in the UK where the introduction of substantial student fees is likely to give rise to a swathe of complaints and, possibly, litigation. This is made more complex by the often indefinite legal status of such teaching staff (Flora, 2007).

In Australia, Marina Harvey *et al.* (2005) have struggled to provide an accurate figure of the numbers of staff involved but looked to an action research approach to develop 'sessional' staff, building on earlier work undertaken by the Australian Universities' Teaching Committee (2003). In 2002 the Learning and Teaching Subject Network Generic Centre (now the UK Higher Education Academy) set up an initiative to build a database of resources to help those new to the role as an academic to find out about appropriate teaching methods for their own disciplines; this programme has been described in greater detail by Sue Burkill and Yolie Knight (2005). In the UK, the great majority of higher education institutions now have Postgraduate Certificates or Diplomas that are accredited by the Higher Education Academy, and increasingly, all new full-time academic staff are expected by their institutions to complete such a programme. However, this approach has largely been confined to those entering the profession on full academic contracts. In some disciplines part-timers take on a very substantial part of the teaching, yet their needs can often be overlooked or neglected.

One specialist institution suggested (privately) that over 90 per cent of its teaching was undertaken by part-time staff. But the statistics for the use of part-timers are difficult to gather and just as difficult to interpret.

Many institutions do run programmes for some of these staff (for example see Williams and Elvidge, 2005) and others permit such staff to participate in courses for full-time academic staff. Without a clear understanding of who these people are, what their needs are and, especially, how many of them there are, it is difficult to plan to provide appropriate support, within the institution or more widely.

Who are they and what do they do?

First, it is important to look at the wide range of people involved. In 2006, I set out to gather a comprehensive list of those involved in university teaching, but who were not counted as full-time academic staff. This was primarily drawn from the UK but additional information was sought from the US and Canada, as well as from Australia and New Zealand. One of the major difficulties was distinguishing differences in role from differences of terminology and the different national styles of role descriptor pose a problem for any sort of analysis both in this chapter and more widely.

The initial list of those involved appears as Table 2.1. However, this table is almost certainly incomplete and some of the job titles probably overlap or simply semantically reflect disciplinary differences. Donna Brown and Michael Gold (2007) point to a significant portion of their sample of 'non-standard academics' as being retired staff undertaking some post-retirement part-time duties. These

Table 2.1 Part-time teaching roles

Role	Includes
Part-time academic staff	Part-time Peripatetic Honorary Visiting
Teaching staff	Teaching Fellows Language teachers PBL facilitators Instructors/Technical instructors Performance tutors Online tutors
Medical, etc. staff	Clinical tutors Clinical facilitators
Workplace-based staff	Practice Educators/Teachers Practice Supervisors Long-arm Practice Supervisors Workplace mentors Work-experience supervisors
Casual	Casual Visitors Hourly paid
Learning support	Learning technologists Educational developers Learning support advisers Computer support Librarians Careers staff Special needs staff
Other staff who teach	Post-doctorate/Research staff Scientific/Experimental Officers Writers-in-residence Artists-in-residence Technician skills instructors Technician Demonstrators
Partner institutions	FE staff Overseas staff
Students supporting learning	PG Demonstrators PG Seminar leaders PG Teaching assistants Peer mentors

would normally be counted as visiting staff in Table 2.1. There is also a category of occasional lecturer that may, or may not, fall outside these categories; some institutions make use of visiting speakers from industry or commerce, usually at a senior level and who may make only a single contribution or two each year.

Christopher Husbands and Annette Davies (2000), also based on UK experience, suggest a slightly different typology, perversely excluding academics on part-time contracts:

- postgraduate students who teach;
- others performing 'hourly-paid' teaching;
- teaching assistants;
- contract researchers who undertake part-time teaching;
- occasional teachers;
- 'interstitial' status employees, e.g. tutorial fellows;
- continuing education tutors;
- Open University tutors.

In the UK, Celia Whitchurch (2008) refers to the development of 'third space' professionals who inhabit a domain between those of the support staff professional and the academic, though in practice, as illustrated above, many individuals are 'boundary spanners' and concurrently perform both academic and professional support roles. Likewise, Bruce MacFarlane (2010) uses the concept of the 'para-academic' in the context of professionals who perform some, disaggregated, parts of the academic role but he goes on to distinguish between those who are appointed to such a role and those academics who choose not to occupy the whole of the academic domain. Although Hong Kong based, much of the background for MacFarlane's view has been garnered in the UK. The concept of 'para-academic' is itself diffuse and including within it some who might otherwise be defined as academic makes it difficult to obtain a clear overall picture. A potential distinction here is between those who undertake some teaching duties in addition to their professional duties and those who take over a disaggregated portion of the work of an academic. But even this distinction is nebulous and practice will vary from institution to institution. However, both of these authors point to a body of full-time university employees whose academic role is only partial as well as the considerable number of people employed part time. A further complication is that some observers include those on full-time but short-term contracts as part of the domain of non-standard academics whereas others do not. This chapter tends to regard such people as full-time academics, though they do present their own developmental challenges, not least in the imaginings of university administrations.

Harvey *et al.* (2005) try to distinguish three overlapping sets of people:

Casual: Employment without leave entitlements. More frequently an employer will offer you hours to fit in with the operational requirements of the organisation, e.g. the days and hours when tutorials are held. There is no expectation of regular or continuing employment.

Contract: Set as a fixed-term period of work or for the duration of a specific task or project, e.g. teaching a unit over one semester.

Part-time: You work a proportion of a 'normal' working week with pro-rata benefits and job security, e.g. if you work a 50 per cent load, you are entitled to 50 per cent holiday pay. A pre-arranged regularity of the hours of work exists.

Why do they do it?

In a study undertaken in the US, Diana Kelly (1990) categorises part-time staff as:

- new and old part-timers;
- hopeful full-timers;
- vocational and academic faculty;
- day and evening faculty;
- moonlighters;
- full-time teachers;
- 'freeway fliers' (i.e. academics who teach in more than one institution).

In Australia, Marina Harvey and colleagues (2005) take a more concise view, with the reasons for working sessionally being boiled down to:

- it suits me;
- it was all that was on offer;
- I do not wish to work full time.

But this is qualified by the advantages of:

- it allows control;
- I can focus on teaching.

In the UK, Brown and Gold (2007) distinguish between male and female responses to non-standard contracts, as follows:

- I always wanted this type of contract;
- there is more money with this type of contract;
- I can avoid administrative duties;
- it was the only contract available;
- it allows variety of occupations;
- I can combine the work with family responsibilities.

Using these motivations, they found family responsibilities to be a greater motivator for taking a non-standard contract among females than among males and the lack of administrative duties a higher motivator among males than among females. However, the overall most pressing reason for taking a non-standard contract was the lack of any other sort.

Despite the different origins of these studies, both nationally and philosophically, there are some common threads. The first of these is the distinction between those who undertake these roles because they align with their personal values and ways of working and those who do so because their preferred type of contract is not on offer. There is also a financial element, with some individuals seeing this as a way of earning more.

These categories may reflect the personal aspirations, or motivations, of those who fall into the categories suggested in Table 2.1 but there is another side to this coin – the motivations of the institutions of higher education. These can be seen as:

- keeping down staff costs by offering poorer terms of service for part-timers;
- providing cover for absence, e.g. due to maternity leave, long-term illness or sabbatical;
- 'hiding' staff who do not then appear in full-time staff statistics or on the roll for such exercises as the UK's Research Excellence Framework;
- providing development opportunities for the next generation of academics;
- utilising the appropriate skills of staff who are not full-time academics;
- enriching the learning of students through learning in social contexts;
- enriching professional courses by engaging teachers who are actively engaged in the practice of their professions or vocations.

In the last instance there may be requirements of professional validating bodies that necessitate a complement of professionally qualified staff that can most readily be met by engaging part-timers.

The issue then becomes more complex with a matrix of interaction of individual motivations and institutional ones.

What do they do?

This group of staff, between them, may cover all aspects of an academic role but each is likely to have a limited brief. As implied by Brown and Gold (2007) the area least likely to feature is that of administrative duties, though even here there are those with primarily administrative roles who also undertake some teaching. The part-time, or visiting, lecturer or professor may differ little in duties from his or her full-time counterpart but other categories of staff may find that they have little to do with curriculum specification or even lesson preparation – they come, they teach, they go.

During the course of the DoPLA project in the UK (see Klapper, 2000) a variety of approaches was uncovered to the use made of language assistants (or lectors or lecteurs/lectrices) and other postgraduates who provide language teaching. In some universities language assistants were given detailed timetables prescribing in great detail what was to be undertaken in each minute of the session, with no discretion for the individual staff member. In other cases the individuals were given broad briefs as to what to cover and were expected to devise their own lesson plans. Moving from one institution to another could be a culture shock! The degree to which individuals were expected to participate in the summative assessment process was also mixed – this could pose particular problems for those new to the UK university assessment culture. The issue of quality of assessment, particularly summative assessment, is a fraught one, but there is considerable variety in attitudes towards teaching staff on non-standard contracts participating in formal assessment of students. These can range from a complete prohibition on such staff conducting formal assessment, through assessment conducted by them in the first instance but moderated by a member of full academic staff, to such individuals making a full contribution to assessment and participating in examination boards.

The perception may well be that the standards of marking of staff who teach part time are inferior to those of their full-time equivalents. But two studies by Bland Tomkinson and Jim Freeman (2007, 2011) suggest that other factors may be more important. Both of these studies concern assessment at postgraduate level and the first found that, in looking at differences between first and second markers of student portfolios, the significant differences occurred when one of the markers was marking this material for the first time. Some of this imbalance can be overcome by discussion and training and it is here that those who teach part time may miss out. The other concern for this group of teachers is that many of them will be moving between institutions and having to absorb new assessment practices. The second study looked at differences between first and second markers of master's dissertations. In this instance the markers were divided into four groups:

full-time staff core to that particular degree; staff in the subject area but not core teachers; 'external' supervisors; and full-time staff from elsewhere in the department. The significant differences here were not between the 'externals' and other markers but between staff peripheral to the subject area and those in other groups. In this case the external supervisors were employed solely to supervise students and to mark their work; they were drawn from professionals in business, former lecturers and academic staff from other institutions.

In laboratory and workshop practice it is not unusual for technicians or postgraduate demonstrators to assess the students' work and for these marks then to be validated or moderated by a member of full-time academic staff. This recognises that those who teach part time possess the necessary skills and knowledge, perhaps more so than the lecturer in charge, while retaining some measure of standardisation across a range of markers. It could be argued that, in many other aspects of professional practice, it may well be that those who teach part time are better informed about appropriate standards than their full-time colleagues.

Some of the tasks undertaken by this group of staff can be regarded as akin to coaching – small group or individual sessions of professional practice. This could be just as true for, say, Ophthalmic Optics students learning to diagnose and prescribe as it is for instrumental music students. In such circumstances a high degree of feedback, or formative assessment, is to be expected. In other cases, staff may be involved in technical instruction, for example graduate demonstrators or technicians giving individual or small group instruction in laboratories and workshops.

One area of concern, expressed by Jill Langen (2011: 191), is that the teaching provided by part-time staff is not subject to the same scrutiny as that of their full-time colleagues: '20% of the higher education institutions studied do not require part-time instructor evaluation on a scheduled basis, and 7% do not require any evaluation of their adjunct faculty.' The impact of this group of staff on student learning is picked up in a later paragraph.

What issues do they face?

One of the key issues raised by some authors is that of gender imbalance: Michelle Webber (2008) suggests that part-time women academics proportionately outnumber their full-time counterparts. This is, however, more complex than mere statistics because of the differences in motivation of part-time staff. Webber also concludes that the use of contingent faculty (a Canadian term) has moved from an instrument of flexibility to a means of reducing labour costs. The concerns about gender and racial imbalance are not the only ones that impact on such staff or on their students. Webber (2008) suggests that one major problem is that part-time staff are often hired at the last minute, when student enrolments are known, and that this causes stress on the individuals, who are constantly engaging in new course preparation, as well as jeopardising the quality of the curriculum. James Monks (2009) also suggests that whereas two-thirds of full-time faculty hold a doctorate or equivalent, only a quarter of part-timers do. This is perhaps unsurprising, given the relatively high proportion of postgraduate students who undertake teaching duties. Issues of curriculum are dealt with below, but the concerns voiced by part-time staff include a range of personal and personnel issues.

One of the keenest issues is that of payment, not just the relatively poor rates of pay but also difficulties in obtaining any payment at all. Part-time staff do not often have any induction of the sort that can help identify processes, procedures and people that can help overcome the bureaucratic hurdles faced by many new employees and which can be particularly irksome for part-time staff. An instance of this is the need to produce documentation to the HR function (e.g. passport, birth certificate, diplomas, proof of social security number) before a contract can be issued, even if the part-timer has been employed in the previous session. For the part-timer who does not habitually attend the university this can require a special journey or two. The issue of a contract can also impact not only on pay but also on access to resources – library access may not be a major issue but registration with the appropriate university information systems may frustrate attempts at teaching online. And this can be exacerbated when one individual is working for two or three institutions, each with their own system. The lack of contract continuity can also impact on key areas like access to university staff websites and email, which may be crucial to lesson preparation. Access to training and development may also be restricted. In the case of university employees with limited teaching duties, training and development may be confined to what their managements deem as 'core' duties; for those with an outside employer, getting time off to attend university training courses, on days other than those devoted to university work, can also be fraught and access to online training may be hampered by firms' internal firewalls.

As has been suggested above, there are many different types of part-time teachers in higher education and so the concerns may differ from situation to situation. For those on temporary contracts because no other is available, career progression can become a major issue; for those undertaking teaching duties while undertaking postgraduate or post-doctoral research, the converse may be true and the part-time teaching may improve career prospects.

James Watters and Patricia Weeks (1999) suggested that the key issues for part-timers are:

- powerlessness – the lack of a voice in the institution;
- co-ordination – the need for senior staff to recognise and coordinate the activities of part-timers;
- relevance – the need to be involved in balancing curricula between real-world practical skills and theoretical frameworks;
- professional development – the lack of appropriate training and development.

The key concerns of this group were identified as a lack of: physical facilities, induction information, marking and teaching guidelines and course organisation and worries about pay and conditions, administrative complexity and delay, quality of teaching and a lack of support for what they do. In the Watters and Weeks study the findings were a prelude to action, trying to identify the issues in order to provide some institutional support for their resolution.

Why are they important?

Part-time teachers are becoming progressively more important in higher education as their numbers grow and their contribution to all levels of teaching increases. Brown and Gold (2007) note that figures from the Higher Education Statistics Agency (HESA) in the UK indicate that 33.7 per cent of the academic staff working at UK institutions of higher education are 'atypical' but this may include those on short-term contracts and almost certainly excludes a swathe of other individuals who either do not appear on the HESA record at all or whose academic contribution is not thus recognised. They go on to cite a newspaper article that suggests that about one-third of undergraduate degrees is taught by staff on non-standard contracts. In a project looking at a limited range of subject areas (Business, Management, Finance & Accounting and Health Sciences & Practice), Colin Bryson and colleagues (Bryson *et al.* 2007) found a serious undercounting of part-time contributions within those subject areas. In a study within one college in the US, Sharron Ronco and John Cahill (2004) found considerable variation in the use of graduate teaching assistants (GTAs) and adjunct or contingent faculty, between subject areas. In the College of Science, GTAs undertook nearly 60 per cent of the teaching of undergraduates and adjunct faculty 15 per cent. This compares with 26 per cent GTA teaching and 31 per cent adjunct faculty teaching in the College of Arts and Letters.

Statistics are not only very hard to come by but also can be very misleading. If a professor asks one of his PhD students to undertake a few of his lectures as part of that individual's career development, it may not be recorded anywhere. On the other hand, if the headcount numbers of part-time staff are taken they can equally misrepresent the total picture. Take an engineering course unit with a cohort of 200 students: they may receive lectures from a single lecturer, attend a similar number of examples classes run by half a dozen PhD students and a similar amount of laboratories and workshops being taught by a score of technicians. If the inputs are taken, it suggests that the lecturer contributes about 4 per cent of the teaching (ignoring the input to the design of the examples classes and workshops) but each student would perceive the teaching to be one-third from a lecturer, one-third from a PhD student and one-third from a technician! Best guesses suggest that there are at least as many individuals in these part-time categories as there are full-time academic staff. A further challenge lies in the tension between part-time teachers providing specialist teaching that could not be achieved as effectively otherwise and concerns about monitoring the quality of their teaching.

In specialist institutions, particularly conservatoires and others in the dramatic and figurative arts, there is a need for coaching from practitioners who will also spend much of their time in performance. This can mean that such institutions rely very heavily on part-time teachers and this should not be taken as implying that such an approach is somehow 'inferior'; on the contrary, it may provide a richer student experience

The underlying question is whether it matters who teaches. As stated above, there are areas where it is important for students to have exposure to professional practice, whether this is within the university or in the workplace. In such cases the involvement of staff whose academic duties are part of their total employment is an important element of the teaching situation. Within the classroom, the question of impact upon the students is not entirely clear. Eric Bettinger and Bridget Long (2004: 24) suggest that, with a couple of exceptions, 'taking a course from an adjunct or graduate student adversely affects the number of credit hours that students subsequently attempt in a subject and the likelihood that a student majors in that subject'. However, these differences, though significant, are still relatively small. Moreover, the effects on subsequent student success are not significant, though there are differences between subject areas. Interestingly, the age of the adjunct staff was found to be a factor, with the under-40s more likely to have an adverse effect on students.

Ronco and Cahill (2004: 18) suggest that there may not be a significant difference in the effects on students between teaching from full-time and part-time academic staff, but qualify this with the suggestion that their accrediting authorities require that all academic staff have 'competencies and achievements that contribute to effective teaching and student learning outcomes' and that it 'is the responsibility of the university to ensure that whomever is in the classroom has the tools to make this happen'. Peter Knight et al. (2007) suggest that

Part-time teachers are a significant resource in higher education, and an important part of the complex ecology of higher education. Their professional formation as teachers often receives less attention from institutions than it merits. Can institutions, facing ever-growing pressures for quality, effectiveness and efficiency, afford *not* to make the best use of the many educational benefits that part-time teachers bring?

(2007: 436)

The real question, then, is what sort of preparation should these 'part-time' individuals receive but, given the diversity of roles and also of motivation to undertake them, how can they be appropriately and effectively supported?

References

Australian Universities Teaching Council (2003). 'Training, Support and Management of Sessional Teaching Staff'. University of Queensland, St Lucia.

Bettinger, E. and Long, B.T. (2004). 'Do College Instructors Matter? The Effects of Adjuncts and Graduate Assistants on Students' Interests and Success'. Working Paper 10370. National Bureau of Economic Research, Cambridge, MA.

Brown, D. and Gold, M. (2007). 'Contracts in UK Universities: Portfolio Work, Choice and Compulsion'. *Higher Education Quarterly* 61(4) 439–460.

Bryson, C., Clark, J., Woodall, J. and Geissler, C. (2007). *HESA Part-time Teaching Staff Statistics: An Analysis and Commentary*. Higher Education Academy Subject Centres for Business, Management, Accounting and Finance and Health Sciences and Practice.

Burkill, S. and Knight, Y. (2005). 'Supporting New Academic Staff (SNAS): Enhanced Support for a Disciplinary Focus'. *Educational Developments* 6 (4) 14–15.

Flora, B.H. (2007). 'Graduate Assistants: Student or Staff, Policy or Practice? The Current Legal Employment Status of Graduate Assistants'. *Journal of Higher Education Policy and Management* 29 (3) 315–322.

Harvey, M., Fraser, S. and Bowes, J. (2005). 'Quality Teaching and Professional Staff'. Proceedings of the 2005 HERDSA Conference. Sydney, Australia, 3–6 July.

Husbands, C.T. and Davies, A. (2000). 'The Teaching Roles, Institutional Locations, and Terms and Conditions of Employment of Part-time Teachers in UK Higher Education'. *Journal of Further and Higher Education* 24 (3) 337–362.

Kelly, D. (1990). 'A Human Resources Development Approach to Part-Time Faculty'. Proceedings of the seventh Annual Conference of Academic Chairpersons: Orlando, FL, February.

Klapper, J. (2000). 'Training Graduate Teachers and Foreign Language Assistants in UK Universities: A Reflective Approach'. In B. Rifkin (ed.) *Mentoring Foreign Language Teaching Assistants, Lecturers, and Adjunct Faculty*. Boston: Heinle & Heinle.

Knight, P., Baume, D., Tait, J. and Yorke, M. (2007). 'Enhancing Part-time Teaching in Higher Education: a Challenge for Institutional Policy and Practice'. *Higher Education Quarterly* 61 (4) 420–438.

Langen, J.M. (2011). 'Evaluation of Adjunct Faculty in Higher Education Institutions'. *Assessment and Evaluation in Higher Education* 36 (2) 185–196.

Macfarlane, B. (2010). 'The Morphing of Academic Practice: Unbundling and the Rise of the Para-academic'. *Higher Education Quarterly* 65 (1) 59–73.

Monks, J. (2009). 'Who Are the Part-time Faculty?' *Academe* 95 (4) 33–37.

Ronco, S.L. and Cahill, J. (2004). 'Does it Matter Who's in the Classroom? Effect of Instructor Type on Student Retention, Achievement and Satisfaction'. Proceedings of the 44th Annual Forum of the Association for Institutional Research, Boston, MA. May.

Schmidt, P. (2010). 'Conditions Imposed on Part-Time Adjuncts Threaten Quality of Teaching, Researchers Say'. *Chronicle of Higher Education*, 30 November.

Tomkinson, B. (2006). 'Supporting Part-time and Other Teaching Staff'. *Educational Developments* 7 (1) 13–14.

Tomkinson, B. and Freeman, J. (2007). 'Using Portfolios for Assessment: Problems of Reliability or Standardisation?' Proceedings of the Higher Education Research and Development Society of Australasia Conference, Adelaide, July.

Tomkinson, B. and Freeman, J. (2011). 'Problems of Assessment'. Proceedings of the International Conference on Engineering Education, Belfast, July.

Watters, J. and Weeks, P. (1999). 'Professional Development of Part-time or Casual Academic Staff in Universities: a Model for Empowerment'. Proceedings of the Annual Conference of the American Educational Research Association, Montreal, April.

Webber, M. (2008). 'Miss Congeniality Meets the New Managerialism: Feminism, Contingent Labour, and the New University'. *Canadian Journal of Higher Education* 38 (3) 37–56.

Whitchurch, C. (2008). 'Shifting Identities and Blurring Boundaries: the Emergence of Third Space Professionals in UK Higher Education'. *Higher Education Quarterly* 62 (4) 377–396.

Williams, E. and Elvidge, L. (2005). 'Training Graduate Students to Teach: an Effective Model'. *Educational Developments* 6 (4) 16–17.

3

DETERMINING THE SUPPORT NEEDS OF CASUAL ACADEMIC STAFF AT THE FRONTLINE

Bronwyn Bevan-Smith, Jayne Keogh and Bruce D'Arcy

Casual, or part-time, academic staff members (referred to throughout this chapter as tutors) have long been a staple part of higher education throughout the world, but their role is often overlooked, and there is a lack of professional development necessary to fulfil their teaching role effectively (Percy *et al.*, 2008a). Tutors are often students themselves (albeit generally postgraduate), often with little to no formal induction into the role, or training in effective teaching techniques, and little previous experience in teaching. To date, little research has been undertaken to investigate the professional development needs of tutors. In order to address this gap in the literature, a quantitative study was recently conducted at a large research-intensive university in Australia to investigate the professional development needs of tutors throughout the institution as perceived by the tutors themselves. This chapter describes the development, dissemination and results of this survey. The chapter then concludes by discussing implications of the findings in relation to supporting the teaching needs of tutors across higher education institutions in general.

Tutors in academia: setting the scene

Globalisation has resulted in workplaces worldwide experiencing an ever-increasing neo-liberal economic and managerial ethos (Currie *et al.*, 2000). Universities in Australia, like many other countries, have experienced an increase in the employment of academic staff on a casual basis who, by definition, are employed on a part-time basis throughout the teaching period and paid on an hourly basis (AIRC, 1998). Statistics from the Australian context suggest that this casualisation of the higher education sector has been more pronounced and accelerated than has been the case for comparable workplaces, with an estimated 40 per cent of academic staff employed casually, compared to a national average of approximately 25 per cent (DEST, 2005, 2007).

Universities often draw heavily on tutors to '*serve as frontline troops. More and more of the interface between the university and the students . . . is happening at the level of genral staff and tutors*' (Eveline, 2004). Indeed, Percy *et al.* (2008b) reported that in two of the universities they investigated, up to 80 per cent of undergraduate teaching was conducted by tutors. Furthermore, studies conducted in the USA (O'Neal *et al.*, 2007) and the UK, France and Australia (Hughes *et al.*, 2010) have found that tutors have an essential role in student retention, especially in the first year of undergraduate studies, and also in ensuring an enjoyable student experience and facilitating student learning. In addition, such evidence indicates that tutors play an absolutely crucial role in student learning in higher education institutes, so much so that Stevenson *et al.* (2006) argue that tutors need to both recognise, and be recognised for, the crucial role they can play in the success of the courses they teach.

Previous studies (Brabazon, 2004; Eveline, 2004; Baranay, 2006; Brown *et al.*, 2006; Junor, 2004) have highlighted some of the joys, challenges and concerns that many tutors experience in relation to aspects of their work conditions. For example, Junor (2004) reported that tutors greatly valued the possibilities of having a choice of when and where they might be employed. One advantage is the flexibility that such employment provides in relation to time off for other pursuits, and the intrinsic rewards of this type of employment in terms of their work–life balance arrangements. However, such advantages are vastly outweighed by reports of the negatives associated with casual employment, including feelings of being ill-informed, marginalised and undervalued, combined with financial insecurity and uncertainties in relation to future employment (Eveline, 2004; Junor, 2004; Brabazon, 2004; Brown *et al.*, 2006; Baranay, 2006). Findings regarding the adverse effects of casualisation have generated a number of studies advocating the implementation of extensive support mechanisms for tutors, including the findings of a large study investigating the contribution of tutors in Australia (Percy *et al.*, 2008a, Percy *et al.*, 2008b). In response to these recommendations, a study was developed to determine those areas in which tutors at one particular large Australian university were felt to need improved support.

Regardless of the key role that tutors play in higher education, the casualisation of the industry has resulted in a somewhat haphazard procedure for the employment of tutors. Rather than emphasis being placed on teaching ability or content knowledge, tutors are often employed based on their availability or who they know (Eveline, 2004). Furthermore, systemic, sustainable and formal employment structures for tutors are rare, and the support of tutors is often intermittent and context-dependent, with few policy-driven practices existent in Australian universities (Percy *et al.*, 2008a). Although training programmes for tutors are sometimes made available, attendance tends to be on a voluntary basis only, and is often unpaid. Additionally, the emphasis of these training programmes frequently focuses on administrative matters, course content or other matters of importance to individual tutor trainers rather than on effective teaching techniques. This has led to concerns regarding the apparent lack of quality assurance in relation to teaching and learning in universities (Percy *et al.*, 2008a). Furthermore, different disciplines seem to have different expectations regarding the working roles of their tutors and, as such, a belief that no one size fits all when it comes to the professional development needs of tutors. Such a situation requires further investigation to identify both institutional-wide and discipline-specific professional development needs and priorities in different schools and faculties across the higher education sector. It is this task that is the focus of this chapter. Specifically, this study was developed to address three key research questions:

1 What do the tutors at a large research-intensive university perceive their professional development needs to be?
2 Which of these perceived needs are of most importance to tutors?
3 How do these important topics differ in relation to different levels of tutor experience in different faculties?

Methodology and methods

A quantitative survey research approach was adopted to answer these research questions and to determine the opinions of a large cohort of tutors regarding their professional development needs. All of the procedures undertaken during this study were approved by the university's Behavioural & Social Sciences Ethical Review Committee (BSSERC) in accordance with the guidelines of the National Health and Medical Research Council.

Context

The study was carried out at a large research-intensive university that offers a comprehensive range of undergraduate and graduate programmes to a student cohort of over 40,000, including almost 7,000 full-time equivalent (FTE) post-graduate students. To teach these students, the university employs more than 2,600 FTE academic staff members and 1,000 tutors. The university is divided into seven faculties; Social and Behavioural Sciences (SBS), Engineering, Architecture and Information Technology (EAIT), Health Sciences (Health), Natural Resources, Agriculture and Veterinary Sciences (NRAVS), Business, Economics and Law (BEL), Science and Arts. Each of these faculties comprised a number of schools and research institutes, and there was a total of 37 schools within the university at the time of this study.

Participants

In January 2009, the academic staff member responsible for employing and managing tutors in each school (here referred to as the tutor co-ordinator) was approached by email and informed of the study, with a request for their consent to participate. A total of 21 tutor co-ordinators representing all seven faculties agreed to be involved in the research project. In February of the same year, a member of the research team attended all of the tutor induction workshops conducted by each of these participating schools, where an anonymous survey was distributed to the attendees. In addition, where not all tutors were required to attend the induction workshop, the tutor co-ordinators circulated an email to their tutors that contained a link to an online version of the survey. Of the estimated 1,000 tutors employed by the university, a total of 439 tutors completed the survey, representing tutors attached to all seven faculties. While personal demographic details such as gender, age and ethnicity were not investigated, the experience level of respondents, the schools and faculties represented, and typical teaching session formats were identified.

Survey

The full research team, consisting of a course co-ordinator, a tutor and three educational researchers, developed a survey comprising three sections of closed and open-ended questions. The first section focused on participants' demographics, while the second section asked tutors to respond to two questions regarding the professional development they would like to receive. The first question in section two asked tutors to indicate their interest in a number of named potential forums for professional development on a four-point scale ranging from not at all (1), to very interested (4). Five forums were offered, including a social coffee club, seminars, discussion groups (online and face-to-face) and a designated office or meeting area specifically allocated for tutors. The second question in this section used the same four-point scale to ask tutors what professional development topics they would be interested in. A total of 17 topics in the general areas of developing teaching and learning skills, assessment and personal development were offered. Following this, the third section of the survey included three open-ended questions where tutors were asked to prioritise their professional development needs from a) the most important and b) the least important by drawing on the possibilities provided in question two of the previous section. Finally, the tutors were asked to identify any actions that the university might take to potentially improve their tutoring experience.

Analysis

Initially, the demographic details of the tutors were documented from the completed surveys. Responses were then separated according to experience and faculty to evaluate whether the tutors' perceived professional development needs were related to the length of their employment and experience, and to identify whether there were any discipline specific similarities or differences. By separating the groups, it was possible to evaluate how universal the needs of the tutors were within this large research-intensive university. Together, the different experience levels and faculties resulted in eight respondent groups which are discussed below, both together and separately. In determining the similarities and differences between each group, the mean response to the level of interest for each forum and topic was calculated. A Kruskal–Wallis ANOVA analysis with Dunn's post test was conducted to determine if tutors were significantly more interested in one forum or topic than in other options offered in each question. This analytic process was conducted for all groups of respondents. Following this, topics that were listed by tutors as being important were identified, and a comparison between the responses of each group was carried out.

Finally, a qualitative analysis of the open-ended questions was implemented using the NVivo software package (QSR International, Victoria, Australia) to identify any common themes identified by the respondents that higher education institutions might consider addressing.

Results

Demographic details of the participants

Approximately half of the 439 respondents (48 per cent) were new to tutoring while a further third (35 per cent) had been tutoring for between one and five years. The majority of tutors indicated that they were employed to teach small tutorial classes of 30 or fewer students (64 per cent of respondents) or laboratory-based practical classes (33 per cent of respondents), indicating that these are the most common teaching session formats for tutoring in this university. A minority of the respondents were employed to deliver computer-based (26 per cent) or field-based (14 per cent) laboratory classes, large tutorial classes (23 per cent), private tutoring sessions (13 per cent) or peer-assisted study sessions (8 per cent). Science was the most highly represented faculty (49 per cent of respondents), followed by EAIT (16 per cent), BEL (15 per cent), SBS (14 per cent), Health (7 per cent) and NRAVS (3 per cent). It is worth noting at this point that only three tutors from the Faculty of Arts responded to this survey. It was felt that such a small sample number was not representative of the entire tutor cohort from this faculty, resulting in the decision to exclude these responses from further analysis.

How should professional development opportunities be delivered?

First, the interest of tutors in a variety of possible forums for professional development was determined from the survey data. It was found that new tutors were significantly ($P < 0.05$) more interested in a social coffee club, online discussion group and access to a meeting area than were the experienced tutors. However, both the new and experienced tutors were significantly ($P < 0.001$) more interested in seminars than in a social coffee club or discussion group. In addition, experienced tutors were significantly ($P < 0.01$) more interested in seminars than in having a meeting area, but they were also significantly ($P < 0.01$) more interested in a meeting area than in a social coffee club and discussion groups. Both the new and experienced tutors were least interested in more casual face-to-face options for professional development, with the social coffee club and discussion group options receiving the lowest overall levels of interest. However, there was no significant ($P > 0.05$) difference between interest in these options and the online discussion board.

Analysis of the faculty-specific responses was then conducted to identify whether tutors from one faculty were more or less interested in each forum. Similar trends were found in each faculty, with tutors in BEL and Science reporting significantly greater interest in a meeting area ($P < 0.05$) compared to all other forums, with the exception of seminars. In addition, Science and SBS tutors were significantly more interested in seminars than in all other options except for the meeting area ($P < 0.001$). Tutors in NRAVS, EAIT and Health did not report any significant preference for or against any forum ($P > 0.05$).

Following this, the comments made by tutors in response to this question were investigated to further understand the lack of interest in social activities. Of the comments made by new (N = 13) and experienced (N = 27) tutors, 38 per cent and 30 per cent respectively indicated that the lack of an office space was important. For example, one experienced tutor stated that 'There is very little room for tutors to prepare, mark assignments, and put the materials that we use for tutorials (or to just have a secure space to work). It would be extremely beneficial to have something like this.' The perceived need for an office space or meeting area will be discussed later in the chapter. Following the findings that tutors were primarily interested in seminars along with the meeting area, the next section investigates the specific topics that tutors perceive as important.

What professional development topics are important for tutors?

Following the question regarding preferred forums for professional development, the survey then asked tutors to indicate their interest in a number of professional development topics. When the mean interest for all tutors was calculated, 'giving effective feedback' was ranked the highest (3.01 ± 0.04). However, there was also a high level of interest in 'learning how to mark assessment items' (2.95 ± 0.05) and in 'coping with difficult classroom situations' (2.90 ± 0.04). Both new and experienced tutors, along with tutors in all faculties except NRAVS, identified 'giving effective feedback' as one of the three most important topics. Another assessment-based topic, 'marking assessment items', was also a high priority for NRAVS and experienced tutors. In addition, two of the personal development topics were ranked as a high priority, with experienced and BEL tutors being interested in 'developing a teaching style' and SBS and Health tutors being interested in 'developing a teaching portfolio'. Further to these topics, 'planning and managing a class' was identified as important by new tutors and those in NRAVS and Science. A similar topic, that of 'coping with difficult classroom situations' was also identified as important by EAIT tutors. There was also a great deal of agreement between respondent groups for the least important topic, with all groups except Health tutors identifying 'managing external students' as a low priority. In addition, all groups except SBS tutors were not interested in 'discussing tutoring literature'. Finally, SBS and Health tutors also agreed that 'managing course co-ordinators' was a low priority.

In the instance that the second section of the survey (encompassing questions regarding possible forums and topics for further professional development) omitted any areas perceived as important to tutors, the final section of the survey invited tutors to identify any area in which higher education institutions could consider providing further professional development to ultimately improve the tutoring experience.

What do tutors really want?

Tutors provided 256 different responses to the open-ended question which were then coded into five categories: better organisation (54), more support (82), more recognition (29), better facilities (79) and social events (12). In terms of organisation, tutors reported wanting a clear policy outlining their roles, improved communication mechanisms with the course co-ordinator, and clear information regarding the criteria used to assess students. The support items identified by the respondents included suggestions of the need to establish discipline-specific support groups with fellow tutors, efficient online training modules, and a handbook of tips for new tutors prepared by experienced tutors.

In relation to recognition, tutors requested better acknowledgment of their efforts, specifically increasing the status of tutoring within academic circles, and formal recognition in the form of an annotation on academic records or a certificate. Further to the interest registered in a meeting area or office space as a forum for professional development, tutors requested an office space where they could store tutoring materials and meet with students and fellow tutors to discuss assessment items. Finally, some tutors requested social events in the form of free coffee, free parking or an end of semester get together with fellow tutors in their discipline.

Discussion and implications

Responses to the survey indicated that all members of participant groups were interested in seminars and having an office or meeting area where they could engage in discussions with fellow tutors. It seems that the majority of tutors employed at this university hold concurrent full-time positions, either as postgraduate students or working to support a family (accurate numbers currently unavailable). As such, tutors may not perceive participation in extensive unpaid casual tutor training sessions to be a priority. Indeed in this study, seminars and workshops where attendance is time specific and reimbursed was an attractive format for receiving professional development, suggesting that higher education institutes seeking to implement professional development opportunities might consider using workshops and seminars as the primary mode of delivery. In addition, a meeting area or office space where tutors could store tutoring materials, print and photocopy resources, mark assessment items and discuss their tutoring experiences with fellow tutors was also highly regarded in this survey. This result strengthens findings previously reported by Smith and Bath (2004) and further advocated by Sparks (1986) who investigated the effectiveness of a range of professional development models, finding that workshops combined with a community of practice where teachers discussed their techniques with peers was the most effective professional development model in ensuring high-quality teaching and learning. Furthermore, Smith and Bath (2004) argue that if tutors are to overcome the general feeling of being undervalued, marginalised and ill-informed by their school, then each school must, at an absolute minimum, provide tutors with access to an institutional email address and office space with computer, printer, photocopier and phone access to facilitate discussions between tutors, and between the tutors and their students, thereby ultimately providing tutors with the opportunity to mark assessment items in a productive, collegial and collaborative environment. It seems logical to suppose that the extensive casualisation of the higher education sector may well have significant implications for the morale of academic teaching teams and, thus, on the quality of teaching and learning in higher education institutions. If the sector is to continue on a path of increased casualisation of their academic staff, findings from this study suggest that higher education institutions should consider implementing professional development opportunities in the form of workshops and seminars as their primary mode of delivery. Furthermore, the provision of an office space with access to general school equipment is a fundamental requirement if tutors are to be able to provide high-quality teaching and learning within the institution.

With regard to the specific topics for professional development, tutors were commonly interested in receiving further training in the area of assessment, and, specifically, in marking assessment items and in giving effective feedback to students. The extensive agreement between participant groups regarding the most and least important topics creates a useful possibility for future tutor professional development. Rather than the perceived no one-size-fits-all situation regarding professional development, the findings of this survey suggest that some forms of professional development might well be generalised for all tutors across different disciplines and experience levels. (See Chapter 6 for an example of this.) This has significant implications for how higher education institutes manage the employment of their tutors. Further to a generalised model of professional development for all tutors within the institution, higher education institutions might also consider a standardised requirement for schools to implement consistent, uniform and transparent methods for recruiting and training tutors. This should also include a clear role statement outlining the expectations of the tutors by full-time teaching, research and administration staff members, as well as by students enrolled in each school, along with an outline of what tutors can expect from the school in return for their teaching.

This study has only investigated the perceptions of tutors, albeit a reasonably large cohort. However, it has not considered the opinions of the tutor co-ordinators responsible for employing and managing tutors within each school, the course co-ordinators responsible for designing and implementing the courses that tutors deliver, or the students whose learning experience depends on the preparedness of the tutor. The research team is currently investigating such matters, with tutor co-ordinators, course co-ordinators, tutors and students being surveyed, interviewed and observed to identify the perceived key roles of tutors in the university, how these roles should be fulfilled, and how these perceptions are actually portrayed in training sessions and a range of classroom environments including tutorials, laboratory-based classes and field-based classes. Thus, future research could investigate any areas in which these groups feel that tutors could develop more effective tutoring techniques and/ or receive further support or training.

Summary and conclusion

Tutors have long been recognised as essential members of the academic team. However, concerns have been raised regarding the quality of teaching and learning in higher education institutions as a result of extensive casualisation of the academic workforce. In response to these concerns, this chapter has described a study conducted at a large research-intensive university in Australia, designed to determine the perceived professional development needs of tutors. The study investigated which of these needs were of most importance to the responding tutors, and examined how differences in tutor-experience level and faculty of employment affected their relative importance. There was a good deal of generalisability between the participant groups in terms of both how professional development should be delivered and the topics of importance. Specifically, the respondents to this survey felt that professional development in the areas of assessment, personal development and classroom management were of greatest importance. Furthermore, when tutors were invited to identify areas in which they wanted further professional development, the provision of an office or meeting area was repeatedly mentioned as a priority, along with the requirement for better organisation, more support and recognition on the part of the institute. Finally, the need to implement a generic and generalised professional development model for tutors at this university was suggested as a means to improve the quality of teaching and learning at higher education institutes.

In conclusion, this study suggests that the professional development needs of tutors with different levels of experience and from a range of faculties are more similar than previously thought, and that higher education institutes might consider creating clear, consistent and transparent requirements for the recruitment and professional development of tutors, including a clear role statement for tutors within all departments throughout the institution. By such means tutors would be able to learn not only from the experiences of others within their own discipline, but also from others within the higher education sector more generally. Thus, it should be the aim of universities to ultimately develop professional development models whereby tutors are embraced and provided with the necessary support mechanisms to enable them to become highly effective educators to the benefit of themselves, their students and the higher education sector.

Acknowledgements

The authors would like to thank Dr Nicholas Baker and Dr Louise Kuchel for their involvement in the research project along with all of the tutors and tutor co-ordinators who participated in this study.

References

AIRC (1998) Higher Education Contract of Employment Award, Australian Industrial Relations Commission. Sydney.

Baranay, I. (2006) 'The academic underclass', *Griffith Review 11: Getting SMART: The battle for ideas in education*, Griffith University.

Brabazon, T. (2004) 'Skirt, cap and gown: how fair are universities to young women in postgraduate study?', *Cultural Studies Review*, 10, 161–175.

Brown, A., Goodman, J. and Yasukawa, K. (2006) 'Getting the best of you for nothing: casual voices in the Australian academy', Melbourne: Australia National Tertiary Education Union (NTEU).

Currie, J., Harris, P. and Thiele, B. (2000) 'Sacrifices in greedy universities: are they gendered?', *Gender and Education*, 12, 269–291.

DEST (Australian Department of Education Science and Training) (2005; 2007) Selection of Higher Education Statistics. Canberra: Commonwealth of Australia.

Eveline, J. (2004) 'Putting the spotlight on ivory basement work: essential and essentially unseen work', conference paper, University of Western Australia.

Hughes, I., Anderson-Beck, R., Atkinson, J., Awabdy, D., Bowmer, C., Colson, N., Cousins, X., Farrand-Zimbardi, K., Good, J., Goodhead, L., Kahler, C., Lluka, L., Moni, R., Nagley, P., Naug, H., Overfield, J., Poutney, D., Sheehan, J. and Wood, D. (2010) 'Improving first year laboratory classes in bioscience – students' views', University of Leeds.

Junor, A. (2004) 'Choice, risk and equity in casual university work: implications for regulation', *Economic and Labour Relations Review*, 14, 276–304.

O'Neal, C., Wright, M., Cook, C., Perorazio, T. and Purkiss, J. (2007) 'The impact of teaching assistants on student retention in the sciences', *Journal of College Science Teaching*, 36, 24–29.

Percy, A., Scoufis, M., Parry, S., Goody, A., Hicks, M., Macdonald, I., Martinez, K., Szorenyi-Reischl, N., Ryan, Y., Wills, S. and Sheridan, L. (2008a) 'The RED Report (Recognition, Enhancement, Development): the contribution of sessional teachers to higher education', Sydney: Australian Learning & Teaching Council.

Percy, A., Scoufis, M., Parry, S., Goody, A., Hicks, M., Macdonald, I., Martinez, K., Szorenyi-Reischl, N., Ryan, Y., Wills, S. and Sheridan, L. (2008b) 'The RED Report (Recognition, Enhancement, Development): the contribution of sessional teachers to higher education', Sydney: Australian Learning and Teaching Council.

Smith, C. and Bath, D. (2004) 'Evaluation of a university-wide strategy providing staff development for tutors: effectiveness, relevance and local impact', *Mentoring and Tutoring*, 12, 107–22.

Sparks, G. (1986) 'The effectiveness of alternative training activities in changing teaching practices', *American Educational Research Journal*, 23(2), 217–225.

Stevenson, J. M., Buchanan, D. A. and Sharpe, A. (2006) 'The pivotal role of faculty in propelling student persistence and progress toward degree completion', *Journal of College Student Retention*, 8, 141–148.

SECTION II

POLICY AND PRACTICE

FIRST PART: DEVELOPING POLICY AND PRACTICE TO SUPPORT PART-TIME TEACHERS

4

POLICY AND PRACTICE TO SUPPORT PART-TIME TEACHERS AT SCALE

THE EXPERIENCE OF THE UK'S OPEN UNIVERSITY

Anne Gaskell

Introduction

The 7,000 part-time associate lecturers[1] (tutors) who work for The Open University (OU) live mainly across all parts of the UK. Of these, 37 per cent work full time for other organisations, 41 per cent work part time elsewhere and 20 per cent have the OU as their sole employer (2 per cent provide no information). Meeting the professional development needs of such a dispersed and diverse group provides a substantial challenge for the institution, while developing as a professional can be a challenge for a part-time tutor. A study based on responses from 2401 OU tutors in 2004 concluded that 'a great deal of professional learning takes place through bringing a lively enquiring mind to bear on the daily business of doing the job' (Tait *et al.*, 2004: 3). This chapter examines the OU's policies and models for the professional development of part-time tutors at scale and provides examples of current practice at the OU, including developments with online media and the use of student feedback to inform professional development. This involves strategic, policy and contractual issues of importance to all higher education institutions particularly as online delivery is driving developments from 'distance education for some to flexible delivery for all' (King 2010: 131).

The structure of distance education at scale

The role of part-time teachers in a single-mode distance teaching institution is very different from that in campus-based institutions. Common to both groups of staff is their role in 'teaching students'; however, the implications of 'teaching' within the OU involve a range of very different skills from those many have found in conventional teaching. Indeed, a survey by Tait *et al.* emphasised 'the need to question any assumption that a "traditional" teaching training, experience or qualification (at whatever level) can be expected to provide sufficient preparation for a role as a [OU] tutor' (2004: 8).

Distance teaching institutions have been characterised by a separation of functions or constituent elements – so that (for example) those who create teaching materials are a distinct group of staff from those who deliver them to students and facilitate student understanding. Peters (1998) has likened this to an 'industrial' mode of teaching, where each constituent element of course production and delivery is undertaken by a different cohort of staff who are often very widely separated in terms of their location. To ensure that this provides a successful experience for students, a 'systems' approach is needed: 'a distance education system consists of all the component processes that operate when teaching and learning at a distance occurs. It includes learning, teaching, communication, design and management' (Moore and Kearsley, 2005: 9). This involves not just the important processes evident in campus-based universities, such as registration, student advice centres and so on, but a wider range of processes which include Educational Technology Units to support the design of teaching materials to ensure that they, whether in print or online, are fit for the purpose of teaching and supporting students at a distance; and particular qualities and skills among staff who support students within the system. It is this separation of functions and the systems approach that have provided a holistic experience for students and enabled the distance 'mega-universities' – the term used by Daniel in 1999 for those distance teaching institutions such as the OU that had enrolled over 100,000 students at the time – to operate successfully at scale.

What implications does this have for OU tutors, and therefore for their professional development? First, it highlights one of their key differences from some part-time teachers in other institutions: the OU tutor's role is to facilitate student learning from materials written or created by other people; it is not to create large amounts of new teaching materials or to deliver traditional lectures (Gaskell and Mills, 2007). As new technologies make the interaction between traditional course teams, OU tutors and students much more flexible, these boundaries between groups are constantly shifting which requires staff in particular to develop new skills and an increased understanding of the importance of new pedagogies of learner support (Thorpe, 2002).

Second, the role of tutor involves a great deal of time spent on marking student assignments; these may number up to seven per presentation on a 60 credit module and form up to 50 per cent of a student's overall final assessment score. As tutors do not see students frequently, or engage with them online necessarily unless it is a requirement of the module, their key teaching role is through providing detailed constructive written feedback and 'feed-forward' on assignments – comments which are designed to enable students to achieve higher grades in future. As such, correspondence tuition remains core to the Open University's interaction with students, both in terms of teaching and in terms of tutor time.

In a survey of 600 tutors in 2004, 44 per cent of tutors said that this accounted for 40–50 per cent of the overall time they spent on their part-time role (Gibbs, 2004).

It also forms one of the most important contributors to professional learning. Drawing on questionnaires from 2401 tutors, Tait *et al.* (2004: 3) report that 'their recent professional learning has been particularly stimulated by tutorials and engaging with students by marking and correspondence tuition'. This has also led to a strong emphasis on professional development for correspondence tuition, which forms a key aspect of new tutor induction, and the development of a range of printed and online resources to support their activity in this area. It would seem that this is paying off; collated information from the Open University's electronic student feedback questionnaires indicate that the questions about assignment marking routinely receive high scores: in 2010, for example, 84 per cent of 82,935 students agreed or strongly agreed with the statement: 'the tutors' comments helped me improve' (Developing Associate Lecturers through Student Feedback 2010).

Third, it emphasises the importance of the role of tutor in student support. This is mainly cognitive and affective rather than systemic – the three key parts of a distance learning student support system (Tait, 2000). Students are at the heart of the OU system, but they may not find their way around it very easily when they are located at a distance from the institution – and the person they are most likely to turn to in the first instance is their tutor. In terms of professional development for tutors, this has meant a reorientation from instruction to facilitation and from a wider range of skills than those based mainly on subject knowledge, especially when tutors are supporting first-year (level 1) students. A range of staff development resources are in place to help support tutors in this role, some of which are discussed below.

The professional formation of OU tutors

Knight *et al.* (2006) argue that the professional learning of HE teachers can be seen as a strategic issue in the sense that 'it is implicated in the development and working through of university policies and strategies' and 'that resources are allocated following a principled view of the ways in which professional teachers learn' (Knight *et al.*, 2006: 336). These in their turn will impact on the possibilities and routes for the professional formation of teachers which will depend on their role within the institution.

University policies and strategies: the role of part-time tutors

The first OU part-time teachers in 1971 were appointed to three separate roles: as class tutors, correspondence tutors and educational counsellors. They 'had in common little more than good academic qualifications and teaching experience in a University or adult education' (Beevers, 1975: 12) – which emphasises the importance of support and development for OU tutors at an early stage.

From 1976 the three roles were combined into two: the tutor-counsellor, appointed to tutor first-level students and then provide support for their progress throughout their OU career; and different course tutors who provided subject-expert academic teaching for each future course a student might follow. Until 2002, all part-time tutors were paid on a piece-work basis, for example in terms of:

- the number of students allocated and the credit points value of the course;
- the number of assignments marked;
- hours allocated for academic support.

(The Open University, 1999: 16)

Maternity and sick pay, etc. were also introduced in line with employment law.

However, a major change was the introduction of a new role and contract in 2002 which provided tutors with a formal salary paid monthly within a standard OU staff scale dependent on the salary banding of a particular module (for example in terms of its ICT requirements). The 2002 contract also (unusually for university part-time staff at the time) included two paid days per year for professional development related to issues of teaching and learning. It also introduced a new compulsory element: from 2004, tutors would be required 'to use information communication technology when appropriate for teaching and supporting students, accessing information, facilitating contact with academic units and administration' (The Open University, 2002–3 Appointments: 11). Both these areas have major professional development implications. From 2004, UK resident OU part-time tutors have also been eligible for University Superannuation Scheme (USS) pensions bringing their role and contract closer to 'internal' staff – that is central and regional academics, student services staff and all office-based staff in the OU, whether full or part time.

The 2002 contract is under review, but since 2010 it has been agreed that a process for 'Career Development and Staff Appraisal' (CDSA) is implemented for all tutors from February 2012. This mirrors the process which is already in place for 'internal staff'. In short, since 1971 OU part-time tutors have gradually gained greater parity with 'internal' staff in terms of salary scales and benefits and these are the latest examples of the process.

This brief survey of the evolving contracts and roles of OU part-time tutors illustrates the ways in which some elements of professional development are driven by institutional policies and strategies, for example:

- In the first years of the OU, much time was spent on encouraging traditional teachers to develop skills in facilitating learning rather than traditional lecturing.
- The tutor's role in student support is very important, particularly for those who teach level 1 (first-year) modules, and this has professional development implications.
- Contractual and university requirements for engagement with ICTs have major professional development implications. Many of these are common to all universities, but use of ICTs in distance education is perhaps of particular importance.
- CDSA requires considerable engagement and development – not just for tutors but also for their managers.

The ways in which professionals learn

A great deal of institutional resource for professional development is often invested in face-to-face events, which can have an important role but are difficult (and expensive) to deliver at scale for part-time tutors at a distance. Records of attendance at such events within the OU suggest that there are a number of individuals who attend everything they possibly can, while other staff attend rarely if at all. Sometimes it is exactly this latter group of staff who might benefit most from opportunities for professional development.

Research by Knight *et al.* on general professional formation as a teacher within the OU, based on surveys of 2401 part-time tutors and 248 'internal' staff, indicated that staff learn to teach in higher education mainly by doing the job; and secondly by the experience of having been taught in higher education (2006: 323). The authors therefore suggest that we should move away from event-delivery methods and pay more attention to informal and non-formal learning – not purely on practical grounds but because 'formal and established methods were reported to be appropriate for learning to take on a specific role, whereas social learning and practice were associated with general formation as a teacher' (2006: 324). This conclusion is supported by Prebble *et al.* (2004) whose synthesis of research confirmed that short training courses had a limited impact on improving the quality of teaching.

In 2012 these findings take on a wider significance as ICTs impact increasingly on all aspects of teaching, learning and professional development globally.

Principles and practice

All development for tutors (as for all other university staff) has a threefold purpose. Expressed in terms of the tutors' role these are:

- to enable tutors to support students in the best possible way;
- to support tutors' own development;
- to support wider university objectives.

All publically funded UK universities are accountable for the use of resources and the quality of the teaching they deliver. Investment in professional development of staff is clearly of vital importance in both these areas. However, what has been of particular importance in relation to the OU's mission to be 'open to people, places and ideas' is the support needed to ensure the success of students from unconventional backgrounds who are often balancing study with other roles. Enabling tutors to support students is therefore of prime importance. However, professionals need support too – the following sections provide examples which show how both of these aims might be achieved. Finally, professional development needs to be aligned with university objectives for all staff – an example of this is also provided.

Professional development is based on a number of principles:

- that professional learning cannot be contained within a one-off event but is something that we are all engaged in all the time – and this involves all staff, not just part-time tutors;
- that it is a collaborative process;
- that developmental activities should model the student experience and so encourage reflective practice (Gaskell and Mills, 2007);
- that student feedback can improve teaching practice, but only if mediated (Gibbs and Coffey, 2001; Brennan et al., 2006).

Development draws on strategies relevant to supporting tutors at scale; for example modelling, cascading and peer support.

It is also supported by a wide range of media – online through, for example, 'TutorHome' (the OU's portal for tutors), forums, Elluminate (a synchronous audio conferencing tool), social networking tools and so on. These are complemented by print-based materials and face-to-face workshops and events, though as a distance teaching institution these may be used only where they are particularly relevant.

The rest of this chapter provides selected examples of how these policies, principles and strategies are illustrated in practice.

Professional development to support students: modelling

The role of the OU tutor in supporting students is of key importance to student success – and also to their perception of the quality of the course/module they are studying. Research by Richardson *et al.* in 2003 using the Course Experience Questionnaire and Academic Engagement Form demonstrated that, for those studying at a distance, 'the role of course tutors in supporting academic engagement was crucial to the students' perceptions of the academic quality of their courses' (Richardson *et al.*, 2003: 37).

There is a wide range of online resources and information to support the core role of student support through the OU's online portal 'TutorHome'. This provides all tutors with their student lists plus additional information that will assist them in their support, for example if students have any disabilities or additional requirements, if they are under 18 and so on. This is the key source of information for tutors with regard to their students and is the most frequently accessed site on the portal. TutorHome also includes a wide range of developmental resources for tutors (Gaskell *et al.*, 2005).

In more general terms, our practices for supporting the development of tutors have been informed by the proposition that

> the principles and practices of learning which have been developed to promote student learning . . . are equally applicable to tutors as learners (and, indeed, to staff developers as learners). Therefore the notion of tutor-centredness as a mirror of student-centredness is crucial in staff development activities.
>
> (Wright, 2001)

This embodies the concept of modelling the student experience to encourage reflection and has been used very successfully in supporting tutors as students in online courses, whether the course is especially developed for OU staff (Macdonald and Poniatowska, 2011) or a student module studied within a tutor cohort (Warren and Gaskell, 2002).

Comments from tutors taking an OU module to develop their ICT skills in the early days of ICT developments illustrate the ways in which the student experience impacts on the professional learning and reflection of tutors:

> I carry very vivid memories of what it feels like to struggle with something which does not come naturally and with which I am getting nowhere despite hours of effort. This is something I shall hold on to when I am trying to help students who are struggling.
>
> (Warren and Gaskell, 2002: 11)

The course, as with many professional development activities and sessions, was for tutors only and run by a fellow tutor and so supportive of peer collaboration.

The principle of modelling also underpins our process of monitoring the marking of student assignments, which forms part of our quality assurance processes. Just as tutors support student learning through constructive feedback, so monitors support tutors in their marking through monitoring reports. From every 'batch' of perhaps 20 assignments marked, up to three will be reviewed by a central academic or senior colleague in the faculty who will comment on whether the grading is accurate and the feedback constructive. As tutors become more experienced, this 'sampling' becomes less frequent, but it is a critical part of the early professional development of new tutors or tutors on new modules. These monitoring reports are then passed to the tutor's immediate line manager who can add comments (and indeed disagree) if they wish.

Professional development to support tutors: cascading, peer support and student feedback

There are a large number of ways in which the OU supports professional development for individual tutors. These include:

- a range of regional and national programmes covering core aspects of the tutor role, such as making the most effective use of the electronic assignment system and supporting disabled students – these are all supported by a cascade model whereby Chairs of Staff development groups (who are usually the Staff Tutor managers of tutors) are provided with the latest information and staff development opportunities in advance of any event.
- a staff development fund for tutors to which they can apply for support to attend conferences, study non-OU courses, etc.;
- a 'buddy system' of regional/national expert tutors who will support individuals with various ICT skills necessary for teaching with the OU, again supported by a cascade model;
- the OU's library providing Information Literacy training for all tutors via a cascade model – interested tutors attend a central briefing and then disseminate outcomes to their own locations;
- a booklet on professional development which includes discussion of ways in which tutors can take ownership of their own development and seek a range of options within the university to develop themselves (Coats *et al.*, 2008);
- the option to take the OU's Certificate in Higher Education Practice at no cost – completion of this entitles a tutor to Fellowship of the UK's Higher

Education Academy, an independent organisation supported by grants from the four UK higher education funding bodies which provides individual professional accreditation routes for academic staff and has been instrumental in developing the UK's Professional Standards Framework for teaching and learning in Higher Education.

(www.heacademy.ac.uk/ukpsf)

Peer support

Comprehensive staff development programmes are put in place for new tutors and include paid face-to-face role briefings and course/module briefings. However, new tutors report that one of the aspects of support they regard most highly is that of their mentor, usually a more experienced tutor who is teaching the same course. Paid mentors are appointed to support each new tutor and provide a continuing source of support and development through the new tutor's first year. They may, for example, visit each others' online tutor-group forums (with appropriate agreement from students) to illustrate and explore ways of supporting students. The mentor role provides an example of the ways in which peer support can be particularly important both for the support and development of new tutors at scale and also involve and develop the expertise of more experienced colleagues.

Further examples of peer and cohort support include two important short courses specially developed for OU tutors which have been designed to develop online skills through a focus on pedagogy rather than technology, and are moderated by experienced tutors. 'Tutor-moderators' provides an introduction to moderating online forums and has proved very successful when undertaken by cohorts of tutors (Macdonald and Campbell, 2010); while 'VLE choices' provides examples of how to select the most useful Web 2.0 tool to support learning by focussing first on the pedagogical objectives of a particular tutorial activity or module design and then on what tool would best meet these aims (Macdonald and Poniatowska, 2011). Again these courses encourage tutors (and other staff) to reflect on their learning and apply it to their support of students through their different roles.

Student feedback to inform professional development

The use of student feedback to inform professional development is well documented. Prebble *et al.* note that 'student assessments are among the most reliable and accessible indicators of the effectiveness of teaching. When used appropriately they are likely to lead to significant improvements in the quality of teaching' (2004: x). How can these be used to inform professional development at a distance?

The provision of a printed 'Toolkit' for tutors in the 1990s entitled 'How do I know I am doing a good job?' (Hewitt *et al.*, 1997) provided a theoretical framework for practitioner engagement and templates for collecting student feedback to inform professional reflection. This was much used and is still in use today, particularly now it is available online and can be customised.

More recently and more extensively, our electronic student survey 'Developing Associate Lecturers through Student Feedback' (DALS), developed by Graham Gibbs and Martin Coffey, provides all students at a distance with the opportunity to provide feedback on their experiences of their tutor. There are 18 core questions, but unlike many standard surveys, tutors can customise the survey in advance in order to gain feedback on any additional aspects of their teaching that they would like to include. They can, for example, add questions from a bank of 53 about their use of telephone or online support if that is relevant to their programme.

Collecting feedback by itself has been shown to have little impact on the quality of teaching. However, if supported by consultation with a colleague or manager, it can have a major impact on an individual's professional development (Gibbs and Coffey, 2000; Brennan *et al.*, 2003). The DALS process enables this through the electronic collation of student responses which are then sent to the tutor's line manager who can add comments, engage in discussion over the telephone and then deliver it to the tutor through TutorHome.

Professional development to support wider university objectives: career development and staff appraisal (CDSA)

Wider university objectives can seem a little remote to a part-time tutor working for three or four hours a week at a distance. The ten English regions and three nations (Scotland, Wales and Northern Ireland) have had a particularly important role to play here in providing the local face of the university for tutors, as tutors provide the local face of the university for students. Increasingly, online interaction and social networking systems are providing more extensive opportunities for communication.

With the increasing use of online resources, the dissemination of university news through TutorHome and the introduction of podcasts from the vice-chancellor which are accessible to all staff are valuable ways of keeping in touch.

Of particular importance in this context is the introduction of 'Career Development and Staff Appraisal' (CDSA) for all OU tutors. The CDSA process is in place for internal staff but its mainstreaming in February 2012 to all tutors provides the opportunity for the OU to align processes for all staff and to ensure that there is a formal and recorded occasion for discussion between a tutor and their line manager within an agreed timeframe. As for other OU staff, CDSA provides tutors with the opportunity to reflect on their past activities in the context of university priorities such as student retention, look forward to new objectives and identify their own development needs. Feedback from tutors so far is very positive about this development:

> I found the process very helpful in clarifying my thoughts and giving me objectives for the near future.

> The process flowed very smoothly. I was reassured that I am doing a satisfactory job for the OU.

> I wanted to ask questions hoping for a few ideas. I left full of ideas and the motivation to carry them out.

Conclusion

In the OU's staff survey 2008, more than 90 per cent of tutors said they were proud to be a member of The Open University staff – described elsewhere as 'the best job in UK Higher Education!' (Simpson, 2009: 1).

The OU's development since the first students were admitted in 1971 has had implications for the role of the tutor – and hence for their professional development needs. University policy and contractual decisions, together with employment law, have increasingly led to tutors gaining terms and conditions of service (such as pensions) some of which are similar to those of internal OU staff – something that is not always available to other part-time teachers in higher education.

The challenges of providing professional development and support for diverse groups of tutors within a distance teaching system have been addressed by the policies, principles and practices outlined above. This has met with some success with tutors claiming that they receive more effective professional development from the OU than they do from other institutions for which they also work.

However, the traditional distance education processes and roles are changing, just as much as they are for conventional institutions who take on dual-mode or online learning. In the case of the OU, some of the major changes involve a reorientation of the traditional distance education distinction between the roles of tutor/facilitator who supports learning and module teams who prepare the materials now that there are far greater possibilities for communication between the two; the use of social networking tools to support collaboration at all levels; an increased need for accredited professional teaching qualifications for staff who may only work on very small contracts; and the affordances for learning and teaching of ever newer technologies which all require staff training and professional development in their use.

Our challenge will be to ensure that that all teaching staff have appropriate support and development for all the future changes in distance education to come.

Note

1   The terms 'associate lecturer (or AL)' and 'tutor' are used almost interchangeably within the OU. For simplicity I use the term 'tutor' in this chapter.

References

Beevers, R. (1975) The function of the part-time academic staff in the Open University teaching system. *Teaching at a Distance* 3: 11–15.

Brennan, J., Brighton, R., Moon, N., Richardson, J., Rindl, J. and Williams, R. (2006) *Collecting and Using Student Feedback on Quality and Standards of Learning and Teaching in HE: a report to HEFCE.* London: Higher Education Funding Council of England (HEFCE).

Coats, M., Gaskell A. and Wiltsher, C. (2008) *Your Professional Development: a guide for Associate Lecturers.* Milton Keynes: The Open University.

Daniel, J.S. (1999) *Mega-Universities and Knowledge Media: strategies for higher education.* London: Kogan Page.

Gaskell, A. and Kelly, P. (2006) Learner support and quality enhancement at the Open University UK. Paper presented to the 22nd ICDE conference Promoting Quality in On-line, Flexible and Distance Education, Rio de Janeiro.

Gaskell, A. and Mills, R. (2007) Professional development for part-time tutors: the changing environment of the Open University UK. Paper presented to the EDEN conference New Learning 2.0: Emerging Digital Territories, Developing Continuities, New Divides. Naples.

Gaskell, A., Gilmartin, K. and Kelly, P. (2005) Towards a networked learning community: using ICTs to enhance learner support, *Indian Journal of Open Learning* 14 (3), 225–234.

Gibbs, G. (2004) Associate lecturers' perceptions of their role. Internal paper, SSRG 89/2004. Milton Keynes: The Open University.

Gibbs, G. and Coffey, M. (2000) What is the training of university teachers attempting to achieve, and how could we tell if it makes any difference? Available online at: www.uni-bielefeld.de/IZHD/ICED/gibbs-lang.html (accessed 12 June 2006).

Gibbs, G. and Coffey, M. (2001) Developing an associate lecturer student feedback questionnaire: evidence and issues from the literature, *Student Support Research Group Report no 1.* Milton Keynes: The Open University.

Hewitt, P., Lentell, H., Phillips, M. and Stevens, V. (1997) *How Do I Know I Am Doing a Good Job? Open Teaching Toolkit.* Milton Keynes: The Open University.

King, B. (2010) Reshaping distance and online education around a national university in regional Australia, *Open Learning* 25 (2), 131–140.

Knight, P., Tait, J. and Yorke, M. (2006) The professional learning of teachers in higher education, *Studies in Higher Education* 31 (3), 319–339.

Macdonald, J. and Campbell, A. (2010) Activity design in online professional development for university staff, *European Journal of Open, Distance and eLearning*. Retrieved from www.eurodl.org/.

Macdonald, J. and Poniatowska, B. (2011) Designing the professional development of staff for teaching online: an OU (UK) case study, *Distance Education* 32 (1), 119–134.

Moore, M.G. and Kearsley, G. (2005) *Distance Education: a systems view* (2nd edn), Belmont, CA: Thomson Wadsworth.

Peters, O. (1998) *Learning and Teaching in Distance Education: an analysis and interpretations from an international perspective*. London: Kogan Page.

Prebble, T., Hargraves, H., Leach, L., Naidoo, K., Suddaby, G. and Zepke, N. (2004) *Impact of Student Support Services and Academic Development Programmes on Student Outcomes in Undergraduate Tertiary Study: A Synthesis of the Research*. New Zealand: Ministry of Education.

Richardson, J.T.E., Long, G.L. and Woodley, A. (2003) Academic engagement and perceptions of quality in distance and e-Learning, *Open Learning* 18 (3), 223– 244.

Simpson, O. (2009) *An Introduction to Your Role with the Open University: a guide for Associate Lecturers*. Milton Keynes: The Open University.

Tait, A. (2000) Planning student support for open and distance learning, *Open Learning* 15 (3), 287–299.

Tait, J., Yorke, M. and Knight, P. (2004) Learning to teach in the OU: associate lecturers' study. Internal paper. Milton Keynes: The Open University.

The Open University. (1999) *Teaching with the Open University*. Milton Keynes: The Open University.

The Open University (2002) *Teaching with the Open University and Course information for 2002–3 appointments*. Milton Keynes: The Open University.

Thorpe, M. (2002) Rethinking Learner support: the challenge of collaborative online learning, *Open Learning* 17 (2), 105–119.

Warren, James P. and Gaskell, Anne F. (2002) Tutors as learners: overcoming barriers to learning ICT skills, paper presented at the European Conference on Educational Research (ECER), Lisbon, 11–14 September.

Wright, T. (2001) Towards a holistic view of staff development of regional tutorial staff at the Open University, *Systemic Practice and Action Research* 14 (6), 735–762.

SECOND PART: DEVELOPING PART-TIME PROGRAMMES TO SUPPORT PART-TIME TEACHERS

5

WHAT MAKES A REALLY GOOD SUPPORT PROGRAMME FOR PART-TIME LECTURERS IN HIGHER EDUCATION?

Anne Lee

The context

There is a fierce debate about whether *full-time* academics should have compulsory or voluntary teacher-training provision (Gibbs 2008; Department for Business, Innovation and Skills (BIS) 2011; Mroz 2011). The picture is even more confused for part-time academics, yet the recruitment of part-time tutors or lecturers is increasing and this group offers essential flexibility to universities when planning their staffing needs. In this chapter I will argue that we need to take a holistic approach to supporting our part-time academics. This group comprises the widest variety of teachers in higher education: they include PhD students and early career researchers who want to build up a teaching portfolio, returning academics who have taken a career break and industrial, commercial or public-sector specialists who have a special expertise and who might work as part-time lecturers and/or co-supervisors. In the USA they are often referred to as 'adjunct staff' (D'Andrea 2002) and graduate teaching assistants who are working part-time are also included in this group.

I have worked with many such staff and the largest sub-group has been the many early career researchers who attended an accredited programme 'Preparing to Teach' at a research-led university in the UK. The time spent studying for a PhD offers a wonderful window of opportunity to inspire our newest and brightest academics to want to get involved in teaching at the highest level, as well as to complete their research. The second group of part-time lecturers were professional engineers who were key in the programme design and teaching of a master's programme in transport planning. This was a ground-breaking programme because it was external practitioners who took the lead. The people with the most up-to-date knowledge were practising transport engineers – but none of them had any experience of teaching at university level; indeed a few of them did not have master's degrees themselves (see the case study at the end of this chapter and Pitt *et al.* 2010). The final group of part-time lecturers that I have worked with were experienced tutors who, for a variety of reasons, did not work full time:

some had family responsibilities, some had portfolio careers and some were waiting for the opportunity to work full time. This last group were difficult to contact: across a large university they can be hired on different terms and conditions and for differing periods of time, but when they were located and invited to participate in staff development activities such as teaching and learning conferences, their enthusiasm for being involved betrayed the isolation they felt from the wider organisation.

I contend that support for these peripatetic but essential teachers needs to be flexible, accessible and inclusive. 'Flexible' to cover the wide range of previous experience that such people bring with them, 'accessible' because they will all have serious time commitments elsewhere (whether it is to their research, professional life or families) and 'inclusive' because this group of employees are the most easily marginalised people in university life.

'Support' can mean many things: there are technical and practical issues that the part-time teacher will need to know about, and many of them may be issues that full-time employees take for granted. Access to an email account, library resources, the relevant (and related) student handbooks, pension arrangements, parking, a desk and computer may all be automatically arranged for full-time staff, and can be forgotten when part-time lecturers start work.

There is the academic life of the department to be considered – are the part-time lecturers or tutors invited to departmental meetings, to briefings by faculty or division heads, to journal clubs and to seminars that may be organised by staff or students? Many departments will ask their senior students and junior researchers to organise and convene conferences, and part-time staff can both find these illuminating and offer their insights as a friendly but critical audience. A simple question to ask is: which email lists are part-time staff included on?

Part-time staff are rarely involved in discussions about curriculum design, development or review, yet their insights can be penetrating. Similarly, they need to be involved in the design of assessment criteria (as well as being invited to any training in marking and assessment) because it is often on the shoulders of these staff that the marking load will land. Some part-time staff will have extensive subject knowledge, and they can be invited to share that with other full-time staff. However, others may be less experienced and assured, so they may be very pleased to be invited to attend lectures given by other members of staff. Many part-time staff have never had the opportunity to question and try to understand the different levels of learning in higher education, so an introduction to a qualifications framework or the equivalent Bologna framework is useful (especially how learning outcomes at bachelor's, master's and doctoral programmes differ from each other (see a UK example at: www.qaa.ac.uk/academicinfrastructure/FHEQ/FHEQCreditStatement.asp).

These generic statements need to be tempered with information about how they are interpreted in different disciplinary and institutional contexts. A useful outline of outcomes-based curriculum design in various disciplinary contexts can be found in a chapter headed 'Organising teaching and learning: outcomes-based planning' (D'Andrea 2003).

Mentoring can offer the most profound and transformative form of feedback, and it can be available to part-time staff through programme leaders and course directors if they see this as part of their role (Clutterbuck and Ragins 2002; Lee 2007). Conversations about how a programme might be taught, focussing on one lecture or seminar, co-teaching and encouraging part-time staff to observe others teach can all be very helpful. Some universities are very good at advertising a public lecture programme – so all it needs is for the programme leader to highlight this as an opportunity for self-development. Other universities may not be so accessible, so a change in the departmental culture needs to be sought, and this can be a helpful development for all staff – not just the part-timers. Changing departmental culture can, of course, be the most difficult task (Seel 2005), yet it is possible to start such a transformation in small ways: perhaps by organising seminars led by doctoral students and inviting all academic staff (full and part time) to attend them. Those in a line-management position can also take the lead by ensuring that part-time staff are included in appraisals, exam boards, invitations to apply for scholarships aimed specifically at part-time staff, staff development opportunities and staff meetings (D'Andrea and Gosling 2000; D'Andrea 2002).

Relationships matter and yet we can easily forget to invite part-time staff to annual parties, or other festivities. Many part-time staff are employed because they already have a relationship with at least one key member of the academic team, and that confers a special responsibility on that member of staff to ensure they are included. They can try to consciously widen the number of contacts that the part-time lecturer has in the department and the university, as well as introducing them to other part-timers, and this all helps to increase a feeling of loyalty towards the institution and commitment to the programme. A policy of inclusion and moving newcomers from the periphery towards the centre, and from apprenticeship to mastery, has been well described by Lave and Wenger (1991) and Wenger (1998).

This overview of the different types of support that can be provided can be formulated into a table which I have argued (Lee 2012) combines organisational, social, philosophical, emancipatory and emotional approaches (see Table 5.1).

Table 5.1 A framework for providing support for part-time academic staff

Functional	Enculturation	Critical thinking	Emancipation	Relationship development
Including part-time staff in teaching awards and staff review processes and ensuring feedback is given on performance.	Involving part-time staff in induction, departmental seminars, teaching and learning conferences, exam boards, departmental meetings, etc.	Involving part-time staff in curriculum design, development and review.	Offering mentoring support in the planning, delivering and evaluation of teaching.	Including part-time staff in departmental social events
Enabling part-time staff to take accredited teaching and learning courses.	Ensuring part-time staff are part of team discussions before giving them assessment tasks.	Involving part-time staff in design of assessment criteria.	Encouraging self-reflection.	Introducing part-time staff to each other
Ensuring part-time staff have relevant course and staff handbooks and are aware of emergency procedures.	Including part-time staff in relevant email circulation lists.	Enabling part-time staff to align their work to national and international standards.	Enabling part-time staff to observe others teach.	Encouraging part-time staff to meet academics working in related disciplines
Ensuring part-time staff have an email account and relevant technical support.	Ensuring part-time staff are comfortable with the learning technologies used and have access to course materials on web-based learning systems.		Offering opportunities for part-time staff to think about how this work contributes to their own career plans.	

Review of provision for graduate teaching assistants across the UK

The UKCGE (United Kingdom Council for Graduate Education) was formed to advance graduate education in all academic disciplines and itself conducts research to map current practice. It was concerned to identify the educational development available for doctoral students (who, when they are recruited as teachers, are often referred to as 'graduate teaching assistants'). A major survey of all its partner institutions identified some sophisticated provision for graduate teaching assistants (GTAs) and the following section is drawn from their report (Lee and Pettigrove 2010).

The gap between teaching as a GTA and becoming a full academic member of staff has been defined as 'the opportunity to exercise significant agency in relation to teaching' (Kahn 2009: 197). There is also a debate about nomenclature: GTAs are often PhD or doctoral students. A common term across Europe is the phrase 'early career researchers', while the Oxford Centre for Academic Practice uses the phrase 'early career academics'.

One of the trends identified in the UKCGE review was the move from developing generic teaching and learning skills to supporting GTAs to work in their disciplinary contexts. Provision might be generic (and thus foster interdisciplinary relationships) but there was often an emphasis on encouraging staff to apply this in their own disciplines. A group of academic staff can be encouraged to focus on one lecture as a case study for improvement. The USA work on lesson study (Dotger 2011) was a good example of this.

Chism (1998) listed nine broad changes that were likely to occur, post-1998, in the skills and knowledge base of graduate student teachers. Lightly paraphrased, these anticipated changes might be an increasing focus on the teacher's deep understanding of their discipline through an increasing appreciation of interdisciplinary connections – whereby the teacher becomes increasingly expert in accessing and evaluating information as it proliferates in their own and adjunct areas of expertise, and in relating ideas and approaches of other fields to their own

- skill in interactive pedagogy, as required by the shift in emphasis from teaching as information transfer toward teaching as the facilitation of learning to learn;
- understanding of student learning, distilled as a model of the variety of ways in which students learn and how to facilitate learning in those ways
- knowledge of instructional design – whereby teachers heighten their understanding of principles of sequencing, as appropriate in face-to-face and virtual or electronically aided interactions;

- teamwork, whereby designing and delivering instruction comes increasingly to include, alongside collegial and pedagogically effective subject experts, the graphic artists, videographers, programmers, systems analysts and others whose contribution will derive more from their technical knowledge and computer competence;
- links with experience, whereby learning (including its material aids, and its evaluation and application by students) is related more closely to the workplace and everyday settings;
- appreciation for difference, whereby the teacher becomes increasingly skilled at allowing for, and drawing advantage from, increasing student population diversity;
- assessment techniques, whereby increased understanding of the principles of assessment give rise increasingly to the delineation of learning outcomes and the development of scoring rubrics and other strategies for assessing learning effects;
- understanding and facility with human relations, requiring development of skills in dealing with interpersonal dynamics within instructional development project teams, and in the facilitation of individual and collaborative student learning.

(Chism 1998: 1–17)

The report identified a persistent 'atomised' mode of preparation (e.g. Lowman and Mathie 1993) which focussed on immediate classroom management techniques. Whilst this may be necessary at the beginning of part-time teachers' experience it needs to be followed by a more integrated holistic approach to development for part-time lecturers where an introduction to teaching and learning in higher education is seen as part of an introduction to academic practice (e.g. Fisher and Taithe 1998). Young and Bippus (2008) move beyond the calming of the novice GTAs' anxiety to the development of 'self-efficacy' (Bandura 1994) in a GTA as a more comprehensive desirable outcome.

Three themes have emerged under the banner of holism and the teacher-scholar:

1 *Academic practice.* The conceptualisation of 'academic practice' and 'academic work' has developed substantially in the most recent decade. It is a contemporary and widely discussed topic. As Blackmore and Blackwell (2006: 375) state: 'In conceptualising academic work, we advocate an explicit concern with the whole faculty role, including teaching, research, knowledge transfer and civic engagement, leadership, management and administration, and with their interrelationships.'

2 *Interplay*. This theme derives from the conceptualisation of the factors that shape, constrain or facilitate academic development as 'interplay between context and agency' (Kahn 2009: 197). When talking about the factors that shape, hinder and help leadership development in academia, Taylor (2005: 31) speaks of the 'interplay of person, role, strategy, and institution'. Knight and Trowler (2000: 69) share Åkerlind's stand (2007) when they say: 'the ways in which academic staff (faculty) experience their work often inhibits them from taking up what the research consensus suggests are ways to be better teachers'. The most frequent locus of interplay is in confrontations with change within an institution, or in and across the higher education sector as a whole. Building on the work of Archer (2003) and Kahn (2009) we can identify three ways in which person, role, strategy and institution can affect part-time lecturers' conceptualisation of their role. First, the structural and cultural factors determining 'how it is done around here'; second, the lecturer's own configuration of concerns and thirdly the lecturer's ability to reflect metacognitively and become agentic. The first is addressed by cultural developments such as those described above and the latter two require an opportunity to develop self-awareness, self-efficacy and skill building.

3 *The integration of GTA training in doctoral training.* This theme suggests a withdrawal from the idea that teaching can or should be dealt with as a separable and self-contained knowledge and skill set. It derives from the re-conceptualisation of GTAs as early career academics who, by virtue of that status, deserve training which provides an induction into the holistic concept of academic practice, and whose training should 'occur during the period of the PhD, because that is when academic identity is being formed within the process of professional socialization' (Gunn 2007: 536, citing Henkel 2000, MacInnis 2000, and Park 2004). There is a call for the creation of 'teacher scholars'.

Orthodoxy, canon and emerging concepts

Kandlbinder and Peseta (2009), drawing on survey responses from 46 certificate courses in higher education teaching and learning across Australia, New Zealand and the UK, identified five concepts that appear to have achieved 'key' status in those courses:

1 Reflective practice as explored by Schon's book *The Reflective Practitioner* (1991) and elaborated by Brookfield's *Becoming a Critically Reflective Teacher* (1995).

2   Constructive alignment as initially explored by Cohen in his article 'Instructional alignment' (1987) and elaborated by Biggs in his article 'Enhancing teaching through constructive alignment' (1996) and his book *Teaching for Quality Learning at University* (Biggs and Tang 2007).

3   Student approaches to learning, in particular the concepts of surface and deep approaches to learning as initially explored by Marton and Saljo in their article 'On qualitative differences in learning: 1. Outcome and process' (1976) and subsequently synthesised and commented on by Ramsden in *Learning to Teach in Higher Education* whose 2nd edition came out in 2003.

4   Scholarship of teaching as outlined in Boyer's *Scholarship Reconsiderate*: *Priorities of the professoriate* (1990) and further explored in Glassick *et al.*'s *Scholarship Assessed*: *Evaluation of the professoriate* (1997), and subsequently by numerous published works including Kreber and Cranton's article 'Exploring the scholarship of teaching' (2000).

5   Assessment-driven learning as explored by Gibbs and Simpson's article 'Does your assessment support your students' learning?' (2004/2005).

The authors are careful to avoid the suggestion that the five identified key concepts constitute the core of an orthodoxy (and in their appendix there is a much longer and more provocative list of 32 concepts), and it is interesting to look at these key concepts in the light of the themes that the UKCGE survey of 68 universities revealed.

Themes included in programmes for GTAs in UK universities 15

Reflective practice	Adult learning
Constructive alignment	Curriculum design
Student approaches to learning	Flexible learning
Scholarship of teaching	Formative assessment
Assessment-driven learning	Student-centred teaching
Student-centred learning	Teaching/research nexus
Student diversity	Conceptions of teaching and learning
Active learning	Diversity in teaching methods
Constructivism	Institutional context
Evidence-based teaching	Learning styles
Academic professionalism	Learning through variation
Experiential learning	Novice-expert learning
Inclusive teaching	Research-informed teaching
Threshold concepts	Student autonomy
Approaches to teaching	Student-focused teaching
Situated learning	Student learning in context

Respondents to the survey gave titles for their provisions which very much focused on words such as an 'introduction', 'induction' and 'preparation' to teaching and learning and assessment. The provision was open variously to postgraduate researchers with some or no teaching experience, teaching assistants, postgraduate teaching assistants, new full-time academics and associate lecturers.

The form of provision was balanced overall between compulsory and optional: 57 per cent of programmes were compulsory and 43 per cent were optional but the newer institutions were more inclined to make their programmes compulsory. Nearly 50 per cent of those responding offered accredited provision, mostly at master's level. There was also a clear movement towards linking provision to the HEA (Higher Education Academy) professional standards and at the time of writing these are under review. All those who were accredited had gained accreditation from the Higher Education Academy at Associate Fellowship level. The provision offered varied from one half-day workshop, seven sessions, a one-week intensive residential and there was one 24-month programme. These programmes required a significant amount of independent study time.

Quality assurance mechanisms included double-marking, external examiners, peer observation of teaching, participant feedback and evaluation forms, liaison committees and reports to teaching and learning committees. The main topics included in development programmes for graduate teaching assistants frequently included the following:

- learning theory;
- student approaches to learning;
- student autonomy – encouraging independent learning;
- equity, fairness and student diversity;
- approaches to teaching: individual, small class, large class, lab, field;
- curriculum development, course design and materials preparation;
- learning technologies and e-learning (blended, distance and face-to-face learning);
- educational taxonomies;
- types of knowledge;
- alignment or congruence of goals, learning activities and assessment;
- types of assessment;
- giving feedback: formative uses of assessment;
- student-led, peer-led and self-evaluation;
- reflection and continuing professional development as a teacher;
- scholarship in and of teaching and learning;
- approaches to teaching in the discipline.

Sixteen institutions reported offering additional curriculum subjects or work-based learning opportunities; the ones listed below include feedback from different types of observed practice, use of learning technologies, recent developments in higher education, personal presentation, team building and some subject specific activities. Additional topics that were mentioned at least once by the institutions surveyed included:

1 observation of teaching practice, peer observations, micro teaching and the opportunity to engage in video interactive guidance (VIG) with a trained VIG facilitator;
2 resources in a handbook and on the web;
3 quality assurance in higher education;
4 team working, communication, working safely and presentation skills;
5 pedagogic research and research informed teaching;
6 'demonstrating' for science PhD students who teach;
7 overview of higher education in the UK, the role of the HEA (Higher Education Academy), JISC and other organisations;
8 auditing your own professional development needs/professional development planning and evaluating your own practice/student feedback to improve provision;
9 analysis of the needs of students from diverse backgrounds, including overseas students; students with disabilities or health problems; students from widening participation backgrounds;
10 contributing to the planning and delivery of teaching, learning and assessment;
11 voice and presentation workshop/video and audio activities;
12 using ICT and e-learning in higher education/participation in StudyZone and e-portfolio activities;
13 subject-based case studies of good practice in higher education;
14 facilitating learning in the laboratory/workshop/ICT suite;
15 ethical issues;
16 dealing with plagiarism;
17 research-related teaching;
18 a portfolio including evidence of participation in StudyZone conferencing.

They are reproduced as lists so that a curriculum designer can check for any omissions that might be relevant in their institutional contexts in their own programmes.

There were also a variety of ways in which these programmes were delivered and these included: lectures, seminars, workshops, online learning, individual tutorials, discipline-based mentoring, action learning sets and enquiry-based learning, role play, micro-teaching sessions, teaching observations, forum theatre, symposiums, guided reading, peer partnering and projects. Some institutions reported using individual tutorials from course team members and faculty academics, induction packs (including the induction pack created by the UK-based professional development body Staff and Educational Development Association (SEDA)), blended learning and an intensive residential programme.

Over half of the programmes were formally assessed and methods of assessment included portfolios, teaching observation, submission of teaching materials, pedagogic research projects, case studies, CPD plans, examinations, essays, learning contracts, annotated bibliographies, journal article critique and demonstration of the abilities to use learning technologies. The methods of assessment used (like the student handbooks, course design and methods of delivery) are an unspoken signal to the participant of 'good practice' and are all described in more detail in the original UKCGE report.

In summary the respondents identified the following elements as the most useful aspects of their provision.

- an enquiry-led process;
- reflective assessments;
- faculty and discipline-based input;
- contributions from (slightly) more experienced GTAs;
- the provision of comprehensive information packs and useful handbooks;
- training in partnership between faculty and educational developers.

Less prominent but still notable were micro-teaching sessions and the opportunity to meet other GTAs from other faculties. The full report also lists the learning outcomes and learning activities that a review of the grey literature included. A final part of the survey was to examine how this provision linked into the opportunities available for full-time staff and it was evident that there needed to be opportunities for accreditation of prior learning (APL) and for a 'ladder of provision' that could enable the participant eventually to complete an MA.

The lists above can be used to create a curriculum plan for part-time lecturers, and a sample of such an approach is shown in Table 5.2.

Immersive learning

One university submitted an evaluation of their first three-day residential programme that had been run for 24 postgraduates who teach. The application process had included requiring them to submit a 150-word statement about why

Table 5.2 A sample matrix for planning a curriculum for part-time lecturers

Topic	Method(s) of delivery	Assessment process
Student approaches to learning	Research project Journal articles critique/symposium	Presentations Posters
Educational taxonomies	Lecture	Submission of own teaching plans as examples
Student, peer-led and self-evaluation, etc.	Case studies Teaching observations	Portfolio assignment

they felt they deserved a place on the residential programme, to submit a £50 deposit to reserve their place and make their own travel arrangements, and it was possible that these expectations encouraged participants to value the experience even more highly. The review of the programme was extremely positive, all participants said that they felt better prepared to support student learning and in particular the participants said how useful it was to work with people from across all disciplines. This approach has resonance with other powerful immersive and experiential learning experiences.

In addition to the work reviewed in the UKCGE report there are three further pieces of work that add to our understanding of what is desirable for part-time lecturers.

Gibbs (2008) in his review of teaching excellence identified 24 different conceptions of teaching excellence (as they underlay teaching award schemes). These included: exhibiting skilful behaviour, being student-focussed, engaging in the 'scholarship of teaching', undertaking reflection, being involved in various aspects of the teaching research nexus, displaying pedagogic subject knowledge, nurturing individuals, creating effective learning environments, creating or collaborating with course teams and innovating.

In the USA, Dotger (2011) writes about using lesson study (originally formulated in Japan) as a technique for supporting the professional development of GTAs. In her example, GTAs attended six three-hour seminars in preparation, co-observed each other's lessons and had a period of reflection. She found that there were small but significant movements towards becoming more learner-focussed, the GTAs began to take prior learning into account and identified areas that students found difficult more readily. The advantage of her situated learning approach is that impact can be more readily assessed, the difficulty is that if the GTAs do not have an opportunity to theorise and conceptualise what is going on, the opportunity for more profound development can be missed.

From Australia, Åkerlind (2011) has explored the differences between developing as a teacher and as an academic holistically. She argues that there is a symbiotic relationship between developing as a researcher and teacher. For example: depth of understanding, self-confidence and the ability to contribute to the field are all aspects of an academic's role that enhance each other and thus link teaching and research. The conclusion we could draw from this is that part-time teachers also need support and encouragement to develop as academics.

Case study: using practitioners as part-time lecturers

In the health sciences and medical studies it is quite usual to use experienced practitioners as tutors. This is a short version of a case study in a different field, transport planning, where an innovative MSc programme was developed and delivered by senior staff in industry in partnership with academia. A full report of this case study is available (Pitt *et al.*, 2010).

Training these experienced transport planning consultants to act as academic lecturers is at the heart of this case study; it required a specific development programme for them and a great deal of acclimatisation through joint consultative and steering group meetings.

First, here is some background about the actual MSc programme itself. The original need for the MSc in Transport Planning was identified by the industry; skills shortages had been reported in several trade journals. Staff from the University of Surrey invited representatives from consultancy firms and local authorities to join a Steering Group whose role was to set out the needs and expectations of the industry, guide the programme content, encourage student recruitment and put forward suitable staff to become practitioner teachers.

The objectives of this initiative were to develop a new industry model of higher education, enhance the relevance of the programme through use of senior industry-based practitioners as associate lecturers and project managers, provide continuing professional development for staff involved in delivering the modules, promote the profession and guide people to professional qualifications, make research facilities and results more readily available to industry, strengthen links between industry and universities and provide a forum for sharing good practice.

Two key principles for the MSc were to maximise the element of work-based learning and to enable distance learning. The emphasis on collecting all the taught material and collating it into course notes meant that international students could enrol and a wider variety of practitioners could come to teach in subsequent years.

The MSc programme was successfully validated in January 2006. The preparation of detailed learning material was then taken on by the module leader responsible together with other practitioners. Each team drafted:

- module notes which would be appropriate as distance learning material;
- summative and formative assessments;
- a session plan for the sections they were responsible for delivering.

All the industry practitioners (who needed also to develop as part-time lecturers) were highly qualified, experienced and up to date in their specialist fields. Some had teaching experience but most did not. Their role was not that of a typical associate lecturer – they were expected to set learning objectives, prepare teaching material, deliver the material, assess progress and give feedback to students about their performance.

Training the practitioners to work as academic lecturers lay at the centre of this case study of employer engagement. To ensure that they would be effective in these new roles a special training course was devised by the academic development unit for practising engineering consultants. The course was delivered over four separate days and covered: identifying appropriate level descriptors, writing learning outcomes, designing learning activities, giving feedback, designing assessment and marking. The practitioners were also introduced to web-based learning management software.

After the training programme for the practitioners had been completed and the MSc had been delivered, an evaluation identified that further work needed to be done by the course team. It was found that part-time lecturers needed to have more realistic expectations of their MSc students' prior knowledge and a greater understanding of different academic levels. In spite of training on marking and assessment, the quality of feedback varied considerably. The mapping of programme content and the work done to ensure a range of different part-time lecturers provided a cohesive learning experience was generally considered good. The university was well aware of potential difficulties for students, and ensured that the Programme Director was a focal point who was always available to liaise with and between the part-time tutors and students. Student feedback from student liaison committees and the university course assessment process revealed a high level of satisfaction. They liked the variety and, most importantly, they appreciated that they were being taught by senior professionals who were up to date, experienced and in touch with the industry.

In addition, there were issues relating to the practitioners:

- How could the large number of associate lecturers be managed effectively?
- How effective was the limited training to enable practitioners to become associate lecturers in a limited time and for limited input?
- How could they juggle priorities of teaching with the day job?
- How could practitioners be properly reimbursed for their input?

The study confirmed that, amongst the practitioners in any organisation, there are some very able teachers. It is also true that amongst academics, there are some very able practitioners and there is an argument for greater flexibility so that practitioners and academics can move more easily between these two roles. It further demonstrated that acclimatisation requires significant inclusion (the part-time lecturers who were recruited as module leaders attended regular meetings for up to two years before the programme commenced); most of the time all the part-time lecturers were included in all the emails relating to the development of the programme – even if they were only teaching a small part of it. All the part-time lecturers had to acquire an understanding of and ability to use the 'tools' of higher education (including level descriptors, constructive alignment, student-centred learning and learning technology). Finally, a key ingredient of the training programme for the part-time lecturers was to enable an open, reflexive attitude towards continuous improvement. There was no space for a blame culture; we had to create a positive learning environment for the part-time lecturers both for them to role-model for their MSc students and for the progress of the MSc programme as a whole.

Conclusions

At the beginning of this chapter it was proposed that a holistic approach needs to be taken to supporting part-time lecturers. However, we have seen that the approach needs to be both holistic, flexible, context-specific and quite detailed. Two-thirds of the programmes for GTAs were delivered by centrally funded departments and about one-third are delivered through discipline-based groups. There is some anxiety about the future of this provision where universities face funding pressures. There are few studies evaluating the impact on the students taught by those part-timers who have completed teaching and learning programmes, and this might be a useful next piece of research.

From the literature that we have reviewed, the survey of the preparation of teaching assistants and the case study where engineering consultants became part-time lecturers, the following conclusions can be drawn:

1   Part-time staff need to be identifiable and contactable and feel included, so they can be invited to attend programmes and conferences on teaching and learning.

    Programmes introducing teaching and learning to new part-time lecturers are very popular and it is a particularly useful and formative stage in doctoral students' careers for them to be able to undertake this type of development. The debate between those who value contextual and discipline-specific programmes, versus those who value generic and interdisciplinary programmes continues. There is a focus at this level on generic provision; it is for example more likely that 'approaches to teaching', 'feedback and assessment' will be included as generic provision. Teaching observations, workshops and micro-teaching sessions tend to be the most preferred discipline-specific forms of delivery. Consultants are occasionally used to deliver workshops and this provision has been well received.

2   There is also evidence from the survey that some international part-time lecturers are particularly strongly motivated to enrol on accredited programmes, and they have a high prestige factor for those returning home. Practitioner-lecturers in the case study were also enthusiastic about their teaching and learning programme, but it was not assessed or accredited. The common factor between these groups is that they are mostly volunteers. Over half the programmes for GTAs were assessed and there is a variety of methods used for that assessment. This is a particularly important feature if we want to use these programmes to model best practice.

    The most common forms of delivery were workshops, key readings and teaching observations; more innovative forms of delivery included action-learning sets, lesson study, forum theatre (where actors demonstrate different approaches to dealing with common problems) and participants creating symposia and giving papers or organising conferences.

3   Learning technologies form an important element of many programmes today. Input on innovative approaches such as the use of wikis, digital stories and virtual classrooms will need to be kept up to date.

4   Provision needs to be flexibly timed because many part-time lecturers have time commitments elsewhere.

5 Whilst many part-timers need and are concerned about teaching and lecturing techniques at the beginning of their study, a holistic approach to becoming an academic is still an important long-term focus.

References

Åkerlind, G.S. (2007) Constraints on academics' potential for developing as a teacher, *Studies in Higher Education*, 32, 1, 21–37.

Åkerlind, G.S. (2011) Separating the 'teaching' from the 'academic': possible unintended consequences, *Teaching in Higher Education*, 16, 2, 183–195.

Archer, M. (2003) *Structure, Agency and the Internal Conversation*. Cambridge: Cambridge University Press.

Bandura, A. (1994) 'Self-efficacy', *Encyclopaedia of Human Behaviour*, 4, 71–81. www.des.emory.edu/mfp/BanEncy.html (accessed 29 November 2009).

Becher, T. and Trowler, P. (2001) *Academic Tribes and Territories: Intellectual Enquiry and the Culture of Disciplines* (2nd edn). Buckingham: Open University Press.

Biggs, J. (1996) 'Enhancing teaching through constructive alignment', *Higher Education*, 32, 3, 347–364.

Biggs, J. and Tang, C. (2007) *Teaching for Quality Learning at University* (3rd edn). Buckingham: SRHE/Open University Press.

Blackmore, P., Blackwell, R. (2006) Strategic leadership in academic development, *Studies in Higher Education*, 31, 3, 373–387.

Boulent, I., Rafiq, I. and Kumar, P. (2011) Improving student learning in engineering discipline using student- and lecturer-led assessment approaches, *European Journal of Higher Education*, 1, 16, 233–248.

Boyer, E. (1990) *Scholarship Reconsidered: priorities of the professoriate*. San Francisco, CA: Jossey Bass.

Brookfield, S. (1995) *Becoming a Critically Reflective Teacher*. San Francisco, CA: Jossey Bass.

Chism, N.V.N. (1998) Preparing graduate students to teach: past, present, future, in M. Marincovich, J. Protsko and F. Stout (eds) *The Professional Development of Graduate Teaching Assistants*. Bolton: Anker, 1–17

Clutterbuck, D. and Ragins, B.R. (2002) *Mentoring and Diversity*. Oxford: Butterworth Heinemann.

Cohen, S.A. (1987) Instructional alignment: Searching for a magic bullet, *Educational Researcher*, 16, 8, 16–20.

D'Andrea, V.-M. (2002) *Professional Development of Part-time Teachers in the USA*. York: LTSN Generic Centre. www.heacademy.ac.uk/resources/detail/resource_database/id117_Professional_Development_of_Part-time_Teachers_in_the_USA (accessed 14 December 2011).

D'Andrea, V.-M. (2003) Organising teaching and learning: outcomes-based planning, in H. Fry, S. Ketteridge and S. Marshall (eds) *A Handbook for Teaching and Learning in Higher Education* (2nd edn). Abingdon: Routledge.

D'Andrea, V.-M. and Gosling, D. (2000) Promoting research in teaching and learning in higher education: two case studies of multi-disciplinary pedagogic research. Conference paper presented at the ESRC Teaching and Learning Research

Programme, First Annual Conference, University of Leicester, November. Available at: www.heacademy.ac.uk/resources/detail/teachingandresearch/Promoting_research _in_teaching_and_learning_in_higher_education (accessed 14 December 2011).

Department for Business, Innovation and Skills (BIS) (2011) Higher Education: students at the heart of the system. White Paper. The Stationery Office. Her Majesty's Government. http://c561635.r35.cf2.rackcdn.com/11-944-WP-students-at-heart. pdf (accessed 11 August 2011).

Dotger, S. (2011) Exploring and developing graduate teaching assistants' pedagogies via lesson study, *Teaching in Higher Education*, 16, 2 157–169.

Fisher, R. and Taithe, B. (1998) Developing university teachers: an account of a scheme designed for postgraduate researchers on a lecturing career path, *Teaching in Higher Education*, 3, 1, 37–50.

Gibbs, G. (2008) Teaching awards: theory, policy and practice. www.heacademy.ac. uk/assets/documents/evidence_informed_practice/Gibbs_Final_Report.pdf (accessed 11 August 2011).

Gibbs, G. and Simpson, C. (2004/5) Conditions under which assessment supports students' learning, *Learning and Teaching in Higher Education*, 1. www.york.ac.uk/ admin/aso/learningandteaching/gibbs%20article.do (accessed 15 August 2011).

Glassick, C.E., Huber, M.T. and Maeroff, G.I. (1997) *Scholarship Assessed: Evaluation of the professoriate*. San Francisco, CA: Jossey-Bass.

Gunn, V. (2007) What do graduate teaching assistants' perceptions of pedagogy suggest about current approaches to their vocational development?, *Journal of Vocational Education & Training*, 59, 4, 535–549

Kahn, P. (2009) Contexts for teaching and the exercise of agency in early-career academics: perspectives from realist social theory, *International Journal for Academic Development*, 14, 3, 197–207.

Kandlbinder, P. and Peseta, T. (2009) Key concepts in postgraduate certificates in higher education teaching and learning in Australasia and the United Kingdom, *International Journal for Academic Development*, 14, 1, 19–33.

Knight, P. and Trowler, P.R. (2000) Department-level cultures and the improvement of learning and teaching, *Studies in Higher Education,* 25, 1, 69–83.

Kreber, C. and Cranton, P.A. (2000) Exploring the scholarship of teaching, *Journal of Higher Education*, 71, 476-495.

Lave, J. and Wenger, E. (1991) *Situated Learning: legitimate peripheral participation*. New York: Cambridge University Press.

Lee, A. (2007) How can a mentor support experiential learning?, *Journal of Clinical Child Psychology and Psychiatry*, 12, 3, 333–340. http://epubs.surrey.ac.uk/info_sci/4/.

Lee, A. (2012) *Successful Research Supervision*. Abingdon: Routledge.

Lee, A. and Pettigrove, M. (2010) *Preparing to Teach in Higher Education*. Lichfield: UKCGE. www2.le.ac.uk/departments/gradschool/about/role/external/publications/ preparing.pdf (accessed 13 July 2011).

Lowman, J. And Mathie, V.A. (1993) What should graduate teaching assistants know about teaching?, *Teaching of Psychology,* 20, 2, 84–88.

Marton, F. and Saljo, R. (1976) On qualitative differences in learning: 1 – outcome and process, *British Journal of Educational Psychology,* 46, 4–11.

Mroz, A. (2011) Hours and hours of reckoning. *Times Higher Education*, 5 August, 11–17.

www.timeshighereducation.co.uk/story.asp?sectioncode=26&storycode=417089&c=
2 (accessed 11 August 2011).

Pitt, J., Lee, A. and Griffiths, B. (2010) Higher education without academics?, *Educational Developments*, 11, 2, 5–9.

Ramsden, P. (2003) *Learning to Teach in Higher Education* (2nd edition). London: Routledge Falmer.

Schon, D. (1991) *The Reflective Practitioner*. Aldershot: Ashgate.

Seel, R. (2005) Culture and complexity: new insights on organisational change, York Higher Education Academy. www.heacademy.ac.uk/resources/detail/resource_data base/id549_complex_change_in_heis_paper4 (accessed 14 December 2011).

Taylor, K.L. (2005) Academic development as institutional leadership: an interplay of person, role, strategy, and institution, *International Journal for Academic Development*, 10, 1, 31–46.

Wenger, E. (1998) *Communities of Practice: learning, meaning, and identity*. New York: Cambridge University Press.

Young, S. and Bippus, A. (2008) Paper presented at the annual meeting of the International Communication Association, TBA, Montreal, Quebec, Canada, 22 May. Online PDF. 2009-06-224. www.allacademic.com/meta/p230028_index.html.

6

STUDENTS WHO TEACH
DEVELOPING SCHOLARLY TUTORS

Meegan Hall and Kathryn Sutherland

Introduction

So much valuable learning occurs in small group teaching environments beyond the lecture theatre: in tutorials, workshops, seminars, laboratory sessions, online, on field trips and so on. Many of the people tasked with facilitating students' learning in these teaching spaces are not permanent academic staff. Rather, they are a part-time, contingent, and impermanent population made up of students (undergraduate as well as postgraduate), industry professionals, retirees, post-doctoral fellows and other adjunct teaching staff. At the university in New Zealand where we work, this teaching population is referred to as the 'sub-lecturer pool' (SLP) and the majority of the SLP are students. This chapter focuses on the under-researched (in New Zealand, at least) population of students who teach in higher education. It considers the challenges and experiences they face, and asks whether we can expect students who teach to become *scholarly* tutors. It concludes by emphasising the need for support and training that enhances the positive aspects of using students as tutors (as well as managing the risks), and suggests ways for helping students to balance their teaching and learning roles and take a scholarly approach to their tutoring.

Background

Tutors

Students who teach are referred to by various names and engage in a wide variety of teaching activities, including, for example: marking; demonstrating; facilitation of seminars, discussion sections and field trips; and sometimes lecturing. For the purposes of this chapter, we refer to students who teach as 'tutors' simply because that is the nomenclature at our institution. This chapter deals only with tutors who are paid, not peer tutors, senior students or student mentors who may or may not receive credit hours or grades for supplemental instruction or peer mentoring activities as part of their undergraduate or postgraduate course work. Elsewhere, the tutors to which we refer may be called teaching or graduate assistants (TAs or GAs), section or seminar leaders, or even assistant lecturers.

Scholarly teaching and the scholarship of teaching and learning

The scholarship of teaching and learning (SOTL) literature has grown exponentially in the last couple of decades, particularly since the publication of Ernest Boyer's (1990) monograph *Scholarship Reconsidered*. Boyer called for a reconceptualisation of scholarship to move beyond a singular focus on scholarship as research to instead embrace four domains: discovery, application, integration and teaching. Academic developers and higher education researchers found this new focus particularly helpful in articulating how teaching might be conceived of as scholarly. In this chapter, we are not specifically interested so much in the *scholarship of teaching and learning* which, arguably, results in 'formal, peer-reviewed communication in the appropriate media or venue, which then becomes part of the knowledge base of teaching and learning in higher education' (Richlin 2001: 58). Rather, we focus on *scholarly teaching*, which embraces the scholarly standards identified by Boyer's Carnegie colleagues in their 1997 monograph *Scholarship Assessed* (Glassick *et al.* 1997). Those six standards are as follows: clear goals, adequate preparation, appropriate methods, effective presentation, significant results and reflective critique. Such results need not always be formal, peer-reviewed scholarship. Indeed, Shulman (2000: 50) has usefully defined scholarly teaching as 'teaching that is well grounded in the sources and resources appropriate to the field. It reflects a thoughtful selection and integration of ideas and examples, and well-designed strategies of course design, development, transmission, interaction and assessment.'

Austin and McDaniels (2006: 56) in their work on the four domains of scholarship in doctoral education claim that 'a key task for graduate students is to develop an identity as a scholar and a member of a discipline', and in a later article, Austin (2009: 179) defines scholarly behaviour as follows: 'As scholars, we have the responsibility to ask questions, to hold ourselves and each other to standards of excellence, and to deepen our abilities to think analytically . . . [and] to be a colleague, which involves supporting and critiquing in productive and respectful ways the work of other scholars.' Such responsibility is a big ask for any academic, but for a student (graduate or undergraduate) juggling the role of classroom learner at the same time as undertaking teaching activities, the responsibility looms large and challengingly.

When those students are not interested in an academic career (Muzaka 2009), the adoption of or socialisation towards a scholarly identity is fraught with tension, and when those students are *undergraduates* who have not yet (arguably) mastered the basics of the discipline, it becomes even more problematic (Sutherland 2009). Yet, these student tutors bring unparalleled enthusiasm to their teaching roles and the benefits to the undergraduates whose learning they influence are immense. While not all student tutors, by simple fact of their lack of discipline knowledge and experience, can claim the mantle of *scholars of teaching and learning* (at least not initially) we can encourage them to begin taking a scholarly *approach* to their teaching. The following section outlines the findings of research conducted with student tutors over the last decade and shows how open they are to developing their scholarly capabilities and identities.

Key challenges and experiences

Over the last decade or so, we have collected survey data from tutors at our university, seeking their perspectives on various aspects of the tutoring experience. These data have helpfully informed the tutor training and development pro-gramme described in the next section, and have also shed an intriguing light on the demographics and opinions of our tutoring population. The data are from the years 2000–2002, 2004, 2007 and 2009, and represent the perspectives of 782 individual respondents. The contingent and devolved nature of this teaching population makes it very difficult to pin down exact numbers of actual tutors employed in any one year, so exact response rates are not possible to determine; however, we estimate that the surveys have averaged around a 40 per cent response rate overall.

Of the 782 respondents, 152 were not currently studying (19.4 per cent) meaning that a very large majority (80.6 per cent) of respondents were students at the time they completed the tutor survey. A surprisingly high percentage of tutors were undergraduate or honours students (42.6 per cent) (see Table 6.1).

Our survey asked respondents to identify agreement with statements on a Likert Scale from 1–5 where 1 represented Strongly Agree, 2 = Agree, 3 = No Opinion, 4 = Disagree and 5 = Strongly Disagree. Of particular interest for our consideration of how we can work with student tutors to develop a scholarly approach to their teaching are the responses to questions around their identity, value and enjoyment.

One of the perceived benefits of using students as tutors is the energy and enthusiasm they bring to the role (Muzaka 2009; Sutherland 2009) and our respondents affirm this claim in that 98 per cent of them indicated that they enjoyed their tutoring role. However, enjoying the role does not necessarily mean that they intend to make a career of it or to develop further as higher education teachers, even if they recognise it as a possibility. Tutoring and teaching assistant-

Table 6.1 Study situation of tutor survey respondents

Study situation during year of survey	Number of tutors	Percentage
Bachelor's	208	26.6
Honours*	125	16
Master's	151	19.3
PhD	108	13.8
Other	38	4.9
Not currently studying	152	19.4
Total	782	100

Notes:
* In New Zealand, students study to gain a bachelor's degree over three years and then study for a further one year to gain an honours degree. This is seen as a postgraduate qualification.
A breakdown of respondents by year of survey is presented in Appendix 6.1

ships have long been considered 'the foundation of future faculty development for the . . . professoriate' (Wimer *et al.* 2004: 2). Indeed, Oxford University research has found that most doctoral students there expect to receive support in developing their teaching skills, and that 'an academic career orientation is maintained throughout the period of doctoral study' (Hopwood and Stocks 2008: 4). Komarraju (2008: 328) also found that 'graduate students who receive quality training and are in a close mentoring relationship with a faculty member are more likely to pursue academic careers'. So, it is clear that the tutoring experience provides an opportunity for future academics to begin developing and/or refining their scholarly practices.

Our respondents generally agreed (76 per cent) that they see tutoring as a key step towards establishing an academic career. However, fewer than half (39 per cent) agreed that they were more committed to pursuing an academic career since tutoring (19 per cent disagreed with this statement and a high 42 per cent had no opinion). Arguably, this finding should make us wary about spending too much time and energy socialising tutors into the academic (read scholarly) community if the majority of tutors have no intention of pursuing an academic career. It also corresponds with Muzaka's (2009) finding in a UK study that 'GTAs . . . did not see themselves as academic apprentices engaged in a meaningful, systematic professional development programme, although most staff perceived GTAs as academic apprentices' (Muzaka 2009: 10).

Yet, a socio-cognitive apprenticeship model (Komarraju 2008) does not merely have to turn out understudies for professors. Rather, such apprenticeship-type approaches to tutor training and development, which aim to induct and/or socialise tutors into the academic community by exposing them to scholarly standards such as reflective critique, clear goals and appropriate methods can have influence well beyond an academic career.

We asked tutors if they thought they had 'developed as a scholar' through their tutoring experience. A subsequent question asked them to explain *how* they had developed as a scholar. Overall, only 8 per cent of all tutors said that they had *not* developed as a scholar, with 68 per cent agreeing or strongly agreeing that they had, and 24 per cent having no opinion. Thus, even if tutors are not intent on an academic career, they still see positive benefits to the development of their scholarly skills – skills that will stand them in good stead beyond the academy as well.

A scholarly training and development programme for tutors

It is common for tutor support programmes to be underpinned by a suite of training workshops, although their quantity and content can vary greatly. The programme offered at Victoria University of Wellington has evolved over the last 15 or so years, adapted by successive academic developers charged with coordinating and delivering the programme. Despite incremental change, the core structure of the programme has essentially remained the same, and comprises workshops, observations, feedback and critical reflection, culminating in the award of a Tutor Training Certificate (TTC).

Core programme
A set of three teaching-related courses are offered frequently to new and experienced tutors, as shown in Table 6.2.

Table 6.2 Elements of the core tutor training programme

Element	Frequency	Description
Teaching skills for new tutors	Multiple offerings twice a year in February/ March and July	Required, paid, three-hour workshop for all new tutors. Introduces basic teaching skills and concepts about learning including ice breakers, getting students involved, common problems encountered in tutorials, and university resources and support.
Marking and feedback	Multiple offerings twice a year in March/April and August	Two-hour workshop offered around the time first assignments are due. Introduces key assessment and feedback concepts, provides strategies for efficient and effective marking, addresses problems related to reliability and shares ideas for giving effective feedback.
Teaching Observation Practicum	Multiple offerings throughout the year, as necessary	Two- or three-hour workshop that provides individual feedback about what tutors can do to enhance their teaching presentation skills. Offers the chance to be digitally recorded while teaching a five-minute mini-lesson and receive practical, constructive feedback from the instructor and other participants.

In addition to these key workshops, tutors are encouraged to complete the TTC by participating in an additional two hours of workshops from the list in Table 6.3 and/or on request from departments or tutors. They are also required to conduct a formal student evaluation of their teaching and discuss that feedback with one of the university's academic developers, and prepare a written reflection or a teaching portfolio. This final component of the certificate requires the tutor to pull together in writing their reflections on their tutoring experience and feedback is provided by an academic developer (although no formal grade is assigned).

Other workshops
All the workshops (core and optional) are open to all of the university's tutors, regardless of whether they have enrolled for the TTC. The workshops are designed to complement any school or discipline-based training and induction sessions. They are delivered by centrally based academic developers, often in conjunction with departmentally based tutor coordinators. The range of other workshops

Table 6.3 Other workshops open to tutors

Title	Description
Motivating your students	Two-hour workshop about how to address issues that affect students' motivation in tutorials and their overall attitude towards learning and teaching.
Teaching critical thinking	Two-hour workshop about the concept of critical thinking and learning and teaching activities that can encourage students to think more critically.
Developing a teaching philosophy	Two-hour workshop focussed on tutors developing a philosophy of teaching which might be included in a teaching portfolio.
Teaching Māori students	Māori are the Indigenous people of New Zealand and Māori students make up 9 per cent of the student population at Victoria University of Wellington. Two-hour workshop introduces key research about Māori-student engagement and offers suggestions to help raise Māori-student achievement.
Teaching international students	Two-hour workshop designed to work through teaching issues that might be encountered in teaching students of diverse backgrounds.
Understanding your teaching evaluations	One-hour workshop about interpreting and using student feedback responses to improve tutoring.
Advanced training for experienced tutors	Two-hour extension workshop to up-skill, refresh and reconnect with other experienced tutors.

usually on offer (beyond the core programme) is set out in Table 6.3. These sessions are usually offered once each trimester, or more often if demand exists.

Scholarly standards

Despite changes made to the workshops' offerings over time, one of the strengths of this programme is its underpinning by Glassick *et al.*'s (1997) scholarly standards of clear goals, adequate preparation, appropriate methods, effective presentation, significant results and reflective critique. This has manifested in the design and facilitation of the workshops and other elements of the TTC, as well as in the way that tutors experience their tutoring work as helping them to develop as scholars. The following section uses Glassick *et al.*'s (1997) six scholarly standards to outline ways in which programmes for tutors can be designed to encourage tutors to take a scholarly approach to their teaching. It includes examples from our own programme to demonstrate what these standards might look like in practice.

Clear goals

Glassick *et al.* (1997) identified the setting of clear goals as the first of their scholarly standards. In accordance with this approach, any workshops in which tutors are involved need clearly defined learning goals. These goals might be articulated to tutors before the workshop in promotional materials, during the workshop in agenda and teaching material provided through Powerpoint, handouts or on the whiteboard. Alternatively, as happens in our workshop on student motivation, in particular, goals can be co-developed with tutor partic- ipants at the beginning of the workshop.

   Tutors respond positively to this emphasis on clear goal setting as emphasised by various survey responses from tutors at our university. One spoke of how tutoring had encouraged her to 'maintain high academic standards' through the 'good practice of preparing lesson plans and lesson materials', while another shared how the tutoring experience 'made me have to think about what I teach and how I teach which gives me a more thorough understanding of the material'. Identifying and articulating clear goals thus benefits both the students being taught and the tutors themselves.

Adequate preparation

Another standard identified by Glassick *et al.* (1997) is that scholars make the time and effort to be adequately prepared. In the workshops that make up the TTC we strongly promote tutorial and individual preparation as a very important scholarly activity. The academic developers involved in delivering the programme regularly keep up to date with relevant new research. They also use, and share with their student tutors, lesson plans that provide structure while still providing room for flexibility and variation. Similarly the tutors reported how they took time to do the necessary 'reading and prep' and even undertook 'additional research . . . in addition to the readings, which were fascinating' which in turn led them 'down pathways [they] hadn't thought about before'. Many tutors wrote about how their preparation for tutorials helped them to deepen their own subject knowledge and consequently improve their performance in their own studies.

This emphasis on adequate preparation can be easily modelled in other tutor training programmes, particularly by encouraging teaching staff to draw on the wealth of learning and teaching literature available to underpin the format, strategies and approaches encouraged in their workshops, and by encouraging their tutors to do the same.

Appropriate methods
A significant aspect of the TTC revolves around sharing and learning effective teaching methods for the tutorial context, and this aligns with Glassick *et al.*'s (1997) emphasis on the importance of using appropriate methods when undertaking scholarly work. As an example, the academic developers who deliver the TTC workshops take the opportunity to model different teaching techniques and approaches, such as 'think, pair, share' (Angelo and Cross 1993) or send-a-problem (Lublin and Sutherland 2009) and other structured group work. Many of these techniques are described in detail in the HERDSA monograph *Conducting Tutorials* (Lublin and Sutherland 2009), which we often use in workshops and promote to tutors as a useful resource.

The tutors appreciate being exposed to a range of techniques, often commenting in the workshops about the usefulness of having different approaches modelled for them in one session. They have also shared their own experiences about seeking to match their tutoring approaches to their students and subjects, with one writing that tutoring 'forces you to present/explain material to people at different levels of knowledge, or who are doing different courses' and another noting that through tutoring he had become 'more aware of different approaches and interpretations to material'. One tutor wrote of having to learn how to 'communicate often complex ideas clearly, breaking down information to concise smaller sections' while another wrote of the skills she had developed in order 'to convey important points in a way (often many ways) that are accessible to students new to the subject'. Finally, in developing a range of approaches in their teaching, the tutors also concluded that they were honing their own academic skills, such as 'critical thinking through discussion with students and colleagues'.

Effective presentation

Just as other research has found that a lecturer's demeanour and enthusiasm affects the way their students engage with a course (Patrick *et al.* 2000, Ramsden 2003). Glassick *et al.* (1997) also promote effective presentation skills as an aspect of scholarly behaviour. Encouraging new tutors to set up peer observation sessions where they sit in on another tutor's class and invite other tutors to attend theirs, and give feedback afterwards, can help tutors to refine their presentation skills. So, too, can teaching practicum opportunities, such as the one in our core TTC programme. In our Teaching Observation Practicum, tutors are given feedback from their peers and an academic developer about their presentation style, including their lesson organisation, oral delivery, non-verbal communication, visual prompts and their ability to engage their audience. This is the best-received workshop of the entire programme, and appears to have really helped tutors to develop not just their presentation skills, but also their reflective capabilities.

For example, one tutor wrote of how this experience 'made me critically aware of how I articulate the concepts and ideas I am discussing with my students, also helping me to increase my abilities to articulate myself in my own work'. Many other tutors noted how tutoring had made them more confident about speaking in public and 'explaining complex ideas in accessible language'. Another noted that they had seen 'how students can interpret directions and questions that are not actually what you intended as a tutor' and that as a result she had become 'a better framer of questions'. Teaching practicums can be helpful for providing direct feedback about tutor demeanour and clarity, but they cannot emulate the more spontaneous, fluid teaching required in an actual tutorial context, which is why we also ask tutors to reflect on what happens in their classrooms, that is, to consider the 'results' of their teaching.

Significant results

Glassick *et al.* (1997) highlighted the significance of results as a key measure of scholarly behaviour, and similarly the tutor training programme provides a mechanism for evaluating the 'results' of the tutors involved. The TTC requires tutors to complete a formal student evaluation of their teaching as one avenue for measuring the impact of their tutoring. The tutors then meet with an academic developer to discuss the evaluation results, which often prompts a conversation about the importance of being organised and clear in communication and the impact that has on the students' perceptions of overall tutor effectiveness.

Ultimately tutors' performances are commonly measured by the degree of their students' success, but, given that so many other factors can impact on those results, another way that tutors can measure the significance of their work is to seek informal feedback from their students throughout their teaching. In the introductory training workshop, tutors are taught about how to collect feedback from students through, for example, the one-minute paper technique (Angelo and Cross 1993: 148) and how to use that feedback to improve their tutoring. This technique can be easily transferred to a variety of tutoring and other teaching contexts.

Reflective critique

To be able to see the full significance of their teaching usually requires tutors to engage in reflective practice. Glassick *et al.*'s (1997) sixth scholarly standard, reflective critique, encourages tutors to reflect on what they do and why they do it, in order to improve their practice. During the workshops in the TTC it is common practice for the academic developers to invite the workshop participants to stop and contemplate an activity or teaching tool in use at that moment, and to ask themselves how they are experiencing that activity or tool as a learner themselves, and how they might adapt it for their own students or into a different context.

Within the TTC programme as a whole, reflective critique is also encouraged by way of a requirement to discuss their student feedback evaluation with one of the university's academic developers and to compose a written reflection piece akin to a mini teaching portfolio. Both the survey responses and these written reflections indicate that the tutors actively and frequently engage in self-reflection about their teaching and their own understanding of the course material. As one tutor put it, 'it has also allowed me to put myself in the shoes of a marker and be more critical of my own work'.

Conclusion

Clearly, there are opportunities for students who teach to develop as scholars through their teaching experience. Using the six scholarly standards described in this chapter, we have created a professional development programme for tutors that encourages them to think in a scholarly way about their tutoring. This approach, our research has shown, has enhanced the student tutors' own learning experiences, as well as enabling them to take a scholarly approach towards their teaching practice and have a positive impact on the learning experiences of the students they teach, also. The last word seems appropriately given to one of these student tutors who recognises the reciprocity that is central to the scholarly tutoring experience: 'Being a good tutor is the beginnings of being a great scholar because you have so many great senior staff to learn from, who enjoy what they do and have a passion. These people enrich the passion in others, which is what any good scholar would want.'

Appendix 6.1: Study profile of survey respondents

Year	Bachelor's	Honours	Master's	PhD	Other	Not currently studying	Total
2000	47	24	55	46	7	43	222
2001	46	21	15	12	8	13	115
2002	21	13	11	8	3	5	61
2004	27	12	9	5	4	14	71
2007	34	25	40	18	12	52	181
2009	33	30	21	19	4	25	132
Total	208	125	151	108	38	152	782

References

Angelo, T. A. and K. P. Cross (1993) *Classroom Assessment Techniques: a handbook for college teachers*. San Francisco, Jossey-Bass.

Austin, A. (2009) 'Cognitive apprenticeship theory and its implications for doctoral education: a case example from a doctoral program in higher and adult education'. *International Journal for Academic Development*, 14, 3: 173–183.

Austin, A. and M. McDaniels (2006) 'Preparing the professoriate of the future: graduate student socialization for faculty roles'. In *Higher Education: Handbook of theory and research*. ed. J. C. Smart, 397–456. Dordrecht, The Netherlands, Springer.

Boyer, E. L. (1990) *Scholarship Reconsidered: Priorities of the professoriate*. Princeton, The Carnegie Foundation for the Advancement of Teaching.

Glassick, C., M. Huber and G. Maeroff (1997) *Scholarship Assessed: Evaluation of the professoriate*. San Francisco, Jossey-Bass.

Hopwood, N. and C. Stocks (2008) 'Teaching development for doctoral students: what can we learn from activity theory?' *International Journal for Academic Development*, 13, 3: 175–186.

Komarraju, M. (2008) 'A social-cognitive approach to training teaching assistants.' *Teaching of Psychology*, 35, 4: 327–334.

Lublin, J. and K. Sutherland (2009) *Conducting Tutorials*. Milperra, NSW, Higher Education Research and Development Society of Australasia.

Muzaka, V. (2009) 'The niche of Graduate Teaching Assistants (GTAs): perceptions and reflections.' *Teaching in Higher Education*, 14, 1: 1–12.

Patrick, B. C., J. Hisley and T. Kempler (2000) '"What's everybody so excited about?": The effects of teacher enthusiasm on student intrinsic motivation and vitality.' *Journal of Experimental Education*, 68, 3: 217–236.

Ramsden, P. (2003) *Learning to Teach in Higher Education*. Abingdon, RoutledgeFalmer.

Richlin, L. (2001) 'Scholarly teaching and the scholarship of teaching.' *New Directions for Teaching and Learning*, 86, Summer: 57–68.

Shulman, L. (2000) 'From Minsk to Pinsk: Why a scholarship of teaching and learning?' *Journal of Scholarship of Teaching and Learning*, 1, 1: 48–53.

Sutherland, K. (2009) 'Nurturing undergraduate tutors' role in the university teaching community.' *Mentoring & Tutoring: Partnership in learning*, 17, 2: 147–164.

Sutherland, K. (2010) 'Supporting scholarly tutors to conduct effective tutorials.' In *An Academic Life*. ed. R. H. Cantwell and J. J. Sevack, 65–74. Camberwell, Australia, ACER Press.

Wimer, D., L. Prieto and S. Meyers (2004) 'To train or not to train; that is the question.' In *Preparing the New Psychology Professoriate: Helping graduate students become competent teachers*. ed. W. Buskist, B. C. Beins and V. W. Hevern, 2–9. Syracuse, Society for the Teaching of Psychology.

7

HOW DO WE KNOW IT WORKS?

DEVELOPING AND EVALUATING A PROFESSIONAL DEVELOPMENT PROGRAMME FOR PART-TIME TEACHERS

Coralie McCormack and Patricia Kelly

Introduction

Sessional, casual, contingent or 'teaching slaves'? Whatever the label, part-time teaching staff have been positioned as the 'academic underclass' (Sharaff and Lessinger 1994: 12) on the 'tenuous periphery' of academia (Kimber 2003: 41). Here, many perform functions, such as unit convening, without commensurate pay or recognition and often under the stresses of discontinuous employment, poor resource access and intellectual isolation (Kelly 2008). This is common across the developed world (Anderson 2007; Brown *et al.* 2006; Bryson 2004; Coat 2006; D'Andrea 2002; May *et al.* 2011; Sharaff and Lessinger 1994; Watters *et al.* 1996).

Peripheral positioning is problematic because universities rely on part-time teachers for much of the day-to-day teaching, particularly of the most vulnerable and demanding large first-year cohorts (Kelly 2008; Martinez *et al.* 2007; May *et al.* 2011; Ryan *et al.* 2011). For example, casual staff undertake over half of all undergraduate teaching in Australian Universities (Percy *et al.* 2008), and they comprise over 60 per cent of all academic staff (May *et al.* 2011: 188). Since 1990, the growth in employment of part-time academic staff has outpaced that of tenured staff (Kimber 2003; Ryan *et al.* 2011). The consequences for universities can include a loss of loyalty and corporate wisdom, uneven quality of teaching (Anderson 2007) and reduced respect for tertiary education among students and staff. Despite this, the Australian Learning and Teaching Council's (ALTC) RED report (Percy *et al.* 2008: 3) found that 'few universities adequately integrate and support sessional teachers in a systemic way'.

The risk to teaching quality has recently become of concern to Australian higher education quality assurance agencies (AUQA 2010; Bradley *et al.* 2008; Coates *et al.* 2009; Ryan *et al.* 2011). The Australian national teaching agenda is focusing on university teaching quality and standards, with an unprecedented resolve for change (ALTC 2010; AQF 2010; Bradley *et al.* 2008; TEQSA 2011), with Australian Universities Quality Agency audits revealing a 'consistent and strong call across the sector' to introduce systematic professional development for part-time teachers (Harvey 2011: 1).

Repositioning part-time staff at the 'core' (Kimber 2003: 41) of university teaching calls for a systematic examination of professional development practices including: institutional policy development (Harvey 2011), induction resources (NTEU 2011), formal professional development programmes (Percy *et al.* 2008), communities of practice (Percy and Beaumont 2007), teaching circles (Blackwell *et al.* 2001; Pearson 2002), mentoring (Hickson and Fishburne 2007) and informal conversation opportunities (Anderson 2007). This chapter contributes by presenting a case study of a formal professional development programme for part-time teachers (Sessional Staff Development Programme (SSDP)), initiated in 2006 at the University of Canberra, a small (approximately ten thousand students) university in Australia's capital city. Part-time staff here are referred to as 'sessional' staff and are defined as 'teachers including any higher education instructors not in tenured or permanent positions, and employed on an hourly or honorary basis' (Percy *et al.* 2008: 4).

Case study: how do we know it works?

After introducing the case study context, including the institutional and programme sessional staff profile, the programme content, staff participation and programme evaluation methods, the rest of the chapter reviews the three phases of its implementation – 'Getting off the ground (2006)', 'The first few years (2007–2009)' and 'Sustaining the momentum (2010–2011+)' – to explore some of the challenges encountered and outcomes achieved. The chapter suggests that the four Rs – respect, recognition, resources and reflection – are critical to sustaining formal professional development programmes for part-time teachers.

Sessional Staff Development Programme overview

For each year between 2003 and 2009, one third of all academic staff at the University of Canberra was classified as either casual or limited-term appointments (University of Canberra Statistical Website http://ucsw.canberra.edu.au/) and most were female. They undertook one or more of the following roles: tutor, lecturer, marker, demonstrator, course convenor, unit (subject) convenor, lab supervisor, course or unit designers, field supervisors, teacher liaison, administration and student consultation.

Similarly, the majority of participants in the initial programme (2007) who responded to a demographic survey was female and had taught for less than one year. Despite their lack of experience, their duties involved a high degree of skill, responsibility and assumed teaching knowledge. For example, 80 per cent of programme participants were marking, which for some, included setting assessment items and moderating grades. Most were practising professionals; few were PhD candidates. Less than half reported having regular meetings with their unit (subject) convenor, suggesting, as Anderson (2007) notes, that support can be a matter of luck rather than good management.

Participation was highest in the pilot programme (Table 7.1, Semester 2 2006). Prior to 2006 there had been only a few irregular professional development opportunities for sessional staff, usually facilitated by enthusiastic course conveners. Following the pilot programme and the initial programme (Semesters 1 and 2, 2007), the number of staff participating has decreased (Table 7.1), partly in response to institutional budget constraints reducing part-time staff. Consequently, tenured full-time teachers have increased the number of tutorials they facilitate. In each year except 2008, the number of programme participants is fewer in the second semester, consistent with the sessional staff hiring timing across the university. Programme completion rates have varied, being highest in the early years and lowest in each semester of 2010 (Table 7.1).

Across the programme's six years, the core content has remained the same (Figure 7.1 and Table 7.2), although the emphasis on student diversity and internationalisation has decreased with professional development opportunities for all staff now focusing on these topics. The programme duration has changed in response to feedback and the availability of the staff member who facilitates the programme.

Table 7.1 SSDP attendance and completion by year and semester of programme

Programme year/ semester	Number of participants	Number completing	Completion rate (%)
2006/2	105	87	83
2007/1	78	56	72
2007/2	39	36	92
2008/1	22	22	100
2008/2	26	14	54
2010/1	46	5	11
2010/2	35	4	11
2011/1	45	16	36

Notes:
1   Changing staff structure led to a much shortened version in semester 1 2008.
2   In 2009 the programme was not facilitated by staff from the Teaching and Learning Centre. No evaluation data is available.
3   The semester 2 2011 programme was under way at the time of writing.

Sources: Donnan 2010, 2011; Kelly 2006, 2008; Kennedy 2008.

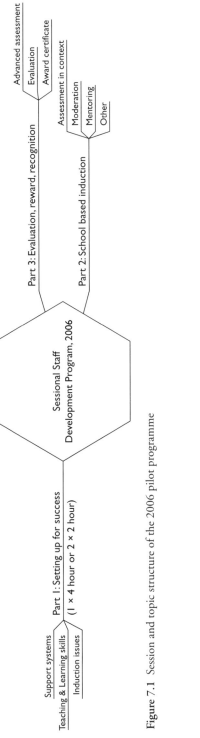

Figure 7.1 Session and topic structure of the 2006 pilot programme

Table 7.2 Summary table of key programme elements: timing, content and recognition, 2007–2011

Year	Content	Hours	Recognition
2007	**Semester 1 programme** *Session 1* [6 hours]: 6 hours offered on one day, with schools given the first two hours for induction. *Session 2* [2 hours]: Performance skills for teaching using acting techniques. **Semester 2 programme** *Session 1* [6 hours]: No school input. Confidence log, planning effective tutorials: working in groups; written and spoken feedback; assessment and policies; connecting students and resources; working with diversity and policies; and evaluation. *Session 2* [2 hours]: Confidence log; teaching portfolios and the scholarship of teaching; writing learning outcomes and assessment rubrics; evaluation techniques and process; and reward and recognition.	Sem 1: 8 hours over 2 sessions	Attendance paid $160 certificates awarded personally Certificates awarded personally
2008	**Semester 1 programme** Session 1: Roles and responsibilities of sessional staff, engaging and supporting student learning, student diversity. Session 2: Assessment policy and practice, feedback to students, student evaluation of teaching. **Semester 2 programme** Session 1: Roles and responsibilities of the sessional teachers, UC resources, engaging and supporting student learning. Session 2: Engaging students in tutorial discussion, linking learning outcomes with assessment tasks and generic skills. Session 3: Assessment policy and practice, feedback to students, student evaluation of teaching.	Sem 1: 6 hours over 2 sessions each of 3 hours Sem 2: 12 hours over 3 sessions	Certificates posted
2009 2010 2011	Session 1: Introduction, orientation and preparation for teaching. Session 2: Engagement, participation and assessment. Session 3: Moderation, feedback and evaluation.	2009, 10 hours over 3 sessions 2010 and 2011, 5 hours over 3 sessions	Certificates posted each year

Sources: Donnan 2010, 2011; Kelly 2006, 2008; Kennedy 2008.

Each year except 2009, both informal and formal evaluation has been undertaken, with participation being voluntary and anonymous. The evaluation methods for 2007–8 are summarised in Table 7.3 and where appropriate, explained in more detail in Appendix 7.1. Three evaluation methods (Harvard one-minute questions during the programme, a formal end-of-programme survey and facilitators' reflections and review for inclusion in a formal report to the director of the Teaching and Learning Centre) were commonly used in subsequent programmes.

Getting it off the ground (2006)

The Sessional Staff Development Programme (SSDP) was initiated by Professor Yoni Ryan, then Director of the University's teaching and learning centre, who gained funding from the University's Teaching and Learning Performance Fund. She appointed a project manager, who undertook an institution-wide consultation process including personal interviews with Divisional Pro Vice-Chancellors, Heads of School and a small group of sessional staff as well as examining a 2005 staff survey and relevant literature (Table 7.3). These were used to identify general issues and to create a snapshot of sessional staff concerns, as well as providing evidence-based justification for the pilot programme. The main problematic areas were:

1 a lack of accessible information about sessional staff, and associated problems with initial employment procedures; time; who appoints and why and finding a work space;

Table 7.3 Evaluation matrix SSDP, 2006–2007

Sources of information	Timing of evaluation		
	Programme beginning	On-going	Programme completion
Participating staff	Demographic survey Pre-programme confidence log (2006 only)	Harvard one-minute evaluations	Formal survey (scaled and open-ended items) Issues of concern workshop Post-programme confidence log (2006 only)
Peers	Pro-Vice Chancellors and Heads of Schools individual interviews	Informal team discussions following each session	Teaching team reflections on evaluation data (process, outcomes, potential impacts)
Facilitator	Literature review Continuous updating	Reflection on one-minute evaluations	Reflections built into draft and final report

2   the need for a coherent induction system for new sessional staff – induction needed dramatic and systematic improvements, while some sessional staff did not realise they should have a staff card;

3   examples of excellent practice existed but were not shared;

4   a constraining ethos of poverty or restraint, in relation to professional development;

5   getting staff to attend programme – payment; incentive, reward, recognition;

6   the lack of guidelines/preparation/support for lecturers to undertake leadership and mentoring roles with sessional staff;

7   quality assurance of teaching;

8   the low awareness/discussion/integration of internationalisation and response to diversity as a teaching, learning and professional development issue.

Sessional staff wanted the 3 Rs: Respect, Recognition and Resources, including basic resources, space and facilities and professional development. Not having access to basic resources caused resentment as well as being an equity issue. Second, they wanted better employment conditions including better opportunities to convert appointments to fractional on-going positions, and more equitable access to leave, professional development and superannuation. They also identified a 'generational gap' in expectations, with the university expecting selfless dedication. Some reported up to 15 hours per week unpaid extra work, with one tutor estimating 100 'donated hours'.

Evaluations showed that 83 per cent of respondents felt the pilot programme was satisfactory and would recommend it to colleagues. Over half described the programme as 'very good' or 'excellent' (Figure 7.2). The majority of participants in the pilot programme (2006) agreed that the programme was well organised and the topics related directly to their teaching (Figure 7.2). Only 19 per cent felt that the programme tried to cover too many topics. A key aspect of the programme likely to influence participants' teaching was the opportunity to network. As one 2006 participant commented, it was an opportunity to 'think together', resulting in recognising common concerns and sharing 'good insights'. In addition, participants reported that their confidence as a university teacher had increased over the programme (Question 5, Figure 7.2).

With respect to the specific aspects of their teaching confidence (reported in Figure 7.3) 2006 participants noted increased confidence in: giving and receiving written feedback, planning a tutorial, working with diversity, managing and marking and assessment, using library resources and understanding important university policies. The greatest increase was in their confidence in understanding university policies (35 per cent), using library resources (19 per cent) and working with diversity (18 per cent) (Figure 7.3). Confidence levels remained much the

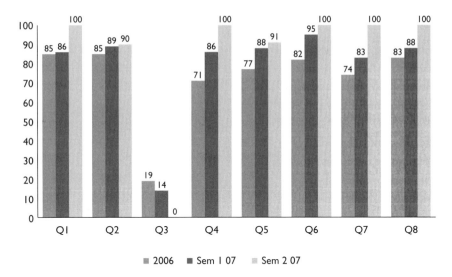

QI The topics covered in the programme related directly to my teaching

Q2 The programme was well-organised

Q3 It seemed to me that the programme tried to cover too many topics

Q4 The opportunities to network with other sessional staff were useful

Q5 Participating in this programme has increased my confidence as a university teacher

Q6 The programme introduced me to ideas and strategies I have used/will use in my teaching

Q7 I feel encouraged to contribute/continue to contribute to my school/unit

Q8 All things considered, would you recommend this programme to other tutors?

Figure 7.2 Participants' per cent agreement with each question in the formal end-of-programme survey, 2006 (n = 54), Semester 1 2007 (n = 64) and Semester 2 2007 (n = 11)

Notes

1   The data for questions 1–7 shows the percentage agreement with each statement calculated by adding the 'agree' and 'strongly agree' responses on a scale of 1 = strongly disagree to 5 = strongly agree. Question 8 shows the percentage satisfaction calculated by adding the 'satisfactory' to 'excellent' responses on a 1 to 7 scale from 'very poor' to 'excellent'.

2   Care needs to be taken when interpreting the Semester 2 2007 data due to the small number of participants responding in that semester.

same for two teaching aspects: using small group activities and giving and receiving oral feedback (Figure 7.3).

Participants agreed that the pilot programme introduced them to ideas and strategies that they had implemented immediately and/or expected to use, particularly in relation to marking and moderation. There were also insights into student learning such as 'the more fun I have the more students will probably enjoy and remember some of the information' (2006 SSDP). Preparation for a teaching career was another outcome. As participants began 'thinking about

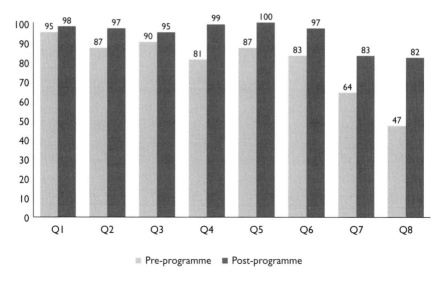

Topics	
Q1 Using small-group activities	Q5 Working with diversity
Q2 Giving and receiving written feedback	Q6 Managing marking and assessment
Q3 Giving and receiving oral feedback	Q7 Using library resources
Q4 Planning a tutorial	Q8 Understanding important university policies

Figure 7.3 Pre- (n = 94) and post-programme (n = 92) per cent agreement with a statement that they had increased their confidence in each of eight aspects of their teaching, 2006 participants

Note: The data for questions 1-8 shows the percentage agreement with each statement calculated by adding the 'agree' and 'strongly agree' responses on a scale of 1 = strongly disagree to 5 = strongly agree.

myself as a developing professional' (2006 SSDP), they appreciated learning about a teaching portfolio and 'moving to a new awareness of teaching scholarship' (2006 SSDP). Importantly, the programme's influence extended to other tutors and to their teaching disciplines (Figure 7.2).

The first few years (2007–2008)

The experiences of 2007 participants were generally similar to those in 2006 (Figure 7.2), in that for most the programme was immediately useful and they were keen to recommend it to peers. For example, in Semester 1, 88 per cent agreed the programme was satisfactory and in Semester 2, 100 per cent agreed the programme was satisfactory (all agreeing it was either excellent or very good) (Figure 7.2).

In both 2007 semester programmes, a higher proportion of participants than in 2006 agreed that the networking opportunities were useful. Similarly, the proportion of participants feeling encouraged to contribute/continue to contribute to their work area was higher than reported in 2006 (Figure 7.2). Feeling encouraged to contribute maintains the goodwill which is the intangible basis for a healthy learning environment. It cannot be bought and is hard to regain once lost.

Programme participants in 2007, like those in 2006, did not feel that the programme tried to cover too many topics (Figure 7.2). One Semester 1 2007 participant noted that 'The topics were very relevant in helping me as a new tutor and the discussions were very useful in discussing ideas for handling various difficult situations' and another added 'many issues I had encountered in my first tutes were covered'. In terms of the programme's impact on participants' confidence as a university teacher, a high proportion in both years agreed their confidence had increased. Similar to 2006, the 2007 programme participants found the opportunities to network with other sessional staff were useful because they realised 'we were not alone' (Semester 1 2007). The programme also 'promoted a collegial attitude – normalised my experience as an inexperienced tutor' (SSDP 2007).

In the 2008 final session, participants developed an evaluation instrument for the SSDP, which they then used to evaluate the programme, their experience of it and the teaching of it. The end-of-programme report for both semesters noted that 'while participants had discussed their feelings of isolation and 'floundering' without appropriate orientation at the beginning of the semester' (Kennedy 2008: 4–5), their final evaluations indicated a better understanding of policy, development of strategies 'which will improve . . . teaching' (Semester 1 2008), and 'more confidence in myself and in my teaching' (Semester 1 2008). Participants in both semesters valued the networking opportunities and the 'ability to share . . . experiences with . . . colleagues' (Semester 1 2008). They also appreciated the fact that the programme delivered on objectives. Participants valued the session on providing student feedback: 'I didn't think about things like how to provide feedback or how the students might see me as someone with the answers, but I feel better prepared for giving feedback next semester' (Semester 1 2008).

Sustaining the momentum (2010–2011+)

The majority of participants in the most recent programmes felt each of the three sessions offered was worthwhile (Table 7.4) and all agreed that the programme would influence their teaching. Only one participant in each of the 2010 programmes neither agreed nor disagreed with the statements about the value of the programme. No participants disagreed.

Like earlier participants, they felt the programme 'met the immediate needs as a sessional staff member' (Semester 1 2011). The programme achieved its

Table 7.4 Participants' per cent agreement with each question in the formal end-of-programme survey, 2010 and 2011

Evaluation item	Per cent agreement semester 1 2010 (n = 12)	Per cent agreement semester 2 2010 (n = 10)	Per cent agreement semester 1 2011 (n = 16)
Overall, Session 1, Introduction, orientation and preparation for teaching, was worthwhile	89	100	85
Overall, Session 2, Engagement, participation and assessment, was worthwhile	100	100	93
Overall, Session 3, Moderation, feedback and evaluation, was worthwhile	100	86	93

outcomes by providing 'a good broad introduction to many of the issues faced by tutors' and suggesting 'ways to deal with these' (Semester 1 2011) which 'helped prepare me for becoming a better tutor' (Semester 1 2010). Growing confidence was again a key outcome for tutors new to teaching and/or new to academia:

> I had not had any sessional teaching experience before attending these sessions, and all 3 [sessions] helped me feel better prepared and more confident going into my classes.
>
> (Semester 1 2011)

> While it may be hard to pin down exactly where these sessions have influenced what I have done in the classroom; I can say for certain that I felt much better, and much more confident, confronting a room full of students knowing I had been able to prepare myself by attending sessions of this kind.
>
> (Semester 1 2010)

Participants in both years appreciated meeting and talking with other sessional staff, particularly from other disciplines. One noted that 'even some long term convenors and lecturers may also benefit' from attending the programme (Semester 2 2010).

Emerging challenges to sustainability include the realities of the future labour market, the changing missions of universities in response to external drivers and a debate about the role of formal university-wide programmes for sessional staff. In the labour market of the future traditionally accepted typologies of part-time staff 'may no longer apply to the higher education sector in Australia' (Gottschalk and McEachern 2010: 48). These authors (2010: 37) note that 'staff employed in casual positions often hold more than one job, at more than one institution and are seeking job security'. Already, traditional career pathways from part-time to full-time teaching positions are less likely to be an option.

> Level A, traditionally the academic career entry point, appears now to be a holding place, confirming staff in either casual or revolving fixed term positions . . . Level B and sometimes Level C, become the career entry point.
>
> (May 2011: 8)

In this context, part-time teachers seeking a career pathway into academia feel 'a sense of disillusionment' as they realise that 'transitioning to full-time work . . . [is] for many an impossible dream' (Gottschalk and McEachern 2010, 48).

Changes in universities' missions are occurring in response to the imperative to improve risk management. Universities continue to see part-time teachers as a risk to be managed because they are a major contributor to students' perceptions of quality teaching, which, in turn, impacts on institutional funding because government funding is now linked to teaching performance. The Australian government expectation that 40 per cent of 25–34-year-olds will have a university degree by 2025 and that previously under-represented groups in university cohorts will increase constitutes an additional external driver.

So, are university-wide programmes the way of the future? This question arises because many of the challenges identified in the pilot SSDP remain, including a lack of support from faculties (previously termed Schools). For example, the second session in the pilot programme (dedicated to School-based induction) proved stressful and labour intensive to administer and despite consultation, received uneven School support, with some criticising it as 'imposed' from outside. Some sessional staff could not arrange the required School-based mentoring and induction, since this work is often not recognised in the workload of full-time staff.

High initial programme attendance has been followed in each year by a falling off at subsequent sessions despite flexible timing. For example, between 10 July and 10 August 2006, 15 sessions of either four hours or two x two hours at varying times and on varying days, were delivered to meet the times suggested by Heads of Schools. In subsequent years flexible programming has continued as this excerpt from the 2008 programme report illustrates.

Sessions 1 and 2 ran on three occasions including a Saturday and two evenings, Session 3 ran on two occasions, one a Saturday, the other an evening. Session 1 was offered in Week 1 and twice in Week 3 to accommodate late arrivals to the

University and those too busy with tutorial preparation to attend earlier . . . Sessions 2 and 3 were scheduled to provide a range of alternatives for sessional staff (Kennedy 2008: 7).

Even this flexible timing clashed with unexpected events, such as student consultations, corridor conversations with their Faculty Dean and other known work commitments. While participants in the pilot and initial programme were paid to attend, this payment, which valued participants' time and efforts, unfortunately ceased with the original funding.

Engaging those sessional staff self-identifying as seeing 'no need' to attend is a common concern of staff in central academic development units. Professional expertise does not guarantee that the sessional staff member has the teaching skills or current understandings to work effectively with diverse groups of students (or staff). Experienced teachers often do what they do naturally and do not take the time to recall their novice teaching years, as was evident in the comments of one experienced participant.

> The session largely consisted of going through a model unit guideline . . . if sessional tutors hadn't already acquainted themselves with the unit guideline for the subject they are teaching then they probably oughtn't be! . . . not bother to attend subsequent sessions.
>
> (Semester 1 2010)

Working with diversity, a strong theme in the 2006–7 programmes, has not survived as a focus, despite increasingly diverse staff and students in terms of age, ethnicity, including Indigenous/non-Indigenous status, ability/disability, gender, sexuality, language backgrounds, work experience, skills and socio-economic status. As Badley (2000) explains, 'globally competent' teachers need not just academic competence or 'knowing what', and operational competence, 'knowing how', but knowing how in different social and cultural conditions, whether teaching onshore or offshore. There are warnings that Australia is now seen as a degree 'shop' rather than a cultural bridge (Lane 2011: 27) and that Australian universities risk being replaced as educational destinations by countries such as Malaysia and Singapore, which is spending millions to improve teacher education and position itself as a quality global education provider (Hill 2006: 28).

A way forward . . .

Despite the challenges, through its individual and institutional benefits the SSDP has laid the foundation for rethinking the role of sessional staff by themselves and by the institution. Personal outcomes include new strategies used creatively, 'It's a great introduction to teaching, and had very strong techniques that I will be able to use immediately and will improve my own quality of life (by reducing my stress!)' (Semester 2 2007); scholarship of teaching, 'Work on moderation was thought provoking – value of good rubrics – specific as opposed to vague or over-generalised' (Semester, 2007); meeting others and realising that they are not alone, and that 'fear and doubt are natural' (personal email, 2007). Institutional benefits include formalised responsibilities for induction of all staff by the Human Resources area and better information on sessional staff. There are now clear pathways for sessional staff into the semester-long programme Tertiary Teaching and Learning (no cost) and the Graduate Certificate in Tertiary Education (GCTE) (study assistance available). In terms of formal reward and recognition, the University of Canberra was one of the first Australian universities to include a sessional staff award in its institutional scheme (McCormack 2010: 1). Since this category was introduced in 2008, two sessional teachers have also won national Australian Learning and Teaching Council Citations for Outstanding Contributions to Student Learning.

In complex contexts, 'one size fits all' professional development is not an option. Sustainable professional development requires a whole of university approach (Chalmers 2003; Coombe and Clancy 2002; Percy *et al.* 2008) through which part-time teachers are treated as part of the solution rather than part of the problem of assuring teaching quality. Scott *et al.* (2008) suggest three possible professional development approaches: formal professional development, practice-based learning and self-managed informal learning. Formal professional development for part-time teachers, such as the SSDP, along with development of unit (subject) conveners' capacity to work with teams of part-time teachers as proposed by Ryan *et al.* (2010) are one way forward. The significance of programmes for convenors is confirmed by Yasukawa's interviewees (in Brown *et al.* 2006), who considered that they worked for their convenor rather than the university and by our demographic survey indicating that only 47 per cent of SSDP participants had regular meetings with their convenor. A complementary session for part-time staff about 'working with your unit (subject) convenor' could be added to a formal programme, to increase their confidence to be pro-active in discussing roles and responsibilities.

Practice-based learning opportunities include formal or informal communities of practice or teaching circles. Brown *et al.* (2006: 44) suggest casual teachers 'want recognition, respect and involvement with their full-time academic colleagues in their "community of practice"'. But can such communities be sustained within the changing higher education environment described in this chapter? McCormack and Kennelly's (2011) evidence-based model suggests a conversation community can be sustained when discussing teaching and learning.

But it must occur within a safe space that fosters on-going connections and con-tinuing reflective inquiry. Self-managed, informal, just-in-time learning oppor-tunities could include online induction programmes, informal conversation groups, one-off workshops timed to meet specific needs at particular points in time (e.g. survival skills workshops at the beginning of semester) and informal mentoring or peer partnerships.

In addition to a flexible approach, there is no substitute for a person whose sole responsibility is sessional staff and their professional development. One example illustrates this. The problem of more participants registering than attending, noted in the 2011 SSDP, was greatly improved in 2007 by the project manager sending personal emails to each participant a week before the session, encouraging them to attend, and asking them to notify if they could not attend.

Final reflections: not three but four Rs

The experience of the SSDP suggests that to the three Rs of Respect, Recognition and Resources should be added a fourth: tutor Reflection. While the SSDP topics do include a skills focus, the programme extends individuals' capabilities by encouraging:

- *critical discussion* through reflecting on applying a particular policy, the benefits and limitations of assessment items, or through using a rubric to mark student work and then discussing the process;
- appreciation and enthusiasm for *diversity* of students and their learning;
- facilitating a *scholarly* approach to participants' teaching – for example, discussing their roles and responsibilities and the conceptions of teaching and learning that underpin university education.

The session drew on students' conceptions of knowledge and learning defined in Session 1 and linked these with Biggs's (2007) notion of constructive alignment (see Kennedy 2008: 7).

The programme's processes pay particular attention to the affective domain to increase participants' confidence in themselves as teachers. With increased confidence came the feeling, and the expectation, that what was learnt prepared them for practice and could be applied in their learning and teaching context. 'Moving beyond' also involves collaborative reflective processes that build a sense of being a *valued* member of a group as illustrated by one Semester 1 2008 programme participant: 'An official feeling of being a teacher (that is, recognition of the role that tutors play, almost like a welcome to the profession)'. Building capabilities, confidence and sense of belonging 'allows' participants to change the way they think about and practise teaching. The SSDP provided a 'chance to reflect or think about broader roles – why I'm doing it and how I fit into the system' (Semester 1 2008) and to 'push boundaries, expand thinking and acceptance of new ideas' (Semester 2 2007).

Part-time staff will remain an embedded feature of university employment in the foreseeable future, so professional development is a long-term imperative. The current focus on quality may be the driver needed to stop part-time teachers being seen as a cheap option. Any 'cost' to the university is a long-term investment in quality that will benefit tertiary education nationally and internationally, since academic staff move between jobs, states and countries.

Appendix 7.1: Description of methods of evaluation

One-minute evaluations

This anonymous, informal strategy uses a one-page sheet which includes two open-ended statements, 'Three things I have learned or am taking away from today's session are . . .' and 'One unanswered question (or muddy area) I am leaving with today is . . .' (Angelo and Cross 1993). Responses were collected as participants left, collated by the facilitator, and discussed with participants at the start of the following session. The benefits include:

- rich, rapid feedback for improving the programme (about 40 things learnt and ten unanswered questions from each session);
- modelling an evaluation and reciprocal feedback strategy;
- foregrounding the positive aspects of learning and not 'blaming' for unclear areas;
- alerting facilitators to problems with teaching or content during the programme, so changes can be made.

Issues of concern workshop

This two-hour workshop (June 2007) responded to requests by sessional staff to discuss problematic issues. A video and a written 'trigger' were used to begin discussion and decide on the main issues. Five were narrowed to three, 'Unpaid work', 'International students' and 'Group work' for detailed discussion. The results were summarised using the headings, Issue, Implications, Problems arising and Strategies to bring about change (Kelly 2008: 29).

Confidence logs

A confidence log is a self-assessment strategy completed by each participant once at the beginning and once at the end of a programme. The SSDP confidence logs asked participants to use a scale (0 = unsure, 1 = not at all confident, 2 = confident, 3 = very confident) to express their confidence level in relation to each of the following teaching activities: using small group activities, giving and receiving written feedback, giving and receiving oral feedback, planning a tutorial, working with diversity, managing marking and assessment, using library resources and understanding of important university policies.

Formal survey

The end of programme survey undertaken in 2006 and 2007 asked each partic-ipant to respond to the following eight questions using a scale ranging from 1 = strongly disagree to 5 = strongly agree:

1   The programme introduced me to ideas and strategies I have used/will use in my teaching.
2   The opportunities to network with other sessional staff were useful.
3   All things considered, would you recommend this programme to other tutors?
4   The topics covered in the programme related directly to my teaching.
5   I feel encouraged to contribute/continue to contribute to my school/unit.
6   The programme was well organised.
7   Participating in this programme has increased my confidence as a university teacher.
8   It seemed to me that the programme tried to cover too many topics.

The final question asked participants to record their overall perception of the programme using a scale ranging from 1 = very poor to 7 = excellent.

In 2010 and 2011, a simpler end-of-programme survey sought participants' responses to four questions, using a scale ranging from 1 = strongly disagree to 5 = strongly agree:

1   Overall, Session 1, Introduction, orientation and preparation for teaching, was worthwhile.
2   Overall, Session 2, Engagement, participation and assessment, was worthwhile.
3   Overall, Session 3, Moderation, feedback and evaluation, was worthwhile.
4   What I have learnt through the SSDP will influence my work.

Acknowledgements

I would like to thank Professor Yoni Ryan and sessional and full-time academic and general staff who have contributed time and energy to the programme since its inception, particularly Dr Peter Donnan, the current facilitator and Dr Monica Kennedy, 2008 programme facilitator.

References

Anderson, V. (2007) 'Contingent and marginalised? Academic development and part-time teachers', *International Journal of Academic Development*, 12(2): 111–21.

Angelo, T.A. and Cross P. (1993) *Classroom Assessment Techniques: A handbook for college teachers* (2nd edn), San Francisco: Jossey-Bass.

Australian Learning and Teaching Council (ALTC) (2010) *Discipline Setting Standards.* www.altc.edu.au/system/files/documents/Standards_100421.pdf.

Australian Qualifications Framework (AQF) Advisory Board (2010) *The Australian Qualifications Framework* (for MCTEE approval 19 November 2010). www.aqf.edu. au/Portals/0/Documents/The%20Australian%20Qualifications%20Framework%20 for%20MCTEE%20approval%2019%20Nov%202010.pdf.

Australian Universities Quality Agency (AUQA) (2010) *Audits: Universities.* www.auqa. edu.au/qualityaudit/universities.

Badley, G. (2000) 'Developing globally-competent university teachers', *Innovations in Education and Training International*, 37(3): 244–53.

Blackwell, R., Channell, J. and Williams, J. (2001) 'Teaching circles: A way forward for part-time teachers in higher education?', *International Journal for Academic Development*, 6(1): 40–53.

Bradley, D., Noonan, P., Nugent, H. and Scales, B. (2008) *Review of Australian Higher Education: Final report.* www.deewr.gov.au/he_review_finalreport.

Brown, T., Goodman, J. and Yasukawa K. (2006) 'Getting the best of you for nothing': Sessional voices in the Australian academy, National Tertiary Education Union. www.nteu.org.au/getinvolved/categories/casual/papers/uts.

Bryson, C. (2004) 'Strategic approaches to managing and developing part-time teachers'. York: Higher Education Academy Learning and Teaching Support Network Generic Centre. www.heacademy.ac.uk/assets/documents/resources/resourcedatabase/id48_ Strategic_Approaches_to_Managing_and_Developing_Part-time_Teachers.pdf.

Chalmers, D., Herbert, D., Hannan, R., Smeal, G. and Whelan, K. (2003) *Training Support and Management of Sessional Teaching Staff*, Canberra (ACT): Australian Universities Teaching Committee (AUTC).

Coat, D. (2006) 'Strategic review of the tertiary education workforce: casual, part-time and contracted staff', Wellington: Tertiary Education Commission.

Coates, H., Dobson, I., Edwards, D., Friedman, T., Goedegebuure, L. and Meek, L. (2009) 'The attractiveness of the Australian academic profession: A comparative analysis'. http://research.acer.edu.au/higher_education/11.

Coombe, K. and Clancy, S. (2002) 'Reconceptualising the teaching team in universities: working with sessional staff', *International Journal for Academic Development*, 7(2): 159–66.

D'Andrea, V.M. (2002) *Professional Development of Part-time Teachers in the USA*. The Higher Education Academy. www.heacademy.ac.uk/resources.

Donnan, P. (2010) *Sessional Staff Development Programme (SSDP) – Evaluation 2010*, Canberra (ACT): Teaching and Learning Centre, University of Canberra.

Donnan, P. (2011) *Sessional Staff Development Programme (SSDP) – Evaluation Semester 1 2011*, Canberra (ACT): Teaching and Learning Centre, University of Canberra.

Gottschalk, L. and McEachern, S. (2010) 'The frustrated career: casual employment in higher education', *Australian Universities Review*, 52(1): 37–50.

Harvey, M. (2011) *Building Leadership with the Sessional Staff Standards Framework*. Australian Learning and Teaching Council successful Leadership for Excellence in Learning and Teaching project proposal. Strawberry Hills, Australia: Australian Learning and Teaching Council.

Hickson, C. and Fishburne, G. (2007) 'Can we help? Mentoring graduate teaching assistants'. www.aare.edu.au/06paper/hic06205.pdf.

Hill, D.T. (2006) 'Southeast Asia seizes the moment', *The Australian,* 12 April: 28.

Kelly, P. (2006) *Draft Report, Sessional Staff Development Project*. Canberra (ACT): Centre for the Enhancement of Learning, Teaching and Scholarship, University of Canberra.

Kelly, P. (2008) *Final report 2008 Sessional Staff Development Programme*, Canberra (ACT): Teaching and Learning Centre, University of Canberra. www.canberra.edu.au/tlc/asd/attachments/pdf3/SSDp-Final-Report14jan-_3_.pdf.

Kennedy, M. (2008) *Sessional Staff Development Programme 2008*, Canberra (ACT): Teaching and Learning Centre, University of Canberra. www.canberra.edu.au/tlc/asd/.../Sessional-Staff-Development-Programme-5.pdf.

Kimber, M. (2003) 'The tenured "core" and the tenuous "periphery": The casualisation of academic work in Australian universities', *Journal of Higher Education Policy and Management*, 25(1): 41–50.

Lane, B. (2011) 'International students see Australia as a shop', *The Australian Higher Education*. www.nlc.edu.au/news2011_sub.php?newsID=820.

Martinez, K., Milton, A., Gannaway, D., Bunker, A., Sparrow, H. and Stracke, E. (2007) 'Theorising multiple positioning of sessionals'. In *Enhancing Higher Education, Theory and Scholarship*, Proceedings of the 30th HERDSA Annual Conference [CD-ROM], Adelaide, 8–11 July.

May, R. (2011) 'Casualisation: Here to stay? The modern university and its divided workforce'. Paper presented at the 25th AIRAANZ Conference 2011. http://airaanz.eventsmart.co.nz/conference-papers/.

May, R., Strachan, G., Broadbent, K. and Peetz, D. (2011) 'The casual approach to university teaching; time for a re-think?', in *Research and Development in Higher Education: Reshaping Higher Education,* ed. K. Krause, M. Buckridge, C. Grimmer and S. Purbrick-Illek, 188–97, Gold Coast, Australia: Higher Education Research and Development Association of Australasia.

McCormack, C. (2010) *ALTC Promoting Excellence Initiative Final Report: Appendix 7*, Strawberry Hills, Australia: Australian Learning and Teaching Council.

McCormack, C. and Kennelly, R. (2011) '"We *must* get together and *really* talk . . .". Connection, engagement and safety sustain learning and teaching conversation communities', *Reflective Practice: International and Multidisciplinary Perspectives*, 12(4): 515–31.

National Tertiary Education Union (NTEU) (2011) Smart Casuals (UC). www.unicasual. or.au.

Pearson, C. (2002) *Teaching Circles as a Response to Staff Development Needs of Part-time Teachers in Higher Education*. York: LTSN Generic Centre. www.heacademy.ac.uk/ resources/detail/resource_database/id120_Teaching_Circles.

Percy, A. and Beaumont, R. (2007) 'Tutor engagement: Working towards an inclusive culture for sessional staff'. In *Enhancing Higher Education, Theory and Scholarship*, Proceedings of the 30th HERDSA Annual Conference [CD-ROM], Adelaide, 8–11 July.

Percy, A., Scoufis, M., Parry, S., Goody, A., Hicks, M., Macdonald, I., Martinez, K., Szorenyi-Reischl, N., Ryan, Y., Wills, S. and Sheridan, L. (2008) *The RED Report: Recognition, Enhancement, Development: The contribution of sessional teachers to higher education*, Strawberry Hills, Australia: Australian Learning and Teaching Council. www.altc.edu.au/system/.../grants_sessional**teachers_report**_june08.pdf.

Ryan, S., Groen, E., McNeil, K., Nadolny, A. and Bhattacharyya, A. (2011) 'Sessional employment and quality in universities: A risky business', in *Research and Development in Higher Education: Reshaping Higher Education,* ed. K. Krause, M. Buckridge, C. Grimmer and S. Purbrick-Illek, 275–84, Gold Coast, Australia: Higher Education Research and Development Association of Australasia.

Ryan, Y., McKenzie, J. and Malfroy, J. (2010) *Coordinators Leading Advancement of Sessional Staff (CLASS)*, Strawberry Hills, Australia: Australian Learning and Teaching Council. www.classleadership.com/.

Scott, G., Coates, H. and Anderson, M. (2008) *Learning Leaders in Times of Change: Academic Leadership Capabilities for Australian Higher Education*. www.altc.edu.au/ carrick/go/home/grants/pid/345.

Sharff, J. and Lessinger, J. (1994) 'The academic sweatshop: Changes in the capitalist infrastructure and the part-time academic', *Anthropology Today*, 10(5): 12–15.

Tertiary Education Quality and Standards Agency (TEQSA) (2011) www.teqsa.gov.au/.

Watters, J., Christensen, C., Ryan, Y., Weeks, P. and Arcodia, C. (1996) *Petpar Project: Part-Time Teachers Improving the Effectiveness of Teaching and Learning through Participatory Action Research*, Brisbane, Queensland: Queensland University of Technology.

THIRD PART: FOCUS ON DIFFERENT
TYPES OF PART-TIME TEACHERS

8

WELCOME ON BOARD

DESIGNING SUPPORT INTERVENTIONS TO MEET THE REAL NEEDS OF NEW PART-TIME LECTURERS

Louise Wilson

You don't know what you don't know.

(Various participants, 2010)

Introduction: the context

Part-time teachers are increasingly making up the numbers of lecturing staff who teach the subject, facilitate learning and who are involved in the creation of a quality learning experience for students studying at different levels. However, little seems to be known about why part-time professionals decide to become teachers within higher education (HE), their development needs or the transition process as they join the academic community. This chapter uses the findings from a small-scale research project to tell the story of how a small group of part-time professionals became teachers in HE. Information is shared about their experiences, expectations and feelings as they make the transition and become a university teacher. These newcomers arrive as confident professionals in their subject area and capable of teaching the content but find that the obstacles formed by the unknown and assumptions lie in the way of an entirely smooth transition. Potential solutions emerge for consideration by those who are designing the support interventions and continued professional development programmes for early-career academic staff using the real needs identified by those who have undergone the transition to become part-time lecturers.

They decide to place themselves on a journey embarking also upon learning about teaching students in higher education and requirements of the 'tribe' they have joined. At the start, these newcomers step onto the verge of an academic community, undergoing a period of transformation as they are submerged into a new culture and way of working. They arrive with their professional know-how and in need of direction, support and useful development interventions. Creating development interventions that fill knowledge gaps, meet the real needs of these professional practitioners helping them get on board quickly, start teaching and to fit into the institution prove key to early success.

Boden *et al.* (2005: 28) highlight various pathways that provide 'entry routes into an academic career' and suggest that 'academics arrive from three main backgrounds' to the world of academia. The three suggested pathways lead from beginnings that are rooted in the traditional route, the professional route or the teaching route. The participants in this study entered university teaching through the professional route, where they have a strong professional background in their field, and are found entering HE with others who have, as Boden *et al.* (2005: 29) highlight, been 'hired for their professional knowledge and expertise'. These people are different to those Becher and Trowler (2001) termed 'gypsy scholars' because they are often engaged part time through personal choice and they are not piecing together an academic livelihood. Instead this group have, for individual reasons, migrated towards university teaching bringing the know-how gained in their primary career with them. These professionals were enticed to this new world, at certain stages of their life, down a route that helped fill institutional gaps as well as to fulfil a personal desire to help others learn from applied practice in what is now their discipline.

My personal experience of joining an educational community to become a lecturer led me to research the transformation process of others who, like me, had made the transition from professional practice to that of teaching adult learners. When I started the investigation, and even now, existing scholarship made reference mainly to staff who were in full-time academic posts. This led to a focus on and to asking questions about the part-time faculty who were entering teaching through the professional route and not via the traditional research paths. How did they come to teach in HE? What was the transition process like? How did it feel? What did they learn from hindsight and could any of the lessons learned be useful to others?

These questions eventually led to a small-scale exploration to find out more. This involved interviewing the knowledge-bearers, those engaged on a part-time basis in the academic community, who had successfully become teachers in HE and survived to tell their tale. Their collective voice enables this chapter to be formed from their stories. It offers information that others who are following on behind will find useful as well as insights for those who are enhancing the quality of the students' experience through academic staff development, policy development and procedures. The chapter aims to provide information that practitioners can use for reflection, action, decision making or just to read.

The project overview

Part-time lecturers increasingly make up the numbers of teaching staff within HE and form an important part of the faculty involved in the delivery of the student-learning experience. With the drive to enhance the quality of teaching and the students' learning experience this chapter considers the transitional experiences of experts who travelled along the professional route undergoing transformation as they became a teacher in HE.

Boden *et al.* (2005) state that universities have a need for people with professional knowledge and expertise to fill a gap and their chapter shows that business people, managers, healthcare specialists and those with specialised skills have entered HE to teach their subject.

New staff had arrived to HE with different perceptions of what they need to know and can find themselves moving into an unfamiliar territory that is culturally different from what they have experienced in the past. A degree of culture shock results for the unprepared. Taylor (1999) points out that the early years are formative and leave a lasting impression while Knight (2002: 37) describes 'the first years in academic work [as] a time when tensions between different calls on our energies and our range of identities resolve into a pattern than can suffuse a career. These years, then, are important for new academics and it is important that they are well guided in their early careers.' If the early experiences of new staff in their first academic appointment 'do not provide a good grounding in these new orientations' then Knight suggests that newcomers 'are likely to use their own experiences of being taught as a template for their own work' and that 'personal frustrations and institutional disappointment may ensue' (2002: 37). This touches on some of the challenges to be overcome through the design of useful support interventions and further insights surface from the investigation, although first of all expectations need to be understood in order to be dealt with. But what are they and what can be learned from those who have already passed through this route?

The chapter reveals that at the heart of the knowledge gap is a need for very basic information about expectations and administration. This void can be filled by the provision of early support interventions, an academic staff induction aimed at helping newcomers to climb on board quickly and provides signposts to the information they need during the early days: a simple survival kit equipped with knowledge supplies, a route map and the tools needed to navigate within the academic community and be successful in their new role.

The group studied proved capable of surviving the early transition phase even if they had found themselves submerged into an unfamiliar culture. They had passed, and in some cases continued to pass, through their own personal learning curve, a learning journey that wasn't always clear, or structured, and which could become unnecessarily extended because basic information or a consistent approach to providing it was not available. Self-directed learning had a part to play too in the speed at which newcomers found the knowledge needed. What did this feel like for a new employee, someone who is not a student and who is not expecting to be involved with self-directed learning? What impact does it have during the transition process?

Answers to these questions, among others, are shared with the reader but first it is worth finding out more about the practitioners who choose to become teachers within HE.

Who are they? Where have they travelled from?

They are professional practitioners who have either fully or partially migrated from professional practice to teach their subject within their discipline. HE teaching is often a second career for them and they can frequently be found simultaneously juggling two careers and undergoing the transition process to become an HE teacher. The majority arrive filled with confidence to teach in their subject. After all, it is their area of expertise and they are already equipped with applied knowledge from practice. They bring skills grounded in and developed from their professional work experience and this enables them to arrive armed with real life examples to share with others. They come from a variety of fields such as business management, health, technology, leadership and consultancy where they have been used to working at different levels and in different types of job roles. Some are employed, others self-employed, enabling them to keep a foot in two camps until they were sure of their future destination.

They come into teaching aware of their capabilities and able to identify themselves in their role as a practitioner but referencing this to their external profession. At the start, it is too early in the process for them to have formed an institutional identity or one as part of an academic community. As Taylor (1999) discusses, identities are achievements that 'attain significance over time' and this social achievement within an academic discipline or community gives 'a sense of belonging, a feeling of personal significance and a sense of continuity and coherence' . . . 'Identities provide the basis for expectations in social interactions – we know what to expect from others, and what/who it is that we are expected to be' (1999: 40). New staff already arrive with a professional identity and it was length of service that helped them to become aware of an academic identity.

Newcomers were not initially aware of how to create an academic identity and often didn't know what one was. They were more easily able to relate their identity to the subject area they taught but during the early stages the expression of an academic identity came after grasping what needed to be understood about University teaching and related activities. In a way, these new staff had not embarked on a journey to become full academics and therefore their expressed identity related to their applied knowledge within the discipline. It was only when tenure was extended or as they became more familiar with HE working that professionals started to become more aware of the significance of identity. In the meantime, teaching outcomes did not appear affected as students were receiving the wisdom these experts had attained from applying practice externally. This enabled students to draw on professionals' real life application of the theories, thus enriching the learning outcomes.

Time and working with others helped professionals gain confidence to form another identity and to articulate this in their new world. The speed at which this transformation and understanding took place was typically associated with the number of allocated teaching hours; the more teaching hours and the greater the exposure to the community of practice the quicker the transition occurred. When it did, part-time lecturers were able to express their identity in a different way such as 'I am a lecturer now' or 'I am an ex-business woman but I lecture'. In being able to state this, their identity had evolved to a point of belonging within the department, discipline and a community of practice within higher education. Here the real transition occurred; the point at which they seemed physically and mentally to leave their old world behind and fuse to the new one, being part of the discipline and the community of practice. Feelings of confidence increased when they felt recognised as part of the core academic team and this helped form a departmental identity.

Part-time lecturers had plunged themselves into a work environment that was not always their primary career and for some it formed a second career. This meant that for the purposes of the investigation it was necessary to select participants from a representative group working in higher education. From a wide population, participation was narrowed down to those engaged on a part-time basis, who had been employed between three months to five years, and who, as professional practitioners were already sharing part of their time, their applied knowledge and their skills with students by working in different Faculties/ Schools. Using the Grounded Theory approach required participants to be selected for what they could contribute to the study (see Denscombe 2007) and for the group size to emerge through theoretical sampling, ending at the point where theoretical saturation was reached. This approach provided a small group of six part-time lecturers, from across disciplines, who had similar transitional experiences and development issues.

Few had prior experience of working in HE, although some did arrive with teaching experience gained in further or secondary education as well as being trainers within the public and private sectors. These people landed in a territory that was unfamiliar. They were equipped with the knowledge and expertise of their subject area. Most were drawn to teaching to share their experience with students entering the profession. The pull towards teaching came about either from receiving encouragement to do so, through advertised vacancies, by a secondment opportunity or simply by chance. They were often initially engaged on a part-time, non-permanent, short-term basis, on the periphery of the academic community and acted as a temporary resource for the institution while using their engagement to trial teaching in HE comfortable in knowing they could return to practice. Often a personal decision, at a pertinent point in their own personal or career life cycle, had brought them into teaching. Most kept a foot in both camps, juggling private or public sector practice and HE teaching and developing their skills through further study and during teaching.

From this group emerged an array of experience, unique skill sets and the applied know-how required to fill institutional gaps. They used their professional knowledge within teaching to enhance the learning experience for students who were entering a profession and studying within the discipline. But what was the learning journey like for these new teachers as they themselves began to adjust and embark upon a period of development in a new role? They were in a new and unknown place. In their life outside HE, they had often reached what Maslow's hierarchy of needs terms self-actualisation and the need to share their knowledge with others became the next motivator. However, the challenges of a new role within education meant these experts also experienced a return to some of the lower needs level and, as Mullins shows through reference to Alderfer's work as a 'progression down the hierarchy' (1996: 492), a necessary regression to satisfy some of the needs that had been met in their previous working life. They have embarked on a journey in what might be termed the shoes of a new apprentice even though they are experienced professionals with external standing. This standing does not always translate across to being a teacher within the context of an established academic community.

Interviewing the knowledge-bearers and analysing data from semi-structured questionnaires shed light on their experiences and feelings and a collective voice surfaced to tell the story of this transformation process, their expectations and the development issues. They had become HE teachers and along the way had added new skills, knowledge and experiences to what was already a repertoire of capabilities.

Hold on tight: the roller-coaster ride begins!

The stories unfolded to tell of an early transition period that likened itself to a roller-coaster ride. Newcomers were familiar with working in very different environments, within different organisational cultures and at different levels. Now they found themselves embarking on a personal learning journey which expected a high degree of self-direction. They were committed to teaching in HE and sharing their experience about the subject with others and the majority had committed to gaining a teaching qualification. They started off confident in their ability to teach the subject and believed that that they could return to practice if the ride faltered. However, in fewer than four weeks, most were at risk of going from feeling like an expert professional in their field to that of a novice teacher in a new environment. The problem was that not all knew what to expect, precisely what they needed to know or where to begin the search to fill knowledge gaps. If these are not addressed, either institutionally or locally, then these early experiences can have a negative impact on newcomers.

This journey is not for the faint-hearted. As the process of on-boarding unfolds and professionals journey towards becoming an established and confident HE teacher emotions are riding high – for example, excitement at the prospect of a new challenge – but the next moment they dip. During the dip, disillusionment can set in along with frustrations about not being told *precisely* about what they needed to know, where they fitted in, exactly what was expected of them and the development support available to understand what is required outside classroom delivery. These dips could be avoided through a planned provision of support interventions which take into account the limited time that these individuals have to find out about the unknown and the use of media to deliver the professional development required at accessible times.

These tutors remained motivated through the feedback received from students, by the help they obtained from peers and from the enjoyment they gained from teaching. Tutors consistently reported that they don't know what they don't know and often simply need directed support during the early stages of the transition period so they can hit the ground running and do not find themselves tripping over the unknown later on.

These starts, stops, up and downs brought about a variety of emotions which included being engulfed by the initial thrill of the new ride, of being lucky, a little unsure and feelings associated with being out of their depth at points: disappointed, happy, comfortable, confident and self-doubting at different stages. For example:

> . . . there were quite a lot of things that you needed to know that were a mystery to me like just how [the place] works, the modules and it's all another language that I am not familiar with . . .

> When I got into it, it felt like second nature.

As the journey continued, newcomers didn't always know what to expect and when unsure they made assumptions and comparison with what they did know – practice in the external world and perceptions held of teaching in HE from observing lecturers when they were students. Some assumptions originated from times spent in professional practice, or from when they had started a new job outside teaching and/or when they had employed staff. These previous experiences had left them expecting certain things from new employers, such as a formal induction, information about administration, service requirements, policies, procedures, employer expectations, to be told from the outset what they needed to know and what support and development opportunities existed. Most found within higher education that they needed to be more self-directed, seeking out for themselves the knowledge needed. This presented a problem when they didn't know that they needed to know something, or if they didn't know which questions to ask, when or of whom to ask. It is around this point that some can experience culture shock as they grapple with a new way of working, thinking and being and a mismatch between expectations and the reality as newcomers settled into the environment and into a different culture. With this came some fear and drops in confidence levels.

> . . . at the moment it is a little bit scary for me because all of a sudden I have got to get into that role and it is like starting at the bottom and working your way up again . . .

> . . . and because someone isn't telling you what to do then you have to kind of be much more self-directed . . . I think [higher education] is very much self directed . . . both from the teaching side of it and the learning side . . . maybe I'm just not quite geared up for it as much as I ought to have been.

> . . . I didn't think I'd have to get so involved with the nitty gritty . . . you don't get the opportunity to do the research . . .

To sum up, newcomers simply wanted to be told what they needed to know and pointed in the right direction to find this new knowledge before they would actually need it so that they had the information to go about constructing new knowledge in a planned and useful way that would enable them to carry out all the tasks associated with the new role. They were keen to make efficient use of the limited time they had available so a 'survival kit' packed with the essential information and a torch to light the way would be helpful. Important elements in the 'kit' included getting to grips with the academic year for the first time, associated administration, teaching and assessment workloads, quality assurance and expectations, so interventions to support this learning activity both locally, institutionally and online were seen to be keys to early success and survival.

The length of time spent on the journey helped part-time lecturers to make sense of things as well as the new environment. Gaining insider experience and self-direction increased consciousness of what needed to be known. The period of adjustment and sense-making helped newcomers to establish signposts, that once found could be used to light up the way forwards. When time was limited getting to grips with the new role became even more challenging and particularly dependent on the number of hours a person is engaged to teach and the frequency of that teaching. Having one day a week vastly differs to that of being engaged to teach for four days. This meant that the time it takes to pass through the learning curve is extended although student expectations of a lecturer remain the same.

Timely and early interventions help minimise the risk of confident practitioners going from feeling like an expert practitioner to that of a novice teacher, in a relatively short space of time. Interestingly, teaching the subject was not identified as a problem. During the interviews, participants identified what had hindered a smooth transition and what they felt were the frustrations or irritations associated with being new to academic life as well as teaching. It became clear that the unknown became a hindrance for most but not for everyone; so too were missing information or misleading assumptions that eventually risked turning into the facts on which new teachers would base their learning and practice.

> I don't know where I have slotted into . . . I think I need to get myself published, get on to applied research . . . I think then I would feel less novice if I had that behind me.

> I don't ever see myself as a novice teacher. Sorry if that sounds arrogant. But judging from the feedback I get from lots of students that isn't an issue . . . it was the bureaucracy and the admin that throws me . . .

Where dips resulted in novice feelings it was for different reasons, for example being unfamiliar with the environment, having only had training experience previously and not having taught in HE, confidence with being able to translate knowledge into the world of academia, not fully understanding how teaching worked in practice or being treated like a novice. These feelings didn't present problems nor did they become show stoppers. However, they impacted on early experiences

> It's like starting all over again. You have got a lot of knowledge in that one area . . . it has always been practical and not [having] to actually think about the theory side and actually delivering it in a way they want . . . it's like starting all over again.

> You know, on our say so [students] are going to pass or fail and that wasn't something that I had actually expected, to be suddenly thrown into but you get there . . .

At the point of theoretical saturation, as previously described as a requirement of using the Grounded Theory approach, the data analysis showed that a one-size approach did not fit all and that part-time lecturers entering from the professional route needed similar knowledge and information to that of other academic staff but did not benefit from this being 'drip fed' at the speed the institution determined. As professionals they had already reached a different stage in their career resulting in the emergence of the requirement for support interventions that took this into account. However, some of the fears and misunderstandings were found to arise at different parts of the process, at points where understanding was forming and this led to an awareness that gave rise to questions such as:

> . . . what [are] the academics actually looking for in that particular thing . . . the marking grids and things like that . . .

> what hindered me was the whole structure and the admin and not knowing what was going on, and it would just have been nicer to have a sit down with somebody . . .

Assumptions about what is known placed a heavy reliance on the part-time lecturers needing to find answers to questions. It required them to know the right questions to ask as they travelled. If knowledge was missing then it took longer to pass through the learning curve making it a steeper climb for some. The emerging remedy was to provide the basic information, in a transparent and easily accessible manner – a road map and survival kit. But what do part-time lecturers want to know, what do they expect and what don't they want? This new model needed to be a little less self-directed and a little more directed without stifling creation of personal learning journeys.

A proposed model

Useful development plans would be ones that had been jointly constructed and where the information was transmitted through a variety of communication methods to ensure efficient use was made of the limited time available. What emerged as valuable were road maps which signposted newcomers to the next stage of knowledge, updated at intervals during the academic year, enabling institutions to communicate key messages. These interventions needed to be designed to start ideally before the person joins, through the induction process (at institutional and local level) and for academic development interventions to be made available at relevant times throughout the cycle of an academic year. A variety of ways to access the information and knowledge was required because part-time staff are not always on campus in the same way that full-time staff are. That way, early-career support interventions that link with continued professional development interventions provide pathways for on-boarding and help to cater for the variety of needs of the different employment terms.

. . . wasn't so much about the academic, or the teaching, [it] was about the admin side . . . for most of my part-time colleagues the questions that they ask me when they're new are about where do you find this, who do you talk to about that, more to do with admin than the teaching and I think most people who come into part-time teaching are confident with the teaching, that's the easy bit . . .

I don't think that I ever knew what was expected . . . so there has [sic] been times when somebody has said well you've not done this, you've not done that and I have just said to them that no-one had told me that I needed to . . .

Supporting the transition: lessons learned

Most new members of staff are faced with the challenges of settling in and establishing what is required. Part-time professionals from practice arrive to teach already equipped with a unique set of practitioner know-how and full of experiences that they are keen to share with others – the students who are entering the discipline to study. They all arrive confident and able to teach their subject areas.

Issues turn into real obstacles when basic information is missing, individuals cannot identify what they need to know and institutions make assumptions about what that knowledge is. Arriving in a self-directed learning environment adds to this. The answer seems simple at first – provide the information needed in a structured way. However, it is not as simple as that. These individuals have their own different needs, they are entering different disciplines and as newcomers they don't know what they don't know. Only when they become conscious of a gap in knowledge can they do something about it. They rely on the institution and those around them to help.

The lessons learned by those who have passed through the transformation process are valuable because they can help others to shorten their own learning journey or to plan training interventions that provide a cushioned landing. A landing that equips new lecturers with a 'survival kit' and a route map as well as removing the time wasted by battling with the unknown, overcoming assumptions and searching to understand expectations.

These professionals did not want to be drip-fed information at a pace that was out of kilter with their own personal learning needs. Neither did they want to be sitting in an induction for lengthy periods of time on arrival. A 'one size fits all' approach was considered inappropriate. Most felt that a week's induction course was too long. All wanted basic information in order to become orientated and to get started in the new role. They were seeking relevant and timely information that would prevent future frustrations arising from the unknown or by finding information out too late. So which early knowledge needs were highlighted as important?

Figure 8.1 Part-time lecturers' early knowledge needs (Wilson 2010)

Figure 8.1 provides an illustration of the information that newcomers expect to be given from the point of arrival. Information around administration, service, policies, procedures and the expectations of their new employer were sought by all and highlighted as key areas to be provided early on. It was suggested that this information could be made available in different formats, through different media and at different times, for example a combination of a face-to-face induction programme, online resources, central training/development sessions and through mentors/buddies locally. This early intervention for part-time teachers is required as they have less frequent contact than new full-time staff with the informal knowledge-bearers.

During data analysis, common-sense thinking challenged the learning needs that surfaced. If part-time teachers were to identify these as the basic learning needs, without really knowing what they needed to know, would this be the same for new full-time academic staff? If one group highlights these as important then it might be deemed likely that other new teachers might also require the same knowledge, signposts, direction and information during their early career. The main difference was that part-time staff did not always have the same amount of time available to dedicate to learning in the workplace and they might not always be on campus during the times training courses are scheduled. They can miss out also on some of the learning that naturally takes place when a person spends time with colleagues from a full-time academic community. Therefore, the support needs of the part-time faculty suggest that this group of staff have needs which might be the same as other new academic staff; however, there is the specific challenge of designing support interventions that are relevant for professionals from practice and that provide the information needed not only in a timely way but in a way that is useful and accessible for part-time staff, on various contracts. This presents a challenge for designers.

In addition, the analysis surfaced that the simple things that happen automatically when a person holds a full-time permanent lecturing post can be missing, causing another obstacle to be overcome. Newcomers require access to teaching resources such as access to teaching rooms, computer access, or systems access early on. Working on the periphery sometimes means that newcomers need to know how to overcome access hurdles as and when they arise. These types of issues may only appear at the point teaching begins. Therefore, part-time lecturers should be equipped with information that helps them to know how to overcome unforeseen situations and with contact details of key personnel especially when delivery happens outside of the usual teaching hours.

Preventive measures can help to reduce the risk of assumptions forming about the unknown at institutional, local and individual levels. Thoughts are offered below for consideration because they provide points at which unhelpful assumptions are likely to start to creep in to the process:

- because the Faculty knows what is going on, that newcomers do too;
- because questions are not being asked by new lecturers, that all is fine;
- that everything would be fine during delivery if part-time lecturers had been told about the session;
- that part-time lecturers know automatically what to look for during assessment, as an academic;
- that part-time lecturers already know what to expect for themselves;
- that they know what to do automatically without being informed and that if they didn't they would ask;
- that they would know how to write for academia;
- that they would get things right;

- that they would automatically be available to teach on dates and times scheduled;
- that they would know about the administration system and institutional policies.

By having development interventions that address these risks and prevent them from arising the transition process can become smoother, especially when development processes align institutionally and locally. Mentoring, support from line managers and academic colleagues are also very important aspects to include in the mix.

In the design of interventions, it should be remembered that part-time lecturers arrive already with a vast array of knowledge, work experience and their own preferred ways of learning. All are unique, carrying their own knowledge gaps to be filled with accurate, timely and relevant information. Care needs to be taken when developing an academic induction programme or development intervention because prescribed solutions can become open to criticism when designed without knowing the facts about what newcomers want, expect or actually need.

A one size fits all approach that is prescriptive and does not take into account the precise facts about the actual knowledge needs of professional practitioners is unlikely to provide the final solution. The capturing of questions from newcomers over time is something that could be used to speed up the transition process and the navigation of individual learning curves. Continued professional development starts from the point of induction. An induction that is designed specifically for new academic staff and supported with other development interventions offered institutionally and locally was considered beneficial. Having materials readily available, the approachability of team members, being able to ask for help without feeling silly or like a novice, the gradualness of secondments and local induction were considered to work well as part of an initial support package.

Without this, part-time lecturers end up using their own initiative to survive, taking the steps they think are right to solve problems and issues as and when they arise. Here an induction programme can be helpful by setting out expectations, providing examples of good practice and aiming to ensure teaching quality from the outset through the provision of supported guidance and signposting.

Hindsight: what does this reveal?

The study asked part-time lecturers to share their learning from hindsight having arrived with the knowledge of their subject and/or discipline but not always with a working knowledge of higher education. A natural gap existed that required the void to be filled. The institutional brain contained this valuable knowledge already, knowledge that newcomers are searching for and trying to grasp hold of as they learn about joining an academic community and teaching practice. The two needed to be connected and matched.

Participants offer hindsight to those wanting to receive it and this formed some handy 'do's and don'ts' (Table 8.1). For the purpose of this chapter these have been condensed to stimulate individual thinking and to help HE practitioners when developing interventions for new lecturing staff.

It is hoped that the information gleaned from the lessons learned and the hindsight offered enables others to receive wisdom that will help them in their practice and to speed up the learning process associated with on-boarding. Some ideas to help create an initial induction surfaced and this unfolds next.

Table 8.1 Dos and don'ts for practitioners (Wilson 2010)

New part-time lecturers	**Do** consider areas such as: • Exactly what you are committing yourself to (workload) • Becoming a qualified teacher • The preparation you need to make the move to HE • Trying it out first (where possible, get some teaching experience) • Being confident in the benefits that you bring to HE education from your professional practice	**Don't**: • Look for perfection • Expect to be told *precisely* what to do in the new role • Make assumptions • Be blindsided when the unexpected pops-up • Try to be something that you are not • Feel intimidated by the environment, the language or being new to an academic community
Institutions and line managers	**Do** aim for best practice by: • Telling newcomers what is expected of them and what is involved • Making the information needed transparent • Providing a consistent induction to all • Investing in training new teachers • Making staff feel valued and included • Improving administration support • Putting things in place before the person arrives • Providing 'how-to' guides • Asking people what they need • Attending to the 'creature comforts' early on	**Don't** • Lose the opportunity of developing people • 'Drip feed' information • Assume there is one answer to everyone's needs • Express a need that leads to a 'dead end' • Raise expectations that could come to nothing • Be woolly • Lose good will • Just say 'you'll be teaching this module' • Assume people know things • Assume people can fill their own knowledge gap • Assume a person knows more than they do irrespective of their length of service

Getting started: ideas for an academic induction and checklist for new lecturers

Induction can provide the first step of an academic development programme and it is worth considering the framework proposed by CIPD (2009). They suggest that all organisations should aim to have an induction programme that is well-considered. However, CIPD (2009) acknowledge the complexity of designing an appropriate and cost-effective package suggesting that 'on-boarding' is used to provide information and to get people up to speed with the job. This thinking matches with some of the findings that part-time lecturers, being new teachers, have highlighted as useful for their journey.

CIPD (2009) recognised that elements of good practice should be included within an induction programme; however, the idea of standardising an induction is considered an inappropriate way forwards, again linking with the thoughts of newcomers. A 'one-size' approach doesn't fit all staff or organisations; however, the elements of good practice can be used to form a basis on which to build or review an academic staff induction programme. It is not suggested to be the glass slipper or that it will fit all needs but it does provide a framework for adjustment and personalisation. It offers a structure that becomes helpful when looking at the bigger picture of how induction aligns institutionally, locally and with the expectations of part-time lecturers.

The website associated with this chapter (www.developingacademicpractice. com) contains three activities. These are designed to encourage bigger picture thinking and to help the reader delve into thinking at different levels and across development processes so that the knowledge needed is identified and designed for.

Activity 1 has been created for those who are reviewing or creating induction programmes and provides a framework to base this on. Activity 2 takes the knowledge needs identified by part-time lecturers and helps you think about your current practice with a view to identifying gaps and areas for action. Activity 3 is designed with new lecturers in mind and offers a prompt sheet to provoke thinking about the knowledge that is likely to be useful during on-boarding and questions that are useful to ask in the early stages. All of these activities can be used by those developing induction programmes. Whatever the activity, you are encouraged to look at it from different angles, either as the individual newcomer, the Faculty/School they are joining or the institutional requirements they will meet there.

Conclusions

This chapter has told the story of the transition experience of a group of part-time lecturers who were new to teaching in education. It has shared facts about the issues associated with the unknown, assumptions, expectations and self-directed learning. Lessons from these experiences have been provided and hindsight offered as wisdom to receive for those who are becoming teachers in HE, for those who are looking to develop induction or academic development interventions and line managers. The real needs, as identified by those who have become HE teachers, are surfaced and made available for others to use and tailor to their own institution or disciplinary requirements. Throughout, the need for a 'road map' and 'survival kit' has been shown to be of importance. Ideally, these should be provided early on to ensure the quality of the students' learning experience and an effective on-boarding for experts as they join the academic community of practice. Induction surfaced as a requirement and the first step of an academic staff development programme. The design of this needs to equip new lecturers with knowledge and information and provide signposts for them to use in order to be successful in their new role and during their early career.

References

Becher, T. and P. R. Trowler (2001) *Academic Tribes and Territories: Intellectual Enquiry and the Culture of Disciplines*, 2nd edn. Buckingham: SRHE and Open University Press.

Boden, R., D. Epstein and J. Kenway (2005) *Building Your Academic Career*. London: Sage Publications.

Chartered Institute of Personnel and Development (CIPD) (2009) Induction available from www.cipd.co.uk/subjects/recruitment/induction/induction.thm?IsSrchRes=1. (accessed April 2009).

Denscombe, M. (2007) *The Good Research Guide for Small-scale Social Research Projects*. Maidenhead: Open University Press. pp. 86–107

Eraut, M. (2008) How Professionals Learn through Work. Online at http://surrey professionaltraining.pbworks.com/f/How+Professionals+Learn (accessed 10 October 2010).

Knight, P. (2002) *Being a Teacher in Higher Education*. Buckingham: SRHE and Open University Press.

Mullins, L. (1996) *Management and Organisation Behaviour*. London: Pitman Publishing

Taylor, P. G. (1999) *Making Sense of Academic Life: Academics, Universities and Change*. Maidenhead: SRHE and Open University Press. pp. 40–45

9

TUTORING ONLINE

PRACTICES AND DEVELOPMENTAL NEEDS OF PART-TIME/CASUAL STAFF

Pam Parker and Neal Sumner

Introduction

'The convergence of social, technical and intellectual forces has pushed higher education to the tipping point of significant transformation' (Garrison and Vaughan 2008: 143). Since these words were written we might add to this convergence development in the economic and political context as further contributors towards profound changes in the structure, design and delivery of higher and further education.

A core feature of these changes is the dramatic increase in online, flexible and blended learning made possible in part through developments in, and the deployment of, digital technologies in universities and colleges worldwide. Beetham and Sharpe have argued that 'these technologies represent a paradigm shift with specific and multiple impacts on the nature of knowledge in society, and therefore on the nature of learning' (Beetham and Sharpe 2007: 4). These rapid changes also impact on the nature of teaching, creating a need for continuing staff development as the modes of knowledge production, distribution and consumption change with increasing speed (Mason and Rennie 2004). This presents a particular challenge for part-time teaching staff striving to balance competing roles and responsibilities.

A recent UK government-sponsored report into the rise of online learning suggests that staff are willing to engage with technology but in order to do this effectively they need development and support (OLTF 2011: 7). This chapter aims to discuss some of the challenges raised by tutoring online, and the skills and support required to be an effective part-time online tutor. How these skills will be acquired will vary from one context to another, but what follows supports the view that online tutoring requires the development of specific technical, social and pedagogic skills.

Terminology

As an emerging field of study there is, as yet, no clear set of definitions which delineate the area of online teaching and learning. Terms such as computer-aided learning or computer-assisted learning have been replaced with online learning, blended learning, networked learning, e-learning and technology enhanced learning, all often used interchangeably to describe the use of digital technologies in the administration and delivery of teaching and learning. More recently the term mobile learning has been coined to describe the use of internet-enabled mobile devices which are used to access and deliver a growing range of education focused digital applications and learning objects. Blended learning can refer to the balance between face-to-face (F2F) and specifically online learning deployed on a particular programme or module, but blended learning is a term also used to describe a multiplicity of teaching approaches and technologies (Littlejohn and Pegler 2007). For the purposes of this chapter a broad definition of online learning will be adopted which will encompass all the above terms: such a definition includes any form of electronically supported learning and teaching. An important characteristic of online learning, one which makes this mode of delivery increasingly attractive to many students and institutions, is the flexibility it offers in terms of the pace and places in which learning can occur. In this respect it is a development of more traditional distance learning approaches. Part-time tutors are themselves increasingly expected to have the skills to deliver online teaching in either a blended or completely online model.

All online learning requires the use of (usually) web-enabled digital tools which can range from personal computers, laptops, tablets, netbooks, iPads to mobile devices, including smartphones and personal digital assisstants (PDAs). Such tools are used to access a growing range of software applications, such as virtual learning environments (VLEs) (also known as learning management systems (LMS)), e-portfolios and multiple-choice quiz tools and these are usually hosted by educational institutions. Other software applications, for example blogs and wikis, are available from the World Wide Web, either as open source or proprietary tools – which may be free or in some cases have a cost attached. It is not intended to discuss in detail the plethora of devices and multitude of applications in this chapter (although these cannot be completely ignored) but to focus on the roles and skills required of the online tutor.

However, the initial task for the online tutor is to establish what tools are available and what technical specifications, in terms of hardware and software, are required by the tutor and students on any particular programme or module. Most higher and further education institutions have some form of support and/or champions for online learning and an important early step is to establish from these sources which tools are supported by the institution and what professional development is provided to enable both staff and students to become skilled in their use. Wherever possible using institutionally supported tools to deliver online tutoring is to be preferred, since there are recent instances where once freely available social networking (e.g. Ning) and social bookmarking (e.g. De.li.cious) applications have either introduced charges for using their applications, or have threatened to do so. Unless the online tutor is developing a new self-authored programme of study outside of any formal institution, it is strongly recommended that institutionally supported tools are used by both staff and students, not least so that the online tutor does not have to develop from scratch technical expertise in any particular tool or application, and students will not have to rely on the online tutor for technical support. The availability of institutionally supported tools will determine what technical and teaching skills the online tutor will need to develop, for example tools which facilitate synchronous and/or asynchronous communication. This does not preclude the use of social networking tools (sometimes collected under the umbrella term Web 2.0) such as Facebook or Twitter, but there are ethical and pedagogic issues surrounding their use of which the online tutor should be aware. How, when and which online tools will be deployed will also to some extent depend on whether the programme or module is delivered entirely online or in a blended model. These issues will be explored more fully later in this chapter.

How part time is part time?

An important consideration for any part-time tutor, whether online or offline, is to clarify what amount of time is available to dedicate to the delivery of the programme of study. Online teaching and learning is widely recognised to involve at least as much time in preparation and delivery as more traditional face-to-face education. The online tutor may be required to develop their own materials or content or, as in The Open University model, deliver the teaching around materials developed by a central academic team. A first step then is to establish what is required in terms of preparation. Do new materials/content have to be developed? Are there re-usable learning objects or open educational resources available to support the development of course content? If the programme or module is hosted by an institution what is its attitude to the use of such materials? Who owns the materials prepared by the part-time tutor? Is it possible or encouraged to engage the students in co-designing the curriculum and assessments, something which the predominantly asynchronous nature of much current online teaching facilitates? Beyond the crucial issue of the preparation of teaching materials, how much time are you expected to spend online and, how much participation is expected from the students? This will be determined by the nature of the programme, the timing of activities and assessments and the levels of interaction expected from both tutor and students.

A very useful introductory activity to undertake with any new group of online students is to discuss the expectations of each other's online participation and where possible negotiate an agreed plan. Students need to know if you are going to respond to emails and discussion board postings or give feedback on assessments on a daily, weekly or monthly basis. There is no straightforward answer to this; it all depends on the teaching context. The management of expectations, both of the students by the tutor, of the tutor by the students, and the students from each other, are central to successful online teaching and learning and will be discussed more fully below. Time invested in making explicit such expectations is not only helpful to all participants, but can serve as part of useful icebreaker activities at the beginning of any online programme of study.

How does online tutoring differ from face-to-face tutoring?

Depending on the structure of the programme of study and the tools available to deliver it, the online tutor must decide on the appropriate blend of online and face-to-face teaching, the balance between synchronous and asynchronous communication and the pacing of activities and assessments throughout the programme. Synchronous tools such as video-conferencing provide a closer approximation of the F2F context, but these are not yet ubiquitous and many programmes feature asynchronous tools as the dominant mode of delivery, since this allows for greater flexibility for both staff and students. Although there is some force to the claim that good teaching is good teaching regardless of whether it takes place in a face-to-face or online environment (Wray *et al.*, 2008) it is nevertheless important from the outset to be aware of the key differences between online and face-to-face teaching, particularly in relation to asynchronous communication in the online environment. Many books and articles have been written on this topic and it is worth repeating Tony Bates's warning that 'technology will never save bad teaching; usually it makes it worse' (Bates, 1995: 12). So what are the key differences between the asynchronous online and F2F context which the online tutor should be aware of? These have been well summarised by Brenda Smith (Smith 2006: 3)

Whether using email, blogs, wikis or discussion boards the text-based nature of asynchronous online communication gives a permanence of record which is lacking in most face-to-face teaching, notwithstanding the growing use of lecture capture software in many traditional campus based institutions! Some participants in online communities can initially find this permanence intimidating, although

Table 9.1 Key differences

Face to face	Online
Emphasis on oral skills	Emphasis on written skills
May include use of humour	May be more formal
Summarising 'on the spot'	Time to reflect on summaries
Single 'conversations'	Multiple 'conversations'
Tutor-directed discussion	Student-directed discussion
Time and space limited	Time and space unbounded
Content ephemeral	Content recorded
Managing equality of student contributions	Encouraging 'lurkers'[1] to participate

Note
1 'Lurkers' is a rather pejorative term – silent witness may be preferred.

it has been argued (Paloff and Pratt 1999) that introverts in face-to-face settings may find the online environment more amenable. An immediate task for the online tutor once a programme commences is to create an environment where all learners will feel comfortable and know what is expected from them in terms of the frequency and length of postings. The absence of visual and verbal clues (and consequent potential for ambiguity and misunderstanding) in the online environment thus requires the online tutor to model the tone and register of online communication. Basic rules of netiquette (discussed below) can also form the focus of early discussions in the online community.

Online tuition can take many forms: one-to-one, small group teaching or large group teaching. It can, as mentioned above, be combined with face to face in a blended model, or online synchronous delivery and each context requires the development of specific skills. However, there is a core set of skills and practices common to each of these settings which can be broadly grouped under the following headings: social and pedagogic. Each of these roles (discussed further below) is also important in the context of face-to-face teaching, but in the asynchronous online context the spontaneity possible in the face-to-face setting and the ability to assess 'how learners are performing, [to] rearrange groups and reassign activities, phrase explanations differently to help learners understand them better, guide discussions and ask questions that challenge learners appropriately' are missing (Beetham and Sharpe 2007: 7). As these authors go on to argue, teaching in the online context 'require[s] forethought and an explicit representation of what learners and teachers will do' (ibid.). It is this aspect of surfacing the hidden assumptions and practices which are taken for granted in face-to-face settings which characterise some of the skills required of the online tutor.

Learning design for online tutors

One consequence of the development of the World Wide Web and online learning over the last 20 years has been the production of an extensive literature (for example Anderson and Elloumi 2004) on the pedagogy of online teaching and learning, as well as new theories of learning and debates about the effects of the widespread adoption of new digital technologies by students of all ages. This chapter can do no more than offer a brief synopsis of the key research in this area, and the next section will focus on drawing out the implications for the part-time online tutor who has the opportunity to design learning for students.

Changing role of the tutor

Much traditional face-to-face education, especially higher education, has focused on knowledge transmission. The formal lecture has been at the heart of higher education delivery hitherto, and remains popular with academics. Can this approach succeed in the online environment? Online lectures can be delivered using a variety of tools and in multiple formats – text versions of lectures can be uploaded either in portable document format (.pdf) or other versions, e.g. Microsoft Word. To replicate the experience of giving a 'live' lecture there is lecture capture software available in many institutions which allows F2F lectures to be recorded and then uploaded to a website or VLE (LMS). Some applications, such as Adobe Presenter, allow an audio file to accompany a PowerPoint presentation, lectures can be delivered as podcasts (see iTunes U) or in other audio file formats. If video equipment is available, vodcasts can be made and uploaded to a website, YouTube or the host institution's Virtual Learning Environment. Where the opportunity to use synchronous communications software exists (such as Adobe Connect or Wimba Classroom) or freely available Skype software then a web-cam and microphone can facilitate the delivery of the online lecture. The degree of interaction between tutor and students in a F2F lecture setting can vary considerably, but, as noted above, the extent to which effective lectures can be successfully replicated in the online environment is diminished by the absence of visual and verbal clues. Are your students paying attention, and how do you know if they have read, heard or understood the information so delivered? Will they discuss the lecture content before or after the event? Where lectures are delivered online, then, the online tutor will have to provide the opportunities for discussion between students in the online environment if they are not to be disadvantaged, and mechanisms for checking understanding developed.

However, there is considerable debate in the literature about whether lectures, online or F2F, are a very effective form of teaching. As Laurillard stated 'What it takes to learn, we now know, is more than being told' (Laurillard 2008: 13). The explosion of information available from the World Wide Web gives students access to vast resources and knowledge which has contributed to the 'decentering' of the tutor as knowledge provider, leading to claims that lectures are becoming redundant. Recent developments in learning theory, particularly those which recognise the growing centrality of learning technologies to the educational experience, emphasise that the transmissive model characterised by the traditional lecture is an ineffective form of teaching. Theories such as constructivism and social constructivism emphasise the importance of designing opportunities for active and collaborative learning in the online environment. One reason for this is to provide opportunities for social and learning interactions between students as well as between tutors and students, in order to compensate for the potential isolation of the online learner, particularly where text-based asynchronous communication is the dominant form of interaction on the programme. A range of other theories and frameworks such as Connectivism (Siemens 2004), Situated Learning, Conversational Framework and Salmon's Five Step model (Salmon 2011) share the basic principle that designing for active learning is the way to approach pedagogic design for successful online communities (see, e.g., Kear 2011: Chapter 2). Another useful model for understanding the role of the online tutor is the Community of Inquiry model developed by Garrison and Vaughan (2008: 18). They identify three elements, social presence, teaching presence and cognitive presence, which overlap to support the educational experience for the online learner and tutor (Figure 9.1).

Designing learning opportunities which engage students, require them to interact with the content, test their understanding, require them to apply their new knowledge in different contexts and reflect on their learning are the core features of these emerging pedagogies for online learning. Most of the tools which can facilitate these kinds of activities have already been mentioned, and the choice of tool will depend on the context and their use will be revised and refined in the light of experience. The affordances of many of the currently available digital tools have been well described by Mason and Rennie (2008: Chapter 4), whose book also includes case studies as to their appropriate use in an educational setting. Tools can be broadly divided between those which deliver content and those which facilitate interaction both with the content, the tutor and between learners. Some, such as virtual learning environments and e-portfolios, can support both content delivery and interaction; tools such as blogs and wikis, normally associated with interaction, can also be used for content delivery. Rather than describe each tool here it is intended to focus more on the roles which the part-time online tutor will need to perform, though tools which can facilitate the performance of these roles will be mentioned.

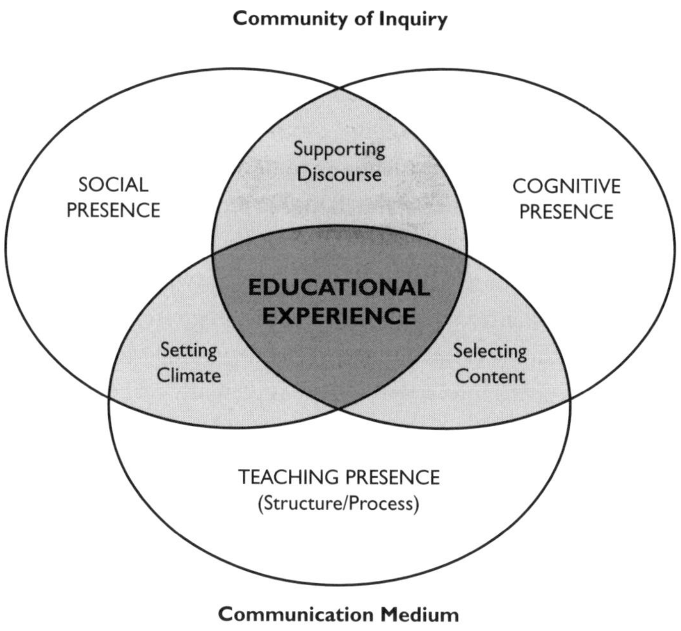

Community of Inquiry

Figure 9.1 Role of the online tutor

The two roles for the online tutor mentioned above – social and pedagogic – do not occur as distinct phases in online teaching, but it is useful to discuss them separately in order to highlight the different aspects of the role. Professional development for the part-time tutor should encompass both aspects and recognise that these are skills which require practice and will benefit from moderation, preferably from experienced online mentors.

The social role

Getting started: icebreakers

Assuming there is no face-to-face contact between the tutor and students at the beginning of a programme the first task for the online tutor is to contact the students using the available technologies and to set up introductory icebreaker activities. There are numerous online resources for icebreaker activities – see, for example, www.southalabama.edu/oll/jobaidsfall03/Icebreakers%20Online/ice breakerjobaid.htm.

The tutor's introductory message can include their own contribution to whatever icebreaker activity is chosen and this is an opportunity to model the tone, length and mode of contribution which students will be expected to fulfil. A well-chosen activity will encourage students to share some personal information and may, if the technology permits, include a personal photograph or an audio file where students can express their expectations of the programme. On a blended programme the icebreaker and induction phases are best covered in the F2F context, although they can be continued online.

This opening activity can form the basis for ongoing social interaction in the online environment which can continue throughout the programme, though this should be kept separate from more academically focused discussions and activities. Many online programmes include a social space or online cafe where students can continue to exchange personal interests as the programme progresses. Tutors must decide for themselves whether they wish to use social networking tools such as Facebook to facilitate such social interaction – there is presently no consensus in the academic community about this. Some commentators have drawn attention to what has been labelled the 'creepy tree-house' effect (http://flexknowlogy. learningfield.org/2008/04/09/defining-creepy-tree-house/) and the part-time online tutor should be careful to check what the institutional policy on the use of such tools is before using them with students. On the other hand, some academics like to use such social networking tools to establish contact with their students and then migrate to a more academic environment once the introductory phase has been completed (Martinez Aleman and Wartman 2009). Whatever tools are chosen the next task is to establish the expectations for how all members of the online learning community will use whatever tools are made available to deliver the programme.

As mentioned above one of the most important tasks for the part-time online tutor is to manage their own time and that of students in the online environment. As Frand (2000) has argued today's Net Gen students expect to be always connected (through digital technology) and they can be intolerant of delays in receiving feedback or answers to questions. This can place an intolerable strain on part-time online tutors who may feel under pressure, given the increasing emphasis on performance and student satisfaction surveys, to be constantly connected and responsive to the demands of their students. This is why a negotiation between staff and students about the frequency of online contact is fundamental to the success of online contact. Where appropriate (and this will depend on the kinds of student, nature of the programme and activities expected) students should be encouraged to share questions, knowledge, ideas, explanations and answers with each other, but here again, students need to be aware of, and to agree their expectations of each other in the online environment. Of course the role of the tutor is to monitor such communications, and to intervene as and where appropriate.

Netiquette (http://en.wikipedia.org/wiki/Netiquette)

Although the term has fallen out of fashion in recent years netiquette is nevertheless important to the success of virtual communities of all kinds, and particularly for communities of learners. The lack of visual and verbal clues in the online environment can lead to misinterpretation and misunderstanding and this can lead to serious disagreements (sometimes called flame wars) which may destroy a good learning atmosphere. Tutors should agree with their students at the beginning of a programme of study what are acceptable rules for behaviour in the online environment, and there are many online sites which offer such guidance. A good place to start is with the advice produced by Gary Alexander of the UK's The Open University (www.adbh.co.uk/tu170/netiquette.php) but this can be tailored to suit the needs of each online community. Such protocols can be developed regardless of which tools are used, and are just as appropriate in synchronous as in asynchronous environments, although for synchronous environments additional protocols such as 'passing the baton' can pre-empt some of the confusion which can arise when several students are trying to make points at the same time.

Developing the learning community.

Having agreed expectations, netiquette and the pace and timing of activities with learners the task of the online tutor is to model through their own contributions the norms that will prevail in each community. Using relevant message headers, demonstrating the appropriate length, adopting a positive tone in messages, giving feedback to learner input, encouraging peer interaction and commending examples of good practice can all contribute to the development of an effective learning community. Especially in the early stages of group formation tutors may need to intervene more frequently, moving misplaced messages in discussion fora, dealing with technical issues promptly as they arise and above all encouraging every member of the community to participate. Ideally the tutor will be able to communicate a genuine enthusiasm for the subject and through this engender a cooperative spirit among participants, where conflict is constructively dealt with and the sense of a learning community established.

The pedagogic role (cognitive and teaching presence)

In setting tasks for the learners to perform the online tutor potentially has a wide range of tools to deploy. Some, such as e-portfolios and blogs, may encourage reflective activities whilst others, such as discussion fora and wikis, may be more useful for group learning. Whichever tools are used the tutor must ensure that all students are comfortable with the technologies and know where to direct students for assistance should they require it. The kinds of tasks which are developed will to some extent be determined by the subject content (further discussion of discipline-specific activities and approaches may be found in Beetham and Sharpe 2007: Chapters 11–14). Nevertheless, some general principles can be described.

We have already established that maximising opportunities for interaction with the teaching materials/content is paramount in the online environment. The expected learning outcomes and timing and nature of assessments should also be made explicit at the beginning of any programme. Opportunities for formative feedback, whether delivered in written or audio/visual format, should be available to students at strategic points in the course of study. Where online discussion forums are available (and these can be delivered through a variety of tools) the online tutor can perform a number of tasks which can help promote and encourage student learning. Weaving together the contributions of individual learners, focusing on key learning points in the materials, probing and challenging responses and summarising each topic discussed are all valuable in sustaining a vibrant online learning community. Activities which promote group learning are particularly valuable in the online environment since they help reduce the sense of learner isolation, as well as exposing students to multiple perspectives and encouraging them to learn from each other. Wikis can be effective for group work – 'the fundamental premise of wiki construction is a belief in the shared construction of knowledge' (Mason and Rennie 2008: 66) – but more important than the tools are the kinds of activities which are designed to facilitate group work. Many of the activities to achieve this can be adapted from the F2F context, such as whole-group discussion, small-group discussion, buzz groups, snowballs, the Delphi technique, debates (with online voting), brainstorming and role plays can all be used, but, as with other aspects of online tutoring already discussed, more planning and the explicit statement of rules and roles and time frames will need to be promoted in advance of the exercise. Encouraging learners to contribute their own research and materials to a resource bank for the programme can be facilitated through the use of RSS feeds, blog rolls, social bookmarking tools, and, where images are important, photosharing (e.g. using Flickr). The mix of such activities will be determined by the time and technologies available, as well as the expertise and confidence of the tutor.

Assessment and feedback

In the same way that designing a range of different activities for the online student to engage with can help to meet the diversity of learning styles and student skills, online assessments should also take a variety of forms. Assessments should be integral to the learning process rather than an end of programme bolt-on, and online tools can facilitate more low-level assessments (for example using Multiple

Choice Quizzes) which demand a more even distribution of effort over the course of study. The growing emphasis on timely feedback can also be met through the use of MCQ tools which can be set up to include the use of sounds, images, or videos, or any combination of them, labelling an item, identifying hotspots or drag and drop, depending on which software application is used. Such tools allow the tutor to give immediate feedback as well as flexibility in how and when the tests are delivered. Some VLEs allow the release of further materials and activities only once such tests have been successfully completed using a selective release mechanism. Audio and audio/visual assessments and feedback are growing in popularity.

There are digital tools which can assist the process of marking assignments online, such as digital pens and these can be integrated with the administrative tools available in VLEs to manage and administer online submissions. Most institutions have specific guidance and policies to deal with the administration, marking and feedback relating to assessment, as well as plagiarism detection tools such as Turnitin which can offer considerable efficiencies for managing and marking assignments. Tools such as VLEs and e-portfolios, wikis and blogs can be used to facilitate group and peer assessments, as well as more traditional essays and projects. Given the high-stakes status of the majority of assessments it is essential that the part-time online tutor is offered the necessary staff development to achieve competence in the use of these tools, and is made aware of any accessibility policies which may be required.

Finding support

It is clear from the preceding sections in this chapter that the part-time tutor faces considerable challenges in accessing and sustaining the levels of support required if they are to be effective in their roles as online course designers and facilitators. Responsibility for supporting part-time staff in these roles varies considerably between and across institutions. In some cases this kind of support can be acquired from centralised teams offering educational development, whilst in others there may be e-learning units or departmental and/or school-based mentors or technology champions who are able to provide training and support in the pedagogic and technology skills identified in this chapter.

When you are applying to take up a role that requires you to participate in online learning, or this has started to become a normal part of your current role, it is essential you are able to reflect on the skills you have and what development you might need so you are able to ask about the support early on. Often in today's digital world there is an assumption that many staff have a good knowledge of this area and the skills necessary to be able to undertake this type of teaching.

As this chapter has argued, these skills are specialised and professional development is needed to acquire and practise them. Ideally sources of support should be identified in the induction offered to part-time staff, but in practice it is often the initiative and enthusiasm of the part-timer who identifies where such support may be accessed. Being allocated a mentor within your department is also a useful form of support and can often help identify the support available for online learning.

In addition most universities have professional development programmes which provide seminars and workshops to develop these skills but also often modules on technology enhanced learning which are part of a postgraduate teaching qualification but can be taken as 'stand-alone' modules. These are also offered to external participants but there are a range of organisations which offer short courses and modules in this area, often online.

Participating in peer-review schemes within your institution also enables you to receive feedback on your teaching activity and enables you to explore what others do and provides opportunities to share good practice.

Conclusion

This brief survey of the core skills required to be an effective online tutor has highlighted the wide range of digital tools and practices which are available to teach in the rapidly evolving online environment. However the availability of staff development opportunities to scaffold and support the acquisition of expertise in the pedagogy and technologies for online tuition is patchy at best. There is currently no widely recognised entry-level qualification in online tuition, though some institutions provide post-graduate qualifications for teaching online (for a UK list see http://wiki.alt.ac.uk/index.php/TEL_Courses). The growing popularity of online programmes, whether blended or fully online, demands that all who are involved in supporting online part-time tutors recognise the need for specific, focused and ongoing staff development if the quality of online delivery is to match or exceed that of more traditional modes of education. The transformation of higher and further education currently under way, in part driven by developments in learning technology, requires a skilled and digitally literate staff, whether full or part time. As more institutions seek to employ part-time staff to deliver their programmes, there needs to be a clear institutional strategy for developing appropriate skills in their workforce.

References

Anderson, T. and Elloumi, F (2004) Theory and Practice of Online Learning. Athabasca University. http://cde.athabascau.ca/online_book/ (PDF or HTML).

Bates T. (1995) *Technology, Open Learning and Distance Education*. London: Routledge.

Beetham, H. and Sharpe, R. (2007) *Rethinking Pedagogy for a Digital Age: Designing and Delivering E-Learning*. Abingdon: Routledge.

Frand, J. (2000) The Information Age Mindset: Changes in Students and Implications for Higher Education. *Educause Review*, September/October. http://net.educause.edu/apps/er/erm00/articles005/erm0051.pdf.

Garrison, D.R. and Vaughan, N. (2008) *Blended Learning in Higher Education: Framework, Principles and Guidelines*. San Francisco: Jossey Bass.

Kear, K. (2011) *Online and Social Networking Communities: A Best Practice Guide for Educators*. Abingdon: Routledge.

Laurillard, D. (2008) Digital Technologies and Their Role in Achieving Our Ambitions for Education. Inaugural Lecture to the Institute of Education. London: Institute of Education.

Littlejohn, A. and Pegler, C. (2007) *Preparing for Blended E-Learning: Understanding Blended and Online Learning*. Abingdon: Routledge

MacDonald, J. (2006) *Blended Learning and Online Tutoring*. Aldershot: Gower.

Martinez Aleman, A.M. and Wartman, K.L. (2009) *Online Social Networking on Campus*. Abingdon: Routledge.

Mason, R. and Rennie, F. (2004) *The Connecticon: Learning for the Connected Generation*. USA Information Age Publishing.

Mason, R. and Rennie, F. (2008) *E-Learning and Social Networking Handbook*. Abingdon: Routledge.

OLTF (Online Learning Task Force) (2011) Collaborate to Compete: Seizing the Opportunity of Online Learning for UK Higher Education. Higher Education Funding Council For England (HEFCE). www.hefce.ac.uk/learning/enhance/taskforce/.

Paloff, R.M. and Pratt, K. (1999) *Building Learning Communities in Cyberspace: Effective Strategies for the Online Classroom*. San Francisco: Jossey Bass.

Salmon, G. (2011) *E Moderation: The Key to Teaching and Learning Online*. London: Taylor & Kogan.

Siemens, G. (2004) Connectivism: A Learning Theory for the Digital Age. www.elearnspace.org/Articles/connectivism.htm.

Smith B. (2006) Teaching Online: New or Transferable Skills? Higher Education Academy. www.heacademy.ac.uk/assets/documents/resources/resourcedatabase/id455_teaching_online.pdf.

Wray, M., Lowenthal, P., Bates, B. and Stevens, E. (2008) Investigating Perceptions of Teaching Online and F2F. *Academic Exchange Quarterly*. http://rapidintellect.com/AEQweb/

Websites

Icebreakers

www.southalabama.edu/oll/jobaidsfall03/Icebreakers%20Online/icebreakerjobaid.htm

Netiquette

http://en.wikipedia.org/wiki/Netiquette
www.adbh.co.uk/tu170/netiquette.php

Creepy treehouse

http://flexknowlogy.learningfield.org/2008/04/09/defining-creepy-tree-house/

Assessment and feedback

www.redpentool.com/
https://turnitin.com/static/index.php

Post-graduate courses in online tuition

http://wiki.alt.ac.uk/index.php/TEL_Courses

10

ALL TAKE AND NO GIVE?

RESPONDING TO THE SUPPORT AND DEVELOPMENT NEEDS OF WOMEN IN CASUAL ACADEMIC ROLES

Karen Starr

Introduction

This chapter discusses the experiences and perceptions of women employed in casual academic roles in a large Australian university. It then canvasses the professional learning and support needs for this segment of the university workforce. The experiences of casual staff in this research correspond with those reported in other Australian studies (see, for example, Dever *et al.* 2006; Eveline 1998; Payne and Shoemark 1995) and those from elsewhere in the world (see, for example, Clark *et al.* 1996; Knights and Richards 2003; Lindsay 1996; Mertz 2009; Morley 1999). The casual workforce is continually expanding, which raises questions about how individuals within it can be supported to grow as academics and professionals within an expanding and more accountable higher education sector.

Extant research across Australian universities reveals gendered statistical discrimination, employee clustering and wage gaps, the operation of the 'glass ceiling', as well as gender equity inhibitors such as intimidation, discrimination, exclusion, violence (including bullying, harassment and physical violence) and stressors from the conflicting demands of work and family life (e.g. Bessant 1998; Delaat 2007; Dever *et al.* 2006; Eveline 1998; Hearn and Parkin 2007; Payne and Shoemark 1995; Shands 1998). The organisational consequences of such inhibitors include a more mobile workforce and lowered personnel retention, reduced productivity, unwelcoming organisational cultures, reputational damage, a reduced ability to attain organisational strategic goals or enact core values, and inhibited human capacity. Concomitant personal and professional consequences include negative health effects, feelings of inadequacy, reduced opportunities for career advancement and professional isolation.

Despite the mandatory adoption of anti-discrimination policies in Australia, gender-based employment and income disparities persist (ABS 2007; Cassells *et al.* 2009; Healy *et al.* 2009). This is created through human capital variables such as a lack of employer-provided training, women's lower qualification levels, occupational segregation based on employment sector (in this case the public sector) and industry (in this case education), discriminatory attitudes and labour-market rigidities (Cassells *et al.* 2009; Healy *et al.* 2009).

Australia's casual workforce is the fastest growing in the world after Spain (Munn 2004). Casual workers are defined by the Australian Bureau of Statistics (2007) as those without an ongoing employment contract or access to usual leave entitlements. Due to the short-term or temporary nature of this work, casual employees have little protection available from unions or industrial awards. While usually receiving a pay loading above the hourly rate paid of that paid to permanent employees, casual academics can be dismissed at short notice with no recourse to severance or redundancy payments (Cassells *et al.* 2009). A lack of job security and employment certainty can make it difficult or impossible to maintain a reasonable standard of living or to secure a mortgage, for example (Forward 2005), and has longer-term implications for superannuation savings. Predominantly, casual academics in Australia are women (Foddy *et al.* 1996; White 2001).

The rapid expansion of the casual workforce in Australian universities is primarily due to budgetary cutbacks as globalisation increases the impetus for organisational 'efficiencies', national and institutional competitiveness and workforce flexibility (Munn 2004). Market-driven principles and corporate managerialism have railed against and diminished equity policies and pursuits (Marginson and Considine 2007), while gendered power relations and masculine organisational cultures persist in the Australian higher education sector (White 2001).

In this research, the great majority of casual workers (also referred to as 'sessionals') held part-time positions, with full-time casual employment being less common. Casuals are positioned at the bottom rungs of the academic hierarchy which in Australia goes from Level A (assistant lecturer) to Level E (professor). The university employs twice as many casual women academics as men. Within this group, three times as many women than men are employed at Lecturer A and B level (see note 1) with the opposite occurring at the highest end of the academic employment spectrum where over twice as many men are employed as professors (Level E) compared to women (73 to 32).

This research sought to identify those aspects of the university's policies, practices and work culture that proved positive for women academics that should be enhanced, and those that had deleterious effects which should be eliminated or improved.

The study privileged the lived experience and voices of all women academics, but this chapter focuses on the responses of those employed in casual positions during 2010. Through anecdotes and very frank accounts of their experiences, perceptions, beliefs and suggestions derived through a university-wide survey and semi-structured interviews, this chapter delineates benefits, common problems and their effects, and canvasses ideas for what should change for the current professional development and support needs of casual staff to be met.

Below the advantages and disadvantages of casual employment are discussed before turning to their implications for professional learning and support, and ramifications for policy change.

The advantages of casual academic work

It is important to state at the outset that the women participating in this research generally stated they 'loved' their jobs, and many appreciated the flexibility and family-friendly hours that were possible through casual academic appointments.

Casual academic jobs are often in demand from those who are not currently seeking permanent employment in academia, such as doctoral students, those undertaking studies in a location that is not going to be their home beyond the short term, those who have caring duties or those from other employment sectors who see it as an avenue to future permanent employment.

The flexibility, self-regulatory and self-directed nature of casual and part-time academic work was reportedly a highly valued feature. For women with children, the ability to work from home and to come and go to meet family obligations was a feature of university working life that they believed would not be available in many other work environments. Similarly, women who had other caring responsibilities, such as aged parents, cited this as a positive aspect. The women who felt the benefits of casual employment believed that their decision to work was in their own hands, casual work provided income or extra income, and provided the flexibility to attend to caring, nurturing or other interests.

Some women cited that through casual work they were able to pursue their own research interests. Some needed to earn extra income while undertaking doctoral or other studies, while others continually undertook part-time contracts because they did not want full-time work and part-time permanent posts rarely come up.

Research respondents believed they required and possessed high-level time-management skills and the ability to juggle many tasks. Many were proud of their achievements and reported having good rapport with students and their permanently employed peers. Some casual women were pleased to have been offered opportunities to assume membership on faculty committees, which they believed would benefit their curriculum vitae.

The disadvantages of casual academic work

Despite the benefits of casual work, many drawbacks were reported which are categorised under two major themes discussed below.

Teaching

When it comes to sessional teaching there are severe disadvantages, both for students and casual academics themselves. Casual academics cannot make long-term plans, often don't know until just before a semester commences whether they have a job or not, do not have a dedicated office or university-supplied computer, and have little access to the collegiality and support of their permanently employed peers or the opportunity to get to know them. Some women explained how they travel to and from work with their materials permanently residing in their car boot (Forward 2005). Hourly payments for sessional staff exclude essential activities such as meeting attendance, preparation, marking, student consultations and the administrative work attached to teaching, but have concomitant costs such as petrol, car-parking, childcare and time.

The women cited feelings of guilt and resentment about out-of-hours work (such as responding to student queries – often online) which was unpaid, although students who are unaware of teachers' part-time, casual employment status expect instant replies. The women therefore expressed the fear of receiving unfavourable survey results in compulsory student course and teacher evaluations. Not only were survey results used to determine future employment, but they were also instrumental in determining relationships with the permanently employed academics who engaged their services.[2] Some illustrative comments were:

> At certain times of year (e.g. marking exams) I have no choice but to mark all weekend to get them done in time to submit results. This is very hard on my family life. It is also hard having lecture times scheduled (e.g. 4–6 p.m.) which do not allow time for me to get from the university to the child care centre.

> I had a course meeting to attend – unpaid, but I showed up because I supposed they have bothered to include me as part of the team . . . There were no car parks left. Eventually I found one, rushed to the meeting, only to find I'd received a parking fine when I returned. There was a sign that I'd missed apparently when I drove in – I wasn't allowed to park there. That meeting cost me $120 and the meeting turned out to be a waste of time anyway . . .

> . . . students are very demanding . . . if only they knew how many students you had and how much work there was to do! They expect instant responses on [the university's learning management system] . . . There's little respect sometimes . . .

However, interviewees believed that since they did more face-to-face teaching than many permanent or full-time staff, they often knew the students better than their peers, and felt they could be of more assistance to students. Timetabling arrangements often didn't suit them, with part-time hours being spread throughout the week rather than in convenient blocks of time, yet for casual academics it's often the case of 'take it or leave it'.[3]

With Australian universities relying increasingly on full fee paying international students, much teaching is conducted online. The demands of online students from around the world with their different time zones can be overwhelming, especially when a failure to respond in a timely way can result in low student evaluations of teaching, as mentioned above. The most invasive part is that online teaching can occur anywhere and at anytime, including at home, after hours. Sessionals reported working much unpaid overtime to keep up with their students' demands, with some courses literally enrolling hundreds of students.

Research participants believed that the university places its emphasis on research over teaching and community service (the three aspects cited as comprising the work of an academic). This palpable emphasis is seen to position casual teaching intensive staff in an inferior category, adding to the low status attached to their non-permanent employment. All complained of too much 'administrivia' such that it is, in reality, a fourth, hidden and time-consuming dimension to academic work.

Working conditions

The most severe aspect of casual employment is the lack of entitlement to any kind of leave, with sick leave and holiday leave cited as being the most difficult downside. Australian university courses typically do not run during the Christmas period, and therefore casuals often don't work from November until March. This situation causes some women to take on more work than they would like during the year to put money aside to cope with this annual 'down time'. However, additional shorter periods of 'down time' occur during the year during semester breaks.

Workloads for most casuals are high during peak teaching periods. Some reported working fewer hours than they would have liked while others who wanted more work reported losing hours due to funding cutbacks, programme discontinuation or research projects coming to an end (that provided money for a permanent academic's 'teaching buy-out' which sessionals fill). Earning sufficient income can be difficult.

Mostly, the women had interrupted careers and had either entered or returned to academia after having children. Many were the primary caregivers to minors and took on the majority of household work in their families, hence family constraints conspired with university workloads to make for difficult working lives.

Many research participants reported being appointed as committee representatives and while there is an upside to this (reported above), the downside is that once on a committee, many eventually saw this as another unpaid task and waste of precious time. With so many other things to do, committee meetings were seen to be boring, unproductive, time-consuming and irrelevant to the work of casuals.

The prevailing perception is that sessionals are at 'the bottom of the heap', earning little respect or encouragement. The women spoke about the individualistic nature of academic lives and feelings of being 'exploited'. They believed that unacceptable workplace behaviours were evident, were tolerated and went unchecked. They felt isolated and invisible with a lack of support and access to information in a competitive environment:

> . . . there's a . . . culture of individualism in academia and looking after yourself rather than working in a team . . . when you do need assistance or you do need someone to go out of their way to do something to help you, it's a very rare individual who will do that and you're . . . left to flounder on your own . . . especially in the early stages . . . there's no one in a senior position actually assisting you or supervising you. It does often lead to a culture of blame and stepping away from problems rather than people helping and assisting to solve the problem.

The women also felt they received little or no recognition, acknowledgement or thanks for their efforts.[4]

While some women valued the freedom and flexibility to pursue self-determined working practices, most expressed a sense of oppression from the university's 'greediness' (Franzway 2001), with expectations and the boundless nature of their work taking no account of their working hours or status.

Some sessionals had received some form of induction while others had none beyond an initial conversation to complete an employment contract. A do-it-yourself (DIY) ethos was acutely experienced by new staff especially, who felt thrown in the deep-end as they were expected to survive with little support. Unfortunately, those who mentioned induction processes saw these as inadequate and unhelpful – they were conducted online and not face-to-face. It was a case of 'sink or swim'.

All interviewees wished to be successful, but saw the only means of achieving this was to work harder and for longer. The women saw that expectations of long hours were exacerbated by too many 'invisible' administrative tasks perpetuated and exacerbated by Web 2.0 technologies and the seemingly universal acceptance of a 24/7 university work culture driven by personal desires for 'success'. They said:

> Most of the time there is no time to do anything but work, otherwise you fall hopelessly behind. So instead you fall hopelessly behind on housework, friends, family, etc.

> While the flexibility of academic life in theory allows me to be available to my family when I am really needed, the pressure of workload means that I rarely take up this opportunity.

> [Work] impacts principally through high stress levels at home, long work hours due to poor managerial decisions on workload balances. I was recently asked to go up to 0.8 employment and was asked to take on more teaching despite the fact that I am already working considerably more than I am being paid for. Evenings become more work time rather than family time.

> [I am] mostly working more than my part-time hours in order to get things done at the level that is expected but at the same time being aware of the unspoken views of more senior staff that part-time staff are not as committed.

> For my first few years . . . I was so stressed that it impacted on my health, and the stress and health issues impacted on my family life. These days I have adopted my stubborn refusal to make [the university] the centre of my world. It impacts in the sense that retirement saving will be constrained by my inability to progress my career . . . But I'd rather get to retirement with my health intact than with more dollars in super and major stress-related health issues.

Compared to other sections of the academic workforce, there are fewer casually employed women who hold doctoral degrees, yet many are doctoral candidates. The women expressed difficulty in finding time for research, publication and furthering their own qualifications due to their employment commitments. This was a universal concern amongst respondents who were looking to become a full-time academic. Many had been appointed in casual positions for many years, and could see little hope of obtaining permanent work. To acquire a permanent position usually requires a PhD and a publication record, but this is a vicious circle, with their current role taking valuable time and energy away from achieving the required pre-requisites. This situation is exacerbated when casual staff members are not permitted to be named in national competitive research funding submissions. And once employed on the lowest rungs of the academic ladder, acquiring promotion entails achieving 'research active' status, although there are few opportunities for teaching intensive staff to obtain a sizable research record and experience:

It is generally research that is shuffled/omitted to make way for both teaching and family commitments which are both required and inflexible.

The women understood that to be successful, they have to make time for the 'important' work that 'counts' in universities, which mostly revolves around research and publications. The following quote demonstrates the constant self-questioning about how time is used and for what purposes and the dilemma that there are always things that get in the way of this 'important' work:

I think the challenge of the job – my aim – is always to step outside the job and see what's important, what will be important next week, not now and try and do those jobs – not the ones that are crowding me for attention. I still have to learn that everybody has to learn that skill everyday to try and shut out all the noise and focus on what really matters in the job.

Casual staff members have few opportunities to attend professional development activities in work time. While continual professional learning is an expectation, such activities are often conducted at the personal expense of sessionals and in their own time.

The casual academics were generally not members of the union and so exploitation and unfairness goes unaddressed. Without job security, leave provisions, regular working hours, professional training, opportunities for career planning or advancement, these women are at a distinct disadvantage (Waddoups 2005).

Health, wellbeing and work/life balance were issues of concern, with many women feeling that their working lives impinged detrimentally on their personal and family lives and their personal health, happiness and sense of wellbeing.

Significantly, the women were sceptical of the importance that the university's corporate leaders placed in gender equity and fair employment issues, and were pessimistic about improvements occurring in the near future.

Implications for professional learning, development and support

The implications of the above information for professional learning, development and support are considerable. The women had many suggestions and ideas that they believed would improve their position and functioning as members of the academic workforce.[5] They believed the following measures would enable and assist their contribution to the effective functioning of the university and their contribution to university life:

- The women argued they needed role models of casual staff who had positive experiences of working in higher education – 'who have learnt how to work the system and get through the red tape, who've coped and pushed through and accomplished to get somewhere for themselves'. Towards the same ends, some suggested the benefits of having mentors who could inform their induction and continued work in academia. Respondents wanted someone who could advise, provide insights, answer questions, encourage and help them to devise positive strategies for their teaching, research, service and future employment.

- A proper induction process is required, preferably with back-up written materials to refer to afterwards. The types of induction components mentioned included learning how to navigate and use university's learning management systems (online teaching and learning programmes which currently sessionals have to 'work out' for themselves); the important policies related to teaching and learning, such as assessment policies, assignment timelines, citation conventions, misconduct protocols, etc.; the university's faculty structures, personnel and their roles and contact details; faculty strategic plans; basic information about administrative requirements; campus maps; how library support can be utilised; sources of technical support, for example.

- Opportunities for further professional learning and development conducted during paid work time and free of cost to contracted sessionals. These opportunities included attendance at faculty retreats, university provided conferences (which were also seen to be a useful means by which fledgling researchers could disseminate and discuss their own research), as well as access to national and international conferences. For these latter, more expensive activities, some suggested that a pool of funds could be allocated through which sessionals could apply for funding on a competitive basis.

- Ongoing 'over-the-shoulder' support for online learning management systems (which appear to be different across universities). Help lines for dealing with difficulties, with their long phone queues, are frustrating and waste more (unpaid) time. (The area of online teaching difficulties and the propensity of academics to engage with constantly changing technologies is so extensive it formed the focus of other research, hence extensive details will not be provided here – see Starr *et al.* 2011; Starr forthcoming 2012.)

- The women called for specialised support from the university's human resources division and for policies that pertained to their particular needs. For example, the women believed the unpaid work issue should be addressed; there is a lack of any plans or policies for casual staff to convert to permanent employment status – it appears as if sessional ranks just keep expanding, with no strategy as to what percentage of staff should remain on an inferior employment footing. There were calls for sessional staff to be represented during enterprise bargaining rounds (which determine pay and work conditions). Some also called for information about leadership development, promotion and career advancement in the university.

- The women called for time to pursue their own studies and research, in much the same way as provisionally employed Level A academics who do not have a PhD are able to access supplementary provisions (time and money). This was seen as being 'pie in the sky' for first time sessionals, but for those who have 'been around for years and are part of the woodwork', this provision would be seen as indicative of the worth of casuals and acknowledgement of their needs for continual learning development as well as opportunities for professional advancement. Women also called for support for their research, publications and grant applications.
- The women believed that networks of casual staff should be developed. Blogs or professional associations or alliances with other academics who supported their needs, were seen to be an idea that could provide support, encouragement and good ideas but which could also provide advocacy and political impetus. This was seen as the major way that university policies could be challenged or changed – through effective, organised, collective action. (While unions perform such roles, some respondents argued they could not afford union fees and were dissuaded from joining when their employment was so uncertain.) (See Waddoups 2005.)
- Some longstanding casuals were aware that their permanently employed peers are encouraged to forge a nexus between teaching and research. To achieve this requires time for academics to pursue both research and teaching enhancement activities. They believed that their circumstances thwarted such ideals, yet they saw that their chances for permanent employment might be enhanced if they could speak to and demonstrate such professionalism.
- The women called for some basics: more chances for collaboration, collegiality and teamwork with all peers and access to proper university facilities such as meeting and office spaces and up-to-date IT resources.
- Lastly, but importantly from a cultural sense, the women called for more respect, recognition, acknowledgement and appreciation from personnel at all levels and from all sectors of the university.

Conclusion

This research revealed many similarities in women's stories and experiences to those reported in other research literature on gender in higher education.

Unfortunately, the same sorts of findings have been reoccurring over decades. These are independent individuals who almost universally experienced a sense of workplace isolation, frustration and invisibility. This corresponds with the stories in Mertz's (2009) book and those cited by Isaac, which resound with 'self-silencing' and working twice as hard as women had to 'walk fast, and catch up' (Isaac 2007). Unsurprisingly, then, the women believed their criticisms and concerns to be general within the higher education sector and not specifically related to their employing university alone.

Due to the power of hegemonic social values some inequalities are so structurally and historically entrenched and naturalised as to be generally invisible (Hearn and Parkin 2007). Despite numerous policies, legislative interventions and workplace practices, gender inequalities continue to operate. The university is perceived to provide gender neutral policies that appear, in reality, to be gender blind. Innate subtle, covert biases still appear to explain gender discrimination; and despite gender-friendly, equity and anti-discrimination policies, the 'difference' prevails. Hence the organisational cultures within higher education institutions perform a similar function to those elsewhere in everyday life. As yet, equity policies and practices have not been totally successful.

The casualisation of higher education with reduced employment conditions and benefits, a greater diversity of students, larger classes and workloads, the atomistic nature of academic teaching and learning, and a plethora of invisible but time-consuming work tasks are the commonly expressed downsides of casual working arrangements (Payne and Shoemark 1995). Feelings of exploitation, work intensification, and lack of acknowledgement and gratification are exacerbated if these essential staff members are not sufficiently supported professionally in appropriate and responsive ways.

Such issues have important ramifications for teaching and learning quality, now an integral component of the Australian higher education policy and funding landscape. From 2012 government funds to universities will be distributed according to students' choices of courses and institutions, creating a more competitive market in higher education based on consumer choice and determinations of 'quality' (Bradley *et al.* 2008). Since large numbers of students are taught by casual staff, some investment in their professional learning and support is urgently warranted. Of concern, however, is that while casual staffing numbers are growing, resources for support and development are inadequate or diminishing or are being relegated as a personal responsibility (Forward 2005).

The positive outcome of this research is that many of the suggestions for improvement nominated by casual women employees would require little in the way of resources or effort to enact. The ideas are sensible, reasonable and quite conceivably could produce effective results for casual staff members and their students, especially at a time when market forces are ramping up with possibly massive consequences for the higher education sector.

Since casual staff members feel marginalised from university decision making and employment provisioning, the suggestions cited above could include one more – that in addressing issues surrounding casual academic employment, incumbents themselves should be the first port of call for ideas for improvement in the development of (much needed) appropriate policies and procedures and their proper and timely enactment in practice.

Notes

1   The academic promotion structure spans Levels A to E: A = associate lecturer, B = lecturer, C = senior lecturer, D = associate professor, E = professor.
2   When academics receive research funds they may include teaching substitution to enable them more time for intensive research work. While they may employ sessional staff to undertake these teaching commitments, student satisfaction survey results are attributed to the permanent teacher.
3   The overall research observed higher levels of work satisfaction the higher women were positioned on the academic promotional ladder. The most satisfied women usually had long academic careers and had learnt to work within the structures and processes governing their work. Women employed at Levels D and E had more discretion in their work, with teaching loads reduced due to their research profile and made up to a large extent by doctoral or masters research students.
4   Such rewards were seen to be missing for the majority of women academics whether permanently employed or casual staff, and were seen to be important to everyone at every stage in their careers. The effects of women academics' labour going unrecognised resulted in feelings of alienation and work atomisation and distant institutional support and allegiance.
5   Naturally the women expressed many ideas and suggestions to ameliorate their circumstances. Here I mention only those related to the topic of this chapter.

References

Australian Bureau of Statistics (2007) *Working Time Arrangements, Australia*, November 2006, catalogue no. 6342.0, Australian Bureau of Statistics: Canberra, ACT.

Bessant, J. (1998) 'Women in academia and opaque violence', *Melbourne Studies in Education*, 39(2): 41–67.

Bradley, D., Noonan, P., Nugent, H. and Scales, B. (2008) *Review of Australian Higher Education: Final Report*. Canberra: Department of Education, Employment and Workplace Relations.

Cassells, R., Vidyattama, Y., Miranti, R. and McNamara, J. (2009) *The Impact of a Sustained Gender Wage Gap in the Australian Economy*. Report to the Office of Women, Department of Families, Housing, Community Services and Indigenous Affairs, Commonwealth of Australia: Canberra, ACT.

Clark, V., Nelson Garner, S., Higouret, M. and Katrak, K. H. (1996) *Anti-feminism in Academia*. New York: Routledge.

Delaat, J. (2007) *Gender in the Workplace: A Case Study Approach*. Thousand Oaks, CA: SAGE Publications.

Dever, M., Morrison, Z., Dalton, B. and Tayton, S. (2006) *When Research Works for Women*. Report to the Vice Chancellor, Monash University, April.

Eveline, J. (1998) 'Naming male advantage: a feminist theorist looks into the future'. In A. Mackinnin, I. Elgqvist-Saltzman and A. Prentice (eds) *Education into the 21st Century: Dangerous Terrain for Women?* London: Falmer Press, pp. 177–188.

Foddy, M., Flannagan, J. and Fry, C. (1996) *Gender and Research at La Trobe University: A Quantitative and Qualitative Study*. Equity and Access Unit, La Trobe University, Melbourne, Victoria.

Forward, P. (2005) Casualisation of the TAFE teaching workforce. Speech by Australian Education Union Vice President, Victorian Branch, 15 November.

Franzway, S. (2001) *Sexual Politics and Greedy Institutions: Union Women, Commitments and Conflicts in Public and Private*. Sydney, NSW: Pluto Press.

Hearn, J. and Parkin, W. (2007) 'The emotionality of organisation violations: gender relations in practice'. In P. Lewis and R. Simpson (eds) *Gendering Emotions in Organizations*. Basingstoke: Palgrave Macmillan.

Healy, J., Kidd, M. and Richardson, S. (2009) *Gender Pay Differentials in the Low-Paid Labour Market*. Report commissioned by the Australian Fair Pay Commission. National Institute of Labour Studies, Flinders University, Adelaide, South Australia.

Isaac, C. (2007) *Women Deans: Patterns of Power*. Lanham, MD: University Press of America.

Knights, D. and Richards, W. (2003) 'Sex discrimination in UK academia', *Gender, Work and Organization*, 10(2): 213–238.

Lindsay, K. A. (1996) 'A critique of the culture of complaint: Trends in complaints of sex discrimination in university employment', *Australian and New Zealand Law Journal or Law Education*, 1(1): 99–110.

Marginson, S. and Considine, M. (2007) *The Enterprise University: Power, Governance and Reinvention in Australia*. Cambridge: Cambridge University Press.

Mertz, N. T. (2009) *Breaking into the All-Male Club: Female Professors of Educational Administration*. Albany, NY: State University of New York Press.

Morley, L. (1999) *Organizing Feminism: The Micropolitics of the Academy*. New York: St. Martin's Press.

Munn, C. (2004) ANZ Economic Update, 13 May.

Payne, A. M. and Shoemark, L. (eds) (1995) 'Women, culture and universities: a chilly climate?' Conference Proceedings of the National Conference on the Effect of Organisational Culture on Women in Universities, University of Technology, Sydney, 12–20 April.

Shands, K. W. (1998) 'Doppler effects: female frequencies in higher education'. In A. Mackinnin, I. Elgqvist-Saltzman and A. Prentice (eds) *Education into the 21st Century: Dangerous Terrain for Women?* London: Falmer Press, pp. 142–152.

Smith, D. E. (1988) *The Everyday World as Problematic: A Feminist Sociology*. Milton Keynes: Open University Press.

Starr, K. (forthcoming 2012) 'Refining pedagogy by reviewing professional learning for online course delivery'. In M. Piscioneri (ed.) *Effectively Implementing Information Communication Technology in Higher Education in the Asia-Pacific Region.* Hauppauge, New York: Nova Science Publishers, Inc.

Starr, K., Stacey, E. and Grace, L. (2011) 'Changing technologies/renewing pedagogies: implications for university teaching and learning'. In G. Trentin and M. Repetto (eds) *Faculty Training on Web Enhanced Learning.* Hauppauge, NY: Nova Science Publishers, pp. 95–108.

Waddoups, C. J. (2005) 'Trade union decline and union wage effects in Australia', *Industrial Relations*, 44(4): 607–624.

White, K. (2001) 'Women in the professoriate in Australia', *International Journal of Organisational Behaviour*, 3(2): 64–76.

SECTION III

IMPLICATIONS AND FUTURE DIRECTIONS

11
BUILDING SUSTAINABLE FRAMEWORKS FOR THE ENGAGEMENT AND DEVELOPMENT OF CASUAL TEACHING STAFF

AN AUSTRALIAN PERSPECTIVE

Muyessur Durur and Jennifer Gilmore

Introduction

Higher education in many countries in the world has undergone significant change in the past 20 years. For example, funding needs in higher education have led management to seek and/or accept a broad range of solutions to meet the rapidly increasing demand for and costs of higher education within a generally decreasing level of real funding per student. Nowhere is this better illustrated than in Australia, with one major consequence being the increased casualisation of the academic workforce. This situation will no doubt resonate with other countries undergoing similar fiscal and other challenges in their higher education sectors. Given this scenario, strategies for building sustainable frameworks that will ensure that a casual academic workforce will maintain and enhance quality teaching and learning cultures in universities is the key focus of this chapter.

In analysing the then current policy pertinent to casual (or 'sessional'[1]) academic staff and practice across sixteen selected Australian universities, a recent report (The RED Report 2008) indicated that:

> Evidence of systemic sustainable policy and practice is rare, that:
> - there is a general lack of formal policy and procedures in relation to the employment and administrative support for seasonal teachers;
> - while induction is considered important in all universities, the ongoing academic management of sessional teachers is not as well understood or articulated;
> - paid participation on compulsory professional development for sessional teachers is atypical; and
> - despite various national and institutional recognition and reward initiatives, many sessional teachers continue to feel their contribution is undervalued.
>
> (The RED Report 2008: 2)

To place the increasing casualisation of the higher education academic teaching workforce into context, it is necessary to identify the major changes that are impacting on the employment patterns of academic staff in Australia. These changes are not unique to higher education in Australia, and the situation in countries other than Australia is addressed in other sections of this book. These changes are also addressed in much of the literature and research on higher education and include, but are not limited to:

- the need for all academic teaching staff to have the appropriate expertise and tools, including Learning Management Systems, in order to cope successfully with the changing demands of teaching;
- real decreases in funding per student funded by government for higher education whilst costs are increasing;
- changing student expectations and the move to have funding 'follow the student' as a consequence of the recent Review of Australian Higher Education, 'The Bradley Review' (2008);
- mass education access, including the growth in both the number of universities and student numbers within universities, has changed the student mix in both ability and interests, with a greater emphasis on 'job readiness' and consequently an increasing vocational orientation of many courses being offered;
- the growth of the 'knowledge economy', the rapidity with which new information is generated and disseminated through ever changing technology and the growth of multi-disciplinary approaches seeking to integrate knowledge across traditional disciplinary boundaries;
- the reliance of universities on fee-paying international students, both at Australian campuses and off-shore campuses.

In Australia, furthermore, a number of demographic challenges have influenced the move to a greater casualisation of the academic workforce. These include the aging of the tenured academic population and the exponential growth in the demand for higher education, neither of which has been matched by a growth in the academic workforce. Despite an increase in the number of higher degree research (HDR) completions, reductions in funding have not led to either the generation of new jobs or the attraction of full-time research staff.

Commenting on this situation, Coates and Goedegebuure (2010: 2) contend that, 'In Australia today, fewer academic staff are available to do a growing amount of work. And the capacity of the workforce is shrinking relative to almost linear growth in the size of the system.' Moreover, Bexley *et al.* (2011: xii) found that, 'Overall, when both short and long-term intentions are taken into consideration, close to half of the academic workforce intend to retire, move to an overseas university or leave Australian higher education at some time in the next ten years.' In addition the report notes a major concern that, 'Younger academics, crucial to regenerating the workforce as older members move towards retirement, reveal high levels of dissatisfaction with their job security and levels of pay' (Bexley *et al.* 2011: xii).

Casualisation of teaching staff in Australian universities

The important contribution of casual academic staff in Australian universities was noted by Professor Rob Castle, Deputy Vice Chancellor, Wollongong University in his Introduction to The RED Report (2008) as follows:

> Sessional teachers are the hidden part of the massification that has taken place in higher education in Australia over the last 30 years. One of the greatest achievements of the Australian higher education system has been the growth of student access to university study, and this could not have been achieved without the massive contribution of sessional staff.
>
> (The RED Report: Foreword)

It is difficult, however, to measure accurately the level of casualisation of the Australian higher education workforce and estimate the number of casual staff, as no separate statistics are collected about the number of non-tenured part-time or casual/sessional staff. As at mid-2008 according to The RED Report (2008), between 20 and 50 per cent of teaching in Australian higher education was carried out by casual staff. A more recent report (Bexley *et al.* 2011: 1) discusses the difficulty in accurately determining the number of casual staff and refers to new research using the superannuation records of university staff that indicates that there are currently 67,000 academics employed on a casual basis, comprising 60 per cent of the academic workforce.[2]

The authors, using full-time equivalent (FTE) data held by the Commonwealth Department of Education, Employment and Workplace Relations (DEEWR), identify the characteristics of casual staff to include:

- positions are typically concentrated in the lower academic classifications, 71 per cent is undertaken by employees at Level A (Associate Lecturer) and 24 per cent at Level B (Lecturer); and
- casual contracts are more common in some disciplines than others, with 30 percent of FTE staffing in the Creative Arts, Architecture and Education

being sessional, compared with 13 per cent in Agriculture and 10 per cent in Society and Culture.

The changes facing the higher education sector, including those identified above, have been instrumental in the increasing use of casual academic staff in higher education in Australia. Casual academic staff in Australia are defined as academic staff who are employed by the hour, and do not include part-time tenured staff who receive pro rata benefits of full-time staff, although the issue of 'unpaid work' and access to and time scheduled for paid professional development are also relevant to this section of the academic workforce.

It should also be noted that for many universities the employment in a casual capacity of currently practising experts in their profession and/or HDR students is a deliberate policy that seeks to enrich and deepen the learning of students.

There is an inherent conflict facing higher education in that universities need to retain flexibility in the employment of academic staff when student numbers and course selection may vary significantly year on year. The dilemma facing higher education institutions is the need to manage the substantive costs of employing a large full-time/part-time staff and ensuring a high level of student engagement and quality learning experiences, when it is difficult to quantify demand.

The significant use of casual staff is also occurring at a time when an academic career is generally not viewed as attractive by a key group of potential academic staff, that is graduating PhD students. A key finding in the report by Bexley *et al.* (2011: iii) notes this as a major concern as their evidence indicates that

'HDR candidates believe a secure academic career is difficult to obtain and academic work is poorly paid.' This is particularly concerning in terms of sustaining a future supply of qualified academic staff with both teaching and research strengths.[3]

(Bexley *et al.* 2011: iii)

There is no magic silver bullet to resolve the situation facing universities in a world of reduced and more directed funding, the changing impact of technology and uncertain student demand and the changing nature of an academic 'career' that poses many challenges for sustaining a viable academic workforce. In this context, human resources (HR) practitioners can offer a range of policies and interventions that seek to balance and mediate the competing needs of higher education institutions and academic staff. Suggested strategies are addressed in the final sections of this chapter.

Prior to determining what policies and processes may be of value, it is important for HR practitioners to understand the needs and aspirations of casual academic teaching staff. It is also important for HR practitioners to actively engage and involve casual staff in developing policies and processes. Casual staff, as with all staff groupings, are not a homogeneous group, and there are significant limitations to taking a 'one size fits all' option to addressing the issues raised. There is a need for much more applied research on the needs and aspirations of academic staff in general, not only casual academic staff. What research has been undertaken on the use of casual academic staff provides some guidance to HR staff in developing policies and frameworks for this group.

For example, Coates and Goedegebuure (2010: 20) suggest that there is a need to develop a typology to recognise diversity within this cohort which would assist in ensuring that responses reflect the cohort's diversity. As a start they suggest the following casual staff typology:

- industry expert – people with substantive professional appointments undertaking teaching or research on a sessional basis, who are highly skilled and address specific knowledge needs;
- faculty freelancer – academics who sustain multiple appointments, potentially to foster a critical mass of employment, for family or personal choice reasons;
- returning retiree – retiring academics who shift to a more contingent form of participation in either teaching or research activities;
- treadmill academic – people with research qualifications, particularly doctorates, who aspire to but cannot secure a substantive academic position;
- academic apprentice – university students, predominantly research post-graduates, who participate in formal teaching and research activities to supplement stipends and gain experience.

In terms of discussions on casual academics, whilst the numbers in each of these typologies are unknown, it is suggested by the authors that most attention has been paid to the 'treadmill academic' and the 'academic apprentice'.

Given this context, one of the challenges for universities is to better understand, at a holistic level, the profile of their casual academic workforce and the diverse range of career aspirations and/or appetites for reward, recognition and status.

For instance, how many universities can confidently answer these questions:

- What proportion of our casual academic staff aspire to 'traditional' academic appointments?
- What proportion are currently practising or recently retired professionals who want to share expertise with, or 'give back' to, the next generation of their professional colleagues?

- What depth and range of teaching, professional and research experience exists within our casual academic workforce?
- How much do casuals seek to develop their teaching and scholarship relating to pedagogy, curriculum development, assessment etc.?

This chapter provides ideas and examples of what human resource departments in universities can offer in managing the challenges of casual staffing and the legislative frameworks within which universities employ staff in the Australian context. It is expected, and indeed hoped, that what is occurring in Australia will have applicability in a much wider setting.

Legal/employment framework under which academic teaching staff are employed in Australia

In Australia, the legal framework that establishes the rights and responsibilities of employers and employees in higher education has since January 2010 been under the Commonwealth Government's Fair Work Act 2009 (the Act). The Act has provided for ten National Employment Standards (NES) and for the Industrial Tribunal, Fair Work Australia, to introduce sector-wide Modern Awards, which establish generic, minimum standards of employment. The relevant Modern Award is the Higher Education Industry – Academic Staff Award 2010 [MA000006]. In addition there is specific employment related legislation in such areas as Discrimination, and Occupational Health and Safety.

More details on the provisions of the Higher Education Industry – Academic Staff Award is contained in note 4.[4] It should be noted that in Australia, higher education institutions are bound by the terms and conditions of this Award and cannot contract out of these provisions.

While the Modern Awards provide for a 'safety net' of minimum pay and conditions, Australian employers may negotiate with the unions represented in the work place, specific Enterprise Agreements (EAs), that expand on the conditions in the Modern Award, including specific and very detailed provisions relevant to the organisation. Fair Work Australia will not approve an EA, unless it passes the 'no disadvantage test', which requires that the employees to be covered by the EA are better off overall than under the relevant Modern Award.

Since 1996, each Australian university has negotiated successive enterprise agreements with the National Tertiary Education Union (NTEU) and a number of unions with smaller representation. These are specific to the particular university, and are generally in force for three years. Enterprise agreements specify additional and quite specific and detailed terms and conditions of employment for staff, including employment conditions for casual academics. Whilst there are differences in the content of EAs between universities there is also a lot of commonality.

A recurring feature in enterprise bargaining in higher education over the years has been the pressure to improve terms and conditions of employment for casual staff and simultaneously limit the use of fixed-term contracts and casual employment. Under the most recent round of enterprise bargaining, provisions have been reincorporated into enterprise agreements severely limiting the use of fixed-term staff, particularly to support teaching. The reincorporation of these provisions, which had been deleted under the Howard Federal–Liberal Government industrial legislation, has been coupled with clauses which allow for cases where, if excessive casual hours are worked, there is a provision for conversion to a fixed-term role. Another attempt to manage casual employment has been the inclusion of ratios of numbers of casual staff to non-casual staff in some enterprise agreements.

Despite bargaining on these issues for over 15 years, neither universities nor the NTEU would regard the issue of casual employment as resolved.

What does this context mean for managing casual academic staff?

Attraction, retention and the ongoing development of suitably qualified academic staff is a general issue for most universities competing for talent in a diminishing pool of resources, due both to the aging of the academic population and younger qualified staff seeking careers outside the higher education sector or internationally. In most universities, engagement of casual staff is done at Faculty or School level; hence how such staff are recruited and managed may differ widely within universities.

Understanding the workforce profile and attitudes will assist in longer term workforce planning. For example, there is evidence that over the last decade one level of Australian academic position that is most difficult to fill is situated at the bottom end of the salary range as Associate Lecturer/casual appointments are clustered at this level (Horsley *et al.* 2002: 4). In addition, there is some general dissatisfaction in the academic community with levels of remuneration, indicating early career staff being more dissatisfied than late career staff (40 per cent early career to 30 per cent late career) (Bexley *et al.* 2011: xi).

In the absence of an entitlement to paid time for casual staff to attend faculty meetings, planning days, seminars and other professional development, the extent to which casual academic staff are engaged in broader School or Department activities varies widely, as does their ongoing attachment to the institution. Casual staff may also work a number of unpaid hours responding to and being available for students even when not on campus, such as responding to emails, discussion boards and other online modes or by phone.

For full-time academic staff there is the attraction of continuing employment including security of income, paid sick leave and annual leave, generous super-annuation benefits,[5] paid time for professional development and conference/seminar fees paid, as well as opportunities for sabbatical leave. In addition, tenured staff have access to a range of support functions provided by the university on an ongoing basis.

In contrast, studies of casual academic staff have found there is considerable stress for some staff due to:

- insecurity of unstable work, which for many casual academic staff is semester to semester, rather than a longer term;
- 'intellectual marginality' vis-à-vis tenured academic staff and a lack of opportunity to be more involved in the university community;
- lack of an ongoing income stream, during university breaks there is no salary paid to casual staff;
- disparity between what is stated to be their role and the reality of being available to students outside paid working hours through demand for meetings and use of technology; and
- little opportunity for professional advancement.

While the increased casualisation of the academic workforce is of concern to university management and academic unions, there has been and will continue to be a range of initiatives designed to rectify this. However, there are very few of the current examples which could be deemed to be successful without further research and enquiry.

Building a sustainable casual academic workforce

Ensuring and maintaining the quality of casual teaching and research staff in order to ensure the continuity of a viable academic workforce in the long term is an imperative that universities cannot and should not ignore. If casualisation of the academic workforce is to continue, a strong academic culture can only be sustained and enhanced by such action.

In building a sustainable learning culture, it is imperative that higher education organisations maintain and improve the student learning experience in order to ensure quality outcomes. This has implications for example for the provision of professional development opportunities for casual staff.

There is also increasing awareness of the need to redefine what is meant by the term 'academic career', a significant component being the move to a higher use of casual academic staff. This raises a number of questions for human resources:

- What can be done to provide casual staff with opportunities to ensure they can build a successful academic career, and so remain within the higher education sector?
- What policies should be developed and implemented to better engage and develop a casual workforce?

There are a range of activities that can be introduced to ensure that casual staff engage more effectively with the university and the skills required to be an effective member of the academic staff including:

1 taking a holistic approach and developing and implementing specific strategies and frameworks for the engagement and management of casual academic staff;
2 ensuring that recruitment and appointment processes are effective, equitable and supported by staff making employment decisions;
3 developing employment approaches that provide greater continuity of income and/or increased job security;
4 ensuring that there is an appropriate introduction to the university including a formal induction programme and relevant on-boarding;
5 ensuring that there are specifically identified managers and support people who have responsibility and availability for casual staff;
6 providing suitable work spaces and resources for casual staff on-campus;
7 ensuring that casual staff have the opportunity to be involved in staff meetings and planning days and are aware of (and where possible involved in) other on-campus activities to promote a richer interaction with students and colleagues;
8 providing opportunities for professional development and access to career development pathways.

Critically, the value to the student experience of these activities must be recognised and a way found for casual staff to be appropriately rewarded for the time required to complete them.

The following sections provide some illustrations that 'bring to life' the list of initiatives taken to improve casual employment arrangements and enhance career prospects, albeit not integrating casual academics into a framework which encompasses a holistic approach to an academic career.

Strategy/framework

Many universities in Australia have sought to address concerns in relation to the employment of casual staff. However, The RED Report (2008) found that few universities have attempted a whole-of-university approach, with few having formalised policies and practices specifically for casual staff and many relying on the policies and processes developed for permanent staff, which may not be relevant to casual staff.

Both the University of New South Wales and the University of Wollongong have sought to develop a whole-of-university approach. The University of New South Wales in Sydney introduced a Sessional Teaching Staff Strategic Action Plan, which is linked to performance indicators and supported by the Sessional Staff Co-ordinator located in the Learning and Teaching Unit (see http://teaching. unsw.edu.au/sessional-teaching).

The University of Wollongong, in 2006, established a Sessional Teaching Project, resulting in a university-wide framework for improving the management, support and enhancement of the contribution of sessional teachers. The framework provides a Code of Practice and Good Practice Guidelines including Faculty operating Procedures and Teaching Team Practices (www.uow.edu.au/ about/policy/uow058668.html).

Recruitment and appointment processes

There is a need to ensure that a sufficiently broad and diverse talent pool of potential staff is created and maintained by more consistently advertising opportunities for casual employment. The need for such a pool has been recognised by many universities but fully implemented by only a few. In too many cases casual appointments are made almost exclusively from within a circle of people known to existing staff and the risks associated with patronage and favouritism remain.

It is important to ensure that there are appropriate structured recruitment and selection processes, including reference and background checking,[6] in the initial employment of any staff member, including casual staff. One key support- ing resource in this context is the development of a database of current and prospective casual academic staff with contact details, employment history and evidence of performance. An example of the development of such a database is that administered by Macquarie University's HR department (see www.mq.edu. au/ltc/sessional_staff).

Income regularity/job security

In relation to the provision of a level of job security, universities could offer casual staff an annual contract with an annualised salary, which would be the number of contracted hours paid at the award rate, but averaged and paid over the 52 weeks of a year. To be able to offer such contracts with some certainty, universities need to be more focused on workforce planning, attempt to be more rigorous in identifying the courses that will attract high student demand and seeking staff on a more regular basis who align with the demand.

For example, the University of Technology in Sydney (UTS) provides the opportunity for 'sessional appointment' (which at UTS is different to, not just another name for, casual employment). Sessional employment means employment for a specific period during the year, which is normally related to teaching session(s). Staff employed on a sessional basis receive the salary and non-salary conditions of a full-time appointment calculated on a pro-rata basis. This includes, but is not limited to:

- incremental progression in pay rates within the salary level;
- all forms of leave (on a pro-rata basis);
- workload allocation in accordance with the Faculty workload policy for tenured staff;
- participation in performance review and development;
- eligibility for progression from Associate Lecturer to Lecturer, and for promotion to Senior Lecturer;
- eligibility for professional experience programme (PEP);
- higher rates of employer superannuation contribution if the sessional academic staff member is employed on a fixed term of greater than 12 months or a continuing basis;
- severance or redundancy provisions, depending on whether the sessional academic staff member is employed on a fixed-term or continuing basis;
- sessional staff may choose to have their salary annualised across the year. This allows them to receive their salary in equal portions over the whole year rather than being paid only during the period that they work.

Despite what at face value seem to be significant advantages in this type of appointment, take-up has been very limited to date, probably because of decisions by faculties/schools not to offer engagement on these terms. This illustrates the need for staff making employment decisions to be supportive of initiatives.

A small sample of casuals in a professional discipline at UTS suggests that these arrangements have the potential to ensure broad parity of remuneration with tenured staff.

Induction and on-boarding

Like many universities, Latrobe University in Melbourne and UTS have a range of core information targeted at new appointees available online. Each includes a 'Survival guide for new academics' and a two-day orientation programme for new academic staff which is also offered centrally each semester and is supplemented by Faculty-specific induction activities.

The RMIT University Collective Agreement provides that a casual academic employee who is:

1 new to the university;
2 engaged for the equivalent of a minimum of one contact hour per week for one semester; and
3 required to apply university policies in his or her academic work

will be provided with induction including introduction to necessary software and academic procedures required to fulfil their duties. The casual academic employee will be paid for up to five hours to undertake the University induction programme (see http://rmit.biz/browse:ID=10zik4xry2xk).

Macquarie University's Learning and Teaching Plan (2008–2012) requires 'all new teaching staff (including casual and adjunct) to demonstrate attainment of the FILT (Foundations in Learning and Teaching) . . . programme goals within two years of commencement: (Goal 1). This programme consists of a total of five days face-to-face training (for staff who do not have prior learning)' (see www.mq.edu.au/ltc/programmes/filt/index.htm).

Managers and support

Recognising that the supervisors of casual academics are often subject co-ordinators with limited experience in inducting or supervising other staff, UTS has recently published a HR resource guide for supervisors of casual academics (see www.hru.uts.edu.au/docs/for/guide_cas_aca_super.doc).

To further guide and support consistent management practice across all Faculties, UTS has developed a guide for management about reasonable paid time allowances for induction activities for new casual academics and for other academic activities including engagement with subject coordinators and professional development for all casual academics.

Beyond the immediate supervisor, UTS has identified specific contact people within each Faculty for casual academics, covering both academic and administrative matters (www.casualacademics.uts.edu.au/faculty.html).

Work spaces and resources (physical and information)

Many universities provide information for casual academics about how to use the IT systems (including learning management systems, plagiarism detector tools etc.) and audio-visual equipment in their preparation for and delivery of teaching and learning experiences.

Consistent with what is provided to tenured academic staff, access to the following resources should be provided for casual staff, who may choose to use some or all of the resources provided:

- office space (often shared or hot-desk style);
- an appropriate area for student consultation;
- photocopying facilities;
- a telephone;
- a location for receiving mail;
- Library access (both physical and remote access); and
- appropriate computer facilities.

Designated areas in which casual staff are encouraged to relax and interact with other academic staff such as a staff lounge or tea/meal room, will assist with casual staff engaging with the university community.

An example of this range of resources can be found in the Faculty specific guide for casual academic staff in the UTS Business School (see http://www.business. uts.edu.au/teaching/staff/CasualStaffManual.pdf).

Engagement with the university, colleagues and students

At UTS there is a range of ways that casual academic staff are included in the community, for example:

- The Vice-Chancellor's Teaching & Learning Awards and citations have a specific category for 'teaching by a casual or sessional academic';
- Periods of casual service are counted towards the 'Recognition of Long-Service Awards' for staff;
- All casual academics are subscribed on the Faculty email groups and 'All staff communications';
- Casual staff may be invited and paid to participate in the prospective student 'Open Day' or 'Information Day' events each year.

The RMIT University commits in the collective agreement that casual academic staff 'will be invited to attend relevant College, Centre, School or workgroup meetings. Casual academic employees will be paid for attendance at meetings where they are required or directed to attend' (see http://rmit.biz/browse;ID=l0zik4xry2xk).

Career development and professional development

The recently concluded La Trobe University Collective Agreement 2009 (EA), includes provisions at Clause 19 of the EA, that a Working Party on Academic Casual employment will be convened to develop recommendations on a series of measures to:

(a) provide greater access to career paths for longer term and well qualified casual academic staff;

(b) ensure that there are appropriate criteria for the use of casual academic staff; and

(c) examine what measures can be taken at reasonable cost to improve the working environment of casual academic staff.

(see www.fwa.gov.au/documents/agreements/fwa/AE872794.pdf)

La Trobe and UTS, among others, have committed to establish and advertise Early Career Development Fellowships (ECDF), the field of applicants for which will be restricted to casual academic staff. This provides casual academic staff with access to professional development and career progression into full-time continuing roles.

In the case of UTS, these are fixed-term appointments for up to two years duration on a full-time or, if requested by the staff member, as a part-time fixed-term appointment (of not less than half-time). Each year, existing casual academic staff may register their interest in, and eligibility for the ECDF scheme with the university. This scheme is due to be implemented in 2012.

Similarly, La Trobe University is also to offer centrally funded Early Career Development Fellowships, the applicants for which are restricted to casual academic staff who have been awarded a PhD and have performed sessional work in three entire teaching periods over the past five years, or are active PhD students for at least two years and have performed sessional work in five entire teaching periods over the past five years. Over the life of the current Collective Agreement, La Trobe is to establish and advertise at least 20 full-time Level A academic positions, which will be standard teaching and research or research-only academic positions for a fixed term of two years (Clause 16.2 (h)).

UTS provides professional development opportunities through Faculty-based workshops for casuals, usually towards the beginning of semester. Typical workshops focus on topics such as tutorial interaction, assessment, group work, student learning and facilitating online learning.

Casual academics are also welcome to participate in the two core subjects of the UTS Graduate Certificate in Higher Education Teaching and Learning without having formally enrolled in the course: student learning and teaching approaches; and course design and assessment. Casuals may formally enrol in the course if they can confirm that they will have teaching commitments during their enrolment. Sponsorship of fees may be made available for longstanding casuals.

UTS also hosts an annual conference specifically designed to provide professional development and networking opportunities for casual academics. Casual academics from across the university share their practices and discuss their experiences and a range of speakers share information and insights into teaching and learning within the UTS community. According to those who have attended, these activities have proved to be an extremely valuable resource.

In 2011, the Queensland University of Technology (QUT) moved away from the annual conference approach to a pilot of a suite of three modules specifically targeted as a 'Sessional Academic Programme', which provides an opportunity to share experiences and showcase good practice, in response to their 2010 Sessional Development Review Report (see www.ltu.qut.edu.au/development/teaching deve/sap/).

The RMIT University provides for casual academic staff to participate in applications for all internal funding opportunities, including grants and professional development funds (see http://rmit.biz/browse:ID=10zik4xry2xk).

At UTS there are Faculty-specific 'Casual Academic Professional Development Grants' offering study trips, travel and accommodation, and comparative studies. (see http://datasearch2.uts.edu.au/casual-academics/news-events/news-detail.cfm? ItemId=22632).

The Queensland Institute of Business and Technology (QIBT) (which was identified by the Australian Universities Quality Agency good practice database for 'Support and Development of Casual Teaching Staff') allocates an overall budget annually, which equates to approximately 0.5 per cent of casual teaching staff salaries, for professional development activities (see www.auqa.edu.au/gp/ search/detail.php?gp_id=3591).

Where to from here?

From the above examples, it is clear that a range of positive steps, when taken in combination, can lay a foundation of robust practice for the employment of casual staff. However, there is still more to do, including undertaking research on the impact of current initiatives as outlined above and to test the sustainability of new methods of employment of academics.

In terms of the scope of development activities, related to but extending the development of traditional teaching and learning skills, there are a range of compliance and quality standards requirements that indicate the need for a number of essential training interventions for causal academic staff because of their direct contact with students, for example:

- Education Services for Overseas Students Act (ESOS) awareness;
- cross-cultural awareness and communication skills;
- equity and inclusive practice, especially around disability including mental illness;
- health and safety, especially risk assessment, self-protection and de-escalation strategies in relation to threatening behaviour as well as specific training relating to high-risk or hazardous work environments (such as laboratories, workshops and some field trips).

One of the challenges for the higher education sector is to build on the examples of actions that have been taken that provide the basis for the employment of casual academics over the coming decade.

Most importantly, further work needs to be done to determine for the twenty-first century what is meant by an 'academic career', and where in that career structure the role of the casual academic fits. The NTEU campaign will have an impact on this too.

Conclusion

From what has been discussed, there is a clear need for universities to build a more granular understanding of the group currently called 'casual' or 'sessional' academics. Workforce and Talent Management Systems are becoming increasingly sophisticated, and are able to provide more quantitative and qualitative information, including about 'regular' casual staff. This data needs to be collected, analysed and utilised. Such data are necessary to inform the development of policies and procedures aimed at increasing satisfaction, engagement levels, retention of talent and enhancing learning outcomes for students.

In conjunction with Faculty/School heads, and a cross-section of academic staff, human resources functions need to develop an understanding of the range of needs and issues in relation to employment modes for both the university and the individual. Once this 'picture' has been agreed, HR can develop and implement policies and procedures that ensure that this large part of the student-facing academic workforce is engaged and providing positive and appropriate student learning.

The contribution of casual staff to their university must be duly acknowledged and their specific needs recognised and catered for. Until this happens, it is not possible for universities to build a sustainable and high-performing casual academic workforce.

Given that casualisation of the academic workforce is now a well-entrenched trend, a priority for universities will be to implement sound strategies that provide appropriate and ongoing support for their casual staff. Such practices need to be aimed at developing a high-performing and sustainable academic workforce that upholds a strong and viable teaching and research/scholarship culture.

Finally, in order to possess a casual academic workforce of the highest quality that will endure in the long term, universities will need to build sustainable frameworks for employing and developing their casual staff. In this respect HR Departments need to consider the following strategies:

1   ensuring a greater rigour in their recruitment and selection practices, so that casual academic staff engagement standards are aligned to those of continuing and fixed-term staff;

2   improving data gathering and analysis on the numbers, nature, composition and aspirations of the casual academic workforce;

3   developing articulated career paths (including promotion standards and opportunities) for casual academic staff;

4   partnering with Faculties and Schools to understand workforce needs, cost benefit analysis trends and the need to develop a sustainable long-term workforce;

5   working with Research Offices/Graduate Studies Schools to ensure that components of HDR study include teaching skills and the benefits of an academic career.

6   developing flexible remuneration structures (analogous to annualised hours) for casual staff;

7   identifying the labour and management cost of casual employment as a means of engendering a broader university-wide discussion on casual academic engagement.

Universities will need to address these strategies as an overall package of issues which should form part of a more sophisticated and integrated workforce planning strategy.

Notes

1   In Australia, and in the literature, the terms 'casual' and 'sessional' when referring to academics are used interchangeably. The term 'casual' will be adopted throughout this chapter for consistency.

2   Under the Federal Government's Superannuation Guarantee Legislation, an employee who earns more than AUD450 per month also receives employer superannuation contributions paid into a nominated fund.

3   Unpublished research indicates that the traditional pattern passing from PhDs to academia remains strong in areas such as science and the arts, but professional disciplines, such as business, accounting and the law, face greater challenges in attracting graduating PhD candidates, who have the ability to obtain interesting and well paid employment outside of academia.

4   The Higher Education Industry–Academic Staff Award – selected provisions relating to casual employees: (1) defines casual employment as employment by the hour and paid a rate that includes a loading related to award-based benefits for which a casual employee is not eligible; and (2) establishes the hourly rate that will apply to casual academics for work performed (clause 18.2), in lecturing, tutoring and marking, and includes for lecturing and tutoring a varying number of hours, depending on the activity, to be paid for what is termed 'associated working time'. Subject to meeting the evidentiary requirements, casual academic staff are entitled to unpaid personal/carer's and compassionate leave (clause 25.3), and subject to earnings in excess of AUD450 gross per calendar month, a casual employee will be entitled to superannuation under the Superannuation Guarantee Legislation for each month they earn in excess of the minimum.

5   In Australia, tenured staff receive 17 per cent employer superannuation contributions vs. the statutory minimum of 9 per cent for casual staff assuming they exceed the income threshold.

6   The Western Australian Corruption and Crime Commission has argued that even criminal records checks are 'insufficient to ensure the protection of students, as criminal checks will not reveal improper or otherwise inappropriate conduct which did not result in a criminal conviction' (p. 69). www.ccc.wa.gov.au/Publications/Reports/Published Reports 2010/Misconduct by Sessional Academic at Curtin University of Technology.pdf.

References

Bexley, E., James, R. and Arkoudis, S. (2011) 'The Australian academic profession in transition: Addressing the challenge of reconceptualising academic work and regenerating the academic workforce'. Online, available HTTP: www.cshe.unimelb.edu.au/people/bexley_docs/The_Academic_Profession_in_Transition_Sept2011.pdf (accessed 25 September 2011).

Coates, H. and Goedegebuure, L. (2010) 'The Real Academic Revolution: Why we need to reconceptualise Australia's future academic workforce and eight possible strategies for how to go about this'. Changing Academic Profession Research Brief – L.H. Martin Institute for Higher Education Leadership and Management, University of

Melbourne. Online. Available HTTP: www.lhmartininstitute.edu.au/userfiles/files/research/the_real_academic_revolution.pdf (accessed 27 September 2011).

Horsley, M., Martin, G. and Woodbourne G. (2002) 'Salary relativities and the academic labour market', Oval Research Centre, UTS – e-publication by the Australian Department of Education, Science & Training. Online. Available HTTP: www.dest.gov.au/NR/rdonlyres/232F627E-33C4-4FE3-9250-F3D3B8FC8508/4913/academic_salaries.pdf (accessed 23 September 2011).

La Trobe University Collective Agreement (2009) Online, available HTTP: www.fwa.gov.au/documents/agreements/fwa/AE872794.pdf (accessed continuously).

Review of Australian Higher Education, 'The Bradley Review' Final Report (December 2008). Online, available HTTP: www.deewr.gov.au/HigherEducation/Review/Documents (accessed 22 September 2011).

The RED Report (June 2008) 'The Contribution of Sessional Teachers to Higher Education' funded by the Australian Learning and Teaching Council – an initiative of The Australian Government Department of Education, Employment and Workplace Relations (DEEWR). Online. Available HTTP: http://cadad.moodlesites.com/file.php/1/RED/index.html.

The RED Resource (June 2008) 'The Contribution of Sessional Teachers to Higher Education', the Council of Australian Directors of Academic Development, Sydney, Australia.

University websites

Australian Universities Quality Agency – Good Practice Data Base

www.auqa.edu.au/gp/search/detail.php?gp_id=3591 (accessed 4 October 2011).

Macquarie University

www.mq.edu.au/ltc/sessional_staff (accessed 2 October 2011).
www.mq.edu.au/ltc/programs/filt/index.htm (accessed 2 October 2011).

Queensland University of Technology

www.ltu.qut.edu.au/development/teachingdeve/sap/ (accessed 29 September 2011).

RMIT University

http://rmit.biz/browse:ID=10zik4xry2xk (accessed 2 October 2011).

University of New South Wales

http://teaching.unsw.edu.au/sessional-teaching (accessed 2 October 2011).

University of Technology Sydney

www.hru.uts.edu.au/docs/for/guide_cas_aca_super.doc (accessed 2 October 2011).
www.casualacademics.uts.edu.au/faculty.html (accessed 2 October 2011).
www.business.uts.edu.au/teaching/staff/CasualStaffManual.pdf (accessed 2 October 2011).
http://datasearch2.uts.edu.au/casual-academics/news-events/news-detail.cfm?Item
    Id=22632 (accessed 2 October 2011).

University of Wollongong

www.uow.edu.au/about/policy/uow058668.html (accessed 2 October 2011).

12
ACADEMIC LEADERSHIP
STRATEGIES FOR BUILDING
EFFECTIVE TEAMS OF ALL STAFF

Shân Wareing

Introduction

This chapter considers some tried and tested ways of integrating part-timers into a team. Some of these approaches can benefit all staff regardless of their full-time/part-time status (for example, by encouraging flexible working across the team, by recognising the need to plan explicitly, and by encouraging regular, clear, effective and timely communication to all team members). Some processes need to be adapted specifically to ensure that part-timers feel that they are valued and integrated fully; for example, by allocating bursaries in a departmental/conference budget to support part-time staff who wouldn't otherwise be able to attend events and meetings, by explicitly encouraging part-time staff to apply for grants, awards and projects, by being prepared to organise partially at least around part-timers' availability, or by holding special events which bring part-time staff together. Some of the suggestions here for building effective teams which include part-timers will also work for staff returning from an extended period of absence, for whatever reason (e.g. ill health, a secondment, or maternity leave). The chapter also recognises some of the management challenges to watch out for, and identifies how to mitigate or evade potential problems.

Why managers should welcome part-time and flexible working

I lead two service departments in a large arts university in London, where many staff work part time or flexibly. Art and Design has an extensive culture of employing part-time tutors who combine their teaching with their creative practice or work in industry. While service departments in universities do not necessarily normally employ large numbers of part-timers, at University of the Arts London many do, and I attribute that to several causes. First, is the analogous effect from academic departments: we think it is 'normal' here to work part time. Second, we sometimes attract practising artists to roles in our services, and they wish to allocate some of their working week to their creative practice so are actively seeking part-time employment to enable this. Third, we have sometimes had enough money for one full-time post, but wanted to draw in a range of skills or expertise that can't be found in a single individual, so we have split the funding to provide two part-time roles, increasing the range of expertise the department can call on. Fourth, in some roles, the size of pool of staff from which you are recruiting increases substantially if you offer a post as part time. The proportion of well-qualified staff in the pool sometimes increases too. We have found this to be particularly true in administrative roles, where two skilled and motivated part-timers provide much more effective support than a less skilful, less motivated full-time staff member. And finally, we aim to recruit and retain excellent staff, and in the process of retaining staff over several years, life happens (to all of us!). People who started work as full-timers on normal office hours seek changes in the terms of their employment to take a PhD or be with their children, reducing their hours, or working 'compressed hours' (e.g. four long days instead of five regular days).

We have a number of different kinds of part-time contracts in the departments, including:

- fractional contracts (e.g. three days a week)
- compressed hours (e.g. full time in four longer days)
- staggered hours (e.g. early start and early finish)
- secondments across two roles (so the person is only available to a particular role for some of their time)
- working from home for one day or half day a week.

Having a large proportion of your staff working part time or flexibly in some way puts particular demands on team building. However, I think the benefits are so great to individuals, leading to a greater potential to recruit and retain great staff, and a possible reduction in sickness and stress amongst staff, that on balance I prefer to work with the complexities of part-timers, and I would never welcome a return to a 'normal' full-time culture now. On this basis I would hope always to approach the development of a job description with an open mind about whether the post holder needs to be full time or not.

The next section of the chapter deals with some evident issues for building effective teams that include part-timers, and possible solutions or mitigating approaches.

Seeing the big picture

One challenge for part-time staff, and their managers, is that it is harder to be clear about big picture issues at work, and understand how your role and contribution fits in with those of others. This is partly a logistical difficulty, from having less time available to spend on general understanding or organisation. It can also relate to professional identity, which can be more complex and ambiguous for part-timers than full-timers, with the consequence that they may be less interested in the overall purpose and strategy of the university or their particular area. This is by no means always the case, but the possible variation in levels of interest for aspects of the organisation beyond the staff member's immediate role, as a consequence of a complex professional identity, is something to bear in mind.

As part of developing and integrating your team, you may hold departmental awaydays, or strategic planning events which you will want all your team to attend, and some of them will be unable to do so, due to being part time. There is no ideal way of addressing this, but if you are considering trying to ensure everyone is there, it may help to remember that even when full-timers commit to attending an event, things happen to prevent this. Public transport incidents, babies born early or burst appendixes do not respect institutional planning. As far as possible, relax about not being able to get everyone there, while doing what you can to include everyone, for example by:

- giving clear advance warning about the purpose of the event and the relevance of the activities, so they can judge the necessity of attending;
- check whether there is anything they wish to raise, or have covered, at the event, if they cannot attend;
- make a record of the event available – technology means this can easily be via video, blogs or tweets, as well as by a written record;
- depending on the nature of the event, consider briefing them in person about what went on.

Professional development

Another difficult area to ensure all staff can participate appropriately in, regardless of whether part time or full time, is professional development. For your team to grow and be effective, group and individual professional development is a necessity, not a luxury, regardless of the full-time or part-time status of individuals.

Some of the key considerations are:

1 Whether part-time staff members have access to the full range of development activities which full-time staff can access;
2 Whether part-time staff end up doing a greater proportion of their professional development on their own time, rather than on paid work time.

3 Whether funds set aside for staff development are made available in proportion to the fraction of the contract (e.g. someone with a 0.5fte contract could access only 50 per cent of the staff development budget of a full-time staff member).

These are genuinely difficult issues to resolve fairly, but my opinion is that, through mutual flexibility on both sides, staff members should be able to access as wide a range of professional development as possible. If a full-time staff member would normally be able to participate in professional development on work time, then a part-time staff member should be paid to participate too. While it would certainly be possible to make an argument for only making 50 per cent of the staff development funds available to someone with a 0.5fte contract, this suggests that the value of individuals to the institution is measurable in the number of hours they work. While this is a logical and fair assumption from some perspectives, sometimes I would consider it reasonable to spend a greater sum on a part-timer's professional development, and anticipate seeing the investment pay off in the contribution to the institution of the individual, irrespective of the number of hours for which they are contracted.

It is also important to consider allocating additional staff development funds for part-timers which can provide bursaries for additional hours or days if needed. I appreciate this may seem difficult in a world of very restricted funding for staff development, but it is certainly one of the most important areas for allocating resources to.

It is also important to include and encourage part-timers explicitly to participate in activities such as internal grant applications, and development projects.

Social activities

Successful teams are often built on extra-curricular networking. Part-timers will want to be involved in social activities and opportunities for networking, but they may feel under much greater pressure than their full-time peers to get their job done and meet deadlines within working hours and they may experience a great deal of tension when invited to events or activities which are not part of their core job during their working day. Also their other commitments may prevent them from attending events outside their normal working hours. It helps to be clear what team members are expected to attend, because it is essential to the work of the team, and what is down to individual choice. The most important thing as a manager is to be aware that they may be experiencing this tension, and seek ways to alleviate it when possible, for example, by building time for socialising into work events.

Communication

A question you must ask about your team is whether people know each well enough to collaborate on tasks, share information, advise or point out problems, or ask each other for help. A major potential problem with part-time working is that colleagues do not know each other well enough to operate as effective team members. Where this is the case, it will manifest itself as coolness, and a tendency to mistrust others or think the worst, particularly in a crisis. This will mean that crucial information about risks or problems is not shared, opportunities for collaboration and sharing intelligence and expertise are not taken, potential solutions are not identified, and rather than working effectively together to address problems when things go wrong, the team will fall into mutual recriminations. Over time, this can lead to a ratcheting-up of mistrust, dislike and blame between sections and individuals. This can of course happen in any dysfunctional team, but part-time working can exacerbate the problem, by reducing opportunities for communication, on which effective teams depend.

Communication is vital in all well-functioning teams, and can be broken down into different categories. Communicating effectively *to* people requires different approaches from facilitating communication *between* people, and both matter.

Communicating to people

Communicating *to* people is necessary at times of emergency, or when there are announcements, structural changes, new starters and retirements, or university news which it is essential to communicate to everyone. If the whole team is seldom or never all in the office, the following are worth considering:

1　Establish email lists which include the whole department, to avoid people you see less often being missed off a circulation.
2　Send letters to home addresses, so everyone receives them at the same time.
3　Ensure departmental or other important meetings are well trailed beforehand with clear published agendas (ideally on a wiki, so it can be accessed online from home), so people can decide if they want or need to reorganise their time to attend.

Communication between people

To support communication amongst team members, effective approaches include:

1　Establish a department wiki, where meeting agendas can be developed with everyone's input, notes can be published, viewed and amended, images published of events which not everyone could attend, and so on. We did this, and people were soon adding images from the Christmas lunch, and the video of a long-standing member of staff's leaving do. It also facilitated the introduction of a rotating chair for staff members, since everyone had access to the same documents.

2 At intervals, and as needed, you may want to hold 'get to know you', and planning events.

Case study

As a result of restructuring, two departments were brought together – the Centre for Learning and Teaching in Art and Design (CLTAD) and Student Enterprise and Employability (SEE). The goal of the co-location was to support the development of student enterprise and employability in the curriculum, using the careers expertise of the one team combined with the change management and curriculum development expertise of the other. To achieve this possible synergy, we needed to get the teams working together. We agreed we'd hold a 'get to know you' half-day event, with the purpose of finding out more about one another as the basis for future collaborative working. We identified two staff members good at organising events, one a full-timer in SEE, one a part-timer in CLTAD. The two organisers had to identify the day of the week when most people could attend (a Thursday), and get it in diaries, which of course always takes longer than anyone expects. They were given parameters (e.g. timing, length, budget, things that have to happen), and came back with the programme below:

Time: Thursday 9.00 a.m. – 1.00 p.m.

Outline:

Breakfast, roundtable introductions, people bingo [i.e. questions on little known facts about individuals];

Presentations by department head & teams (5–10 mins each);

Group activity 1: Groups of 10 – identify/summarise core activities across CLTAD & SEE;

Group activity 2: Groups of 5 – identify broad areas for cross-service initiatives/collaboration;

Group activity 3: Groups of 3 – develop and present 1 potential project;

VOTE: all vote for the best suggestion & give prize to winner;

Lunch – each area/team designated a food to bring.

This programme achieved many of the desired objectives:

1 The event-planning process introduced two dynamic, positive staff members to each other, who would be able to work together in future, and link up other staff across the two departments.
2 It involved a part-timer centrally in a departmental planning event, who would be able to bear the perspective of other part-time staff in mind during the planning.
3 It combined a necessary, and potentially dull, process of sharing basic information about the structures, staff and purposes of both departments, where senior staff would take a lead, with some lively, fun, personal activities which would involve everyone in both departments.
4 It explicitly focussed on our goal for joint projects across the two departments, with the potential to identify viable projects at the event.
5 It communicated aspects of the desired culture of the two departments – focussed, purposeful, professional, inclusive and fun.

Beginnings and endings

New starters, and leavers, can both present challenges to team building, and in each case, the presence of high numbers of part-timers presents additional challenges. There are also particular considerations around communication and team building.

New starters

When new people start, in a team with part-timers, it can take longer to assimilate them, because some people in the normal course of things may never meet if their times in the office do not overlap. As a part-timer, if you come into the office after someone new has started who is also on part-time hours, it can seem that everyone's talking about someone you have never met, and it can make you feel peripheral from the rest of the team.

To avoid this situation, consider taking some of the following actions:

1 Before the new member of staff starts, ensure that everything is in place to ensure they have the equipment, facilities and information they need (e.g. a telephone extension, an email address, IT log on and password).
2 When a new member of staff joins the team, prepare an email introducing them by name, when they work and how to contact them, what their role is, their start date, whether they will be working with particular people and how their area of work interacts with others.
3 Arrange a morning coffee, lunch or afternoon tea, a drink after work, whatever is most applicable in your organisational culture, for a day when a large proportion of staff are available to enable the newcomer to meet as many of their colleagues as possible.

Leavers

Although someone leaving the institution may not present the obvious challenges of a new starter, it is in fact very important to many team members, who will need to mark the departure of a colleague in an appropriate way, in order for the team to continue to function well. Again, marking a departure is much harder if you have a high proportion of part-timers on the staff.

We have tended to hold events, at lunch time, or tea time, on days of the week when the majority of staff are in. These are low key, but give people a chance to say their farewells, and for staff who are leaving to hear from people who have appreciated them and valued working with them. When one particularly long-serving staff member left, her leaving do was videoed and stills and the video published on the departmental wiki. We usually do a collection and sign a card, which includes comments from people who cannot be present at the event itself.

Teams are always changing, with people joining them and leaving. Individuals deal with this differently, but it seems to me to be important to the functioning of the team and the satisfaction of individuals within the team, that both arrivals and departures are dealt with formally, that information is available about both, and the emotional issues of meeting new people who will disturb existing patterns of working and loyalties, and saying goodbye to people who have been part of the fabric of our working lives need to be dealt with attentively.

Quick check list for communicating within teams with part-timers

- always include part-timers in all communications and correspondence;
- formally introduce part-timers (name, role, the hours they will work) to the rest of the team;

- clarify with staff members from the beginning of their contract your expectations of them attending team events, and clarify whether they are able and willing to change their days or hours of work if needed to attend a particular activity or event, provided enough notice is given;
- involve people in different groupings on projects, or organising staff development and social activities, wherever possible;
- send round announcements and updates regularly about starters, leavers, achievements and other news;
- involve people across levels in tasks to ensure you don't have divisions caused by hierarchies;
- give people responsibility for cross team tasks, and work in cross team groupings wherever possible.

What can go wrong with part-time working in terms of team building?

A surprisingly important issue is around expectations of working hours and the culture around unexpected absences. This applies across all teams, regardless of whether predominantly full time or part time, but as with other issues discussed in this chapter, some of the issues become particularly pertinent when many staff are part time.

Formal flexible working agreements should be available for the whole team in the interests of fairness, with parameters around start and finish times and the proportion of time normally spent in the office, so there is a degree of transparency and fairness about arrangements and the need to have formal meetings and casual conversations is recognised.

Case study

When I started in my current post, there were a number of practices which made effective team working difficult (as well as presenting challenges to the effective, professional running of the department in other ways). There was a great deal of variety in how often staff came into the office, in normal working hours, and in how 'working from home' and sickness absence were managed. A few staff had a tendency towards so called 'duvet-days', i.e. taking a day of unplanned absence due to oversleeping or feeling slightly unwell, sometimes in combination with a request to 'work from home'. There were two negative effects on team working and general effectiveness resulting from these patterns of behaviour. First, teams do depend on regular contact (at least initially) and, second, if some team members suspect others of slacking, it is detrimental to trust and respect. However, in mitigating the negative effects on the team of unregulated flexibility, we did not want to prevent or reduce appropriate flexible working.

What we did was to consider the parameters to flexible working in a management team meeting, and identified limits which we felt would be conducive to good team working, as follows:

1 core day of 10 a.m.–4 p.m.; no one can start their regular day in the office later than 10 a.m., nor finish earlier than 4 p.m.;
2 no more than one day a week working from home.

All staff in the department were then invited to apply for flexible working if they wished, within those parameters. Staff who were already working flexibly were asked to reapply within the agreed parameters, and some staff who had never applied were encouraged to do so. The management team reviewed the applications and most were approved, although some staff members were asked to submit revised proposals that would comply with the agreed parameters. This equalised out the variations in working across the department, reduced the sense that some staff were taking advantage of others, and made organising meetings easier. One member of staff who had previously had a high number of 'duvet days', ringing in at short notice to ask to take a day's leave when he'd overslept or felt under the weather, changed his working week from five normal length days to four longer days and had Fridays off, which significantly improved his sickness absence and efficiency at work. Over a three-year period, average sickness absence in the department decreased from an average of six days per year per person to three days per person per year, equivalent to a saving of £18,000.

Managing part-time staff

Most people at some point will be unclear about how to progress their work, or will lack the skills they need to complete an activity. This can happen when someone is new in a post, or when their responsibilities change or increase. It is not unusual to recruit someone into a post where it appears they have done something very similar before very competently, and to find that in the new environment, they struggle (either because there is less similarity between the previous role and the present one than it appeared, or because the standards or expectations are different). It is very stressful for most people to feel they do not understand or are not sufficiently skilled to undertake their new role, and as a consequence, they may well instinctively try to cover up their problems.

A manager would normally hope to pick up on these situations and deal with them (by providing more support, clearer guidance, mentoring, resetting the objectives, and so on) but particularly with many part-timers, an unclear system of recording absences lends itself to covering up problems and can make it much harder for the manager to spot problems early enough to sort them out. Someone who would have thrived if given clear guidance or support when they needed it, though working in a collaborative environment, may become a stressed, evasive and disgruntled colleague who has neither the skill nor the motivation to do their job because they were allowed to become too isolated. A very small number of people appear to exploit unclear systems in order to do their own work (e.g. run a separate business) or just not to work at all. From a team working perspective, it is very important that team members trust one another to work hard and be reliable. No one wants to feel they are carrying an unfair workload, or being taken advantage of. These are complex issues requiring complex solutions, but one aspect which is fundamental is to be clear and consistent in the way different kinds of absence are described and recorded, and being clear about differentiating different kinds of leave, particularly between those which are planned in advance with the approval of the line manager, and those which are unplanned.

Again, these are issues in any team, but with large numbers of part-time staff, it is normal to have many empty chairs at work. This can make it harder to identify staff who are having some kind of personal or professional troubles which manifest themselves through absence, or possibly are taking advantage of the arrangements to avoid working.

Clarity around the following helps:

1   Annual leave (holidays) is planned in advance, and must be approved by the line manager. The line manager has the right to refuse annual leave requests which interfere with operational needs (e.g. you can't plan leave in the middle of the busiest time of your year).

2   Working at home is arranged in advance, and is either part of a formal flexible working arrangement, and on a specific day of the week or part of a day, or is an occasional event which relates to a specific activity (such as a report which must be written). Again, the line manager can refuse the right to work at home based on operational need.

3 An unplanned absence must normally be taken either as sick leave or as 'special leave'.

We have found this is important to prevent people from becoming too casual about coming to work, and to be clear that it matters to their colleagues that we see them in the office.

Technology and part-time working

Technology brings dramatic possibilities for facilitating part-time working and integrating individuals into teams. Telephones, chat, texting, emails, wikis, document sharing and video conferencing can all enable staff in different locations to participate in an event synchronously, or those working different hours to participate asynchronously. However, it is important to have a discussion about boundaries and expectations beforehand, to be sure that technology is not a stressful intrusion on their life outside work hours. The negative side of technology and flexible working is often documented in the press. One person's dedication and perfectionism is another person's pressure and harassment. While it may sometimes be convenient to work late at night, if you are working in the hours when other people are asleep, you may want to consider the effect of sending very late or early emails, and delaying until a more civilised hour. Middle of the night emails can make the sender appear very anxious, and the recipient can be made to feel lacking because they are not working at 2 a.m., or bullied because they are being asked for responses at 11 p.m. or 5.30 a.m.

While it is important to recognise and welcome activities done outside work time, and see the other activities of part-timers as valuable, it is also important to find out how all your team prefer to communicate, and what boundaries they expect around communication outside office hours/off site. Also be clear if you expect staff to keep electronic diaries up to date, and to share these with the rest of their team, to facilitate arranging meetings and conversations, to know when to expect someone to be back in contact, if you need to ask them something.

Individual support and interventions

Not all the actions you can take to ensure successful teams revolve around whole teams. Sometimes individuals need personal support to help them participate fully in teams.

For example, when staff who previously worked full time return to work after maternity leave, it may be appropriate to offer them personal coaching. There are a number of common fears about returning to work following maternity. One is that one has forgotten all one's professional expertise and one's brain will no longer conduct the necessary speedy and fine-tuned actions required of the role (and that this will be obvious to everyone!). Another is that one will never manage the demands of the job in balance with motherhood. A further possible fear is that one cannot take part in the activities which establish a successful career trajectory. Having had three periods of maternity leave, and witnessed other colleagues make this transition, I would say that the feelings are real and terrifying, but that the transition is utterly possible. However, it is the kind of life change that coaching is very useful for, in terms of reducing the returner's anxiety, and in terms of speeding up development of coping mechanisms.

Conclusion

As discussed at the outset of this chapter, there are few aspects of team building which are unique to teams with a high proportion of part-time staff, but some issues become exacerbated, or harder to fix, with part-time staff. Part-time staff can be an enormous asset to a team, and nurturing them with appropriate activities to integrate them and give them opportunities for development will pay off in the quality of their work. Clarity of communication and expectations goes a long way to reducing potential problems.

13

FUTURE DIRECTIONS IN PROFESSIONAL DEVELOPMENT
IMPLICATIONS FOR INDIVIDUALS AND ORGANISATIONS

Fran Beaton

In his foreword to this book, Tony Brand identified part-time teachers in higher education (HE) as 'the lost or invisible tribe'. This telling phrase sets the context for our contributing authors to consider the extent to which these teachers, all too aware of their responsibilities in relation to their students, feel and function on the fringes of institutional life and support, unless specific efforts are made to remedy this. Thought and mindfulness about making such efforts are threads which have run through preceding chapters. This concluding chapter has three main aims. First, to identify the common threads which have emerged and, second, to summarise the characteristics of effective interventions so that the reader can consider how these can be applied in their own context. Finally, it will identify the implications for those in HE institutions with responsibility for planning and supporting the career development of all staff, including part-time teachers, and to consider both the initial steps and broader strategic actions needed to make this a sustainable longer-term model.

The lived experiences of part-time teachers are to be heard throughout much of the book and their stories show the extent of the sorts of engagement they have with universities. This engagement goes far beyond the apparently procedural aspects of being an employee. This is not to decry the need for basic procedural and practical knowledge which enables the part-time teacher to embark on their HE teaching career. Rather, it raises the broader issue that presence or absence of these sources of information colours how part-time tutors feel they are recognised and valued by their institution as professional practitioners. 'The student experience', and in particular the experience of would-be and first-year students making the transition into HE, has been the subject of inquiry for some years. While teaching staff entering HE for the first time may be expected to have more life experiences on which to draw, the tutors' voices we have read here suggest that their transition process may have striking similarities with that of their students: transition into a different role, uncertainty about expectations, a sense of isolation and invisibility which is allied to part-timers' genuine desire to contribute to the understanding of their subject. Part-time teachers' experiences of their engagement with institutions influence both how they carry out their work within the university, what that role involves and their sense of identity.

Key issues

It is worth reminding ourselves at this point of the key issues for part-timers which were identified in our opening chapter and which have resonated throughout, namely:

- powerlessness: a lack of voice in the institution;
- co-ordination: the need for senior staff to recognise and co-ordinate the activities of part-timers;
- relevance; the need to be involved, for example designing curricula which bridge real-world practical skills and theoretical frameworks;
- professional development: access to appropriate training and development opportunities.

Experienced professionals, employed because of their expertise in another field, for example as performing artists, health or social care practitioners, find themselves back in the position of a novice when embarking on HE teaching for the first time. Those with previous experience of HE may have garnered this as a none-too-recent undergraduate at a time when approaches to teaching were different. At the other extreme, postgraduates who teach may be very conscious of being all-too-recent graduates. Both groups have common ground: individuals are simultaneously attempting to get to grips with different organisational practices, new approaches to teaching and a raft of implicit expectations of the role. This last aspect is a powerful theme which emerges from several chapters. The 'holistic aspects of becoming an academic', to which Anne Lee refers, embrace both becoming familiar with different attitudes, beliefs and behaviours at the same time as developing or maintaining the skills required in an age of digital literacy. There are challenges for all university teachers in considering the exemplary role (modelling for students the habits of thought and behaviours of the discipline) which can be particularly acute for part-time teachers who are still in the process of trying to discern this for themselves. These considerations are underscored by the circumstances in which part-time teachers are employed. Karen Starr refers to the 'revolving door' for many part-time women teachers, who may function in an environment which makes heavy demands, often at short notice, but which offers limited or no support or scope for career or personal development. Anne Gaskell, Pam Parker and Neal Sumner, in considering the further dimension of teaching and tutoring online, bring us valuable messages about the challenges for institutions in ensuring that tutors have sustained and accessible support to develop the particular skills required to work effectively and sensitively in the online environment. Karen Starr and Shân Wareing both warn of the potential risk that part-timers work significantly more than their contracted hours, whether involved in online teaching or simply coping with the higher student expectations of 24/7 electronic availability and at the expense of other aspects of their lives.

We suggest that, while part-time teachers' roles and motivations undoubtedly vary, their needs more unite than divide them. So while there may be particular skills which teachers need to develop in response to a specific context in which they are working, it is more important to have a deliberated, timely and coherent approach to the professional development of all staff and a thoughtful consideration of how this can be managed to include part-timers. Based on our authors' findings, what are the key factors to consider? It is our contention that there are three aspects to this: the first aspect which can be broadly termed procedural and organisational; a second which considers the development of scholarly behaviours; and a third, the wider application of both these to the quality of part-time staff and the quality of their own career and professional development.

Procedural and organisational aspects

It is important to stress that these aspects need to be considered by all concerned in the institution to avoid either over-duplication or their complete omission. It is not only part-time teachers whose sense of isolation is exacerbated by a feeling that the left hand does not know what the right hand is doing. There are four main elements to this: timeliness, flexibility, accessibility and inclusivity.

Timeliness

All concerned parties need to consider which interventions are most effective in relation to what part-time staff are expected to know and be able to do, both initially and at different points in their employment. This involves a combination of practicalities such as knowing their way around the department and where and from whom to seek help and more conceptual aspects, such as expectations of HE teaching and assessment practice. Timing in this case refers both to the point in time (e.g. pre-service; in the first week; mid-term) and timing in the working day. If full-time staff are allocated time out to attend relevant events or courses held during the 'normal' working day (and bearing in mind that 'normal' means different things in different institutions), how can this be extended to part-time staff juggling multiple professional and familial responsibilities? Can relevant interventions be offered at different times?

Flexibility

In which ways can relevant information be accessed? There will be occasions when there is no substitute for face-to-face interaction but what complementary activity, information repositories or sources of help can be accessed in different ways? This is key for the part-timer who is not routinely on campus and, when they are, it is primarily to teach. Offsite access to email, to the institutional Virtual Learning Environment where all teachers can, for example, seek information, post questions to a forum or otherwise engage with the activity of their home department are all helpful, with the proviso that offsite activity does not become a further unrecognised burden for the part-time teacher. In recent conversation with new part-time teachers leading seminars for the first time about their induction, a story emerged of a combination of interventions run by their home department specifically for part-timers which covered the survival kit (contracts, claim forms) and central information (timetabling, room facilities) before moving on to subject-specific questions about the indicative content for seminars, trouble-shooting possible problems, boundaries around the role. They had expected the first two elements but welcomed the subject-specific discussion as getting to the heart of what they felt they were there to do. I will return to this theme in the section considering the ways in which part-timers can develop an understanding of the importance of a scholarly approach to their work.

Accessibility

This is related to the previous heading and similarly requires attention to the practical arrangements. If part-time teachers are to get access to, for example, the VLE, this involves registering for usernames and passwords. The opening chapter referred to the breathtaking slowness of acquiring these being matched only by the breathtaking speed with which they were removed at the end of the contract, and we have also read about how part-timers may be employed when term is about to start and may not even feature on institutional radar. Are these compelling reasons for access to virtual spaces to appear difficult? Particularly in the early days, how are part-timers kept informed of what they need to do or be aware of?

Inclusivity

This concerns the extent to which part-timers are or feel integrated in the work of their department and, more broadly, within the institution. Shân Wareing's observation that institutional leaders, having made every effort to keep the integration/information loop as tight as possible, should not anguish if not everyone can come to everything (or indeed that some will choose to participate very little) goes to the heart of this. However, it can only be constructive if part-time staff are routinely informed of, and invited to, events which may be of interest. If they are further invited to contribute their views and expertise to discussions within their department or academic team this too promotes a valuable sense of agency. A further important aspect of this, which also relates to professional development, is to give part-timers opportunities to make choices and suggestions about their own professional development.

To this sense of voice should be added practical strategies to give a sense of belonging. This can relate to being involved in the non-formal 'social glue' activities which help build teams but also includes basic facilities such as a room which part-time staff can collectively call their own. Space is at a premium in many universities but is it really so difficult to find a space where part-timers in a department can have access to a computer, hold an office hour, meet each other and keep some of their belongings? One group of part-timers recently commented that they felt they were being taken seriously by the institution when they no longer had to keep their professional materials in a cardboard box, backpack or car boot but were given space in a dedicated room which contained several hotdesks and lockers. If we accept that a sense of belonging is an important aspect of part-timers feeling valued by and committed to an institution, and more likely to want to give of their best, finding such a space is a necessity rather than a luxury.

A further aspect of inclusivity is for the institution to be responsive and open in its relationships with staff. This can be at a local level, for example, asking tutors who were new in post the previous year (so who can remember what they wished they had known) their experience of the various interventions. As Coralie McCormack and Patricia Kelly ask: 'How do we know it works?' Asking tutors is not enough in itself to evaluate the impact of what is offered particularly where needs vary, but getting feedback from tutors is a possible triangulation point and exemplifies critical reflection on our own practice in relation to all staff, including part-time teachers.

Developing scholarly behaviours

As several contributing authors have pointed out, the number of part-time teachers has risen steadily over the years, matched only by an increase in both student numbers and student expectations. In the UK, for example, there has been an ongoing debate about the extent to which the increase in undergraduate fees further raises students' expectations, not just about what they are getting for their money but how much contact time, and with whom, they can expect. This is not the place to consider the detail of the argument about students as consumers; nor is it suggested that these are not challenges for all university teachers. What is relevant is how part-time staff in particular can be encouraged to develop the scholarly approach to their work and thinking which pervades all disciplines and begin to apply these to their own context, both from the perspective of student expectations and in relation to part-timers' professional development.

Challenges for developing a scholarly approach

Not all part-time teachers aspire to build a full-time career as academics, quite apart from the fact that the changing face of student recruitment and the continuing trend for fixed-term or part-time work in HE may mean that there are fewer such jobs available. Traditionally, academic careers are built on a combination of research output and (depending to some extent on the kind of institution) teaching, outreach or enterprise activities. The part-timer risks being caught in a Catch-22 situation where they 'only' teach and have no access to developmental support (such as scope to apply for grants, for study leave to undertake research or to initiate links with external bodies) which would help them build up a profile and reputation. Furthermore, while some part-timers may from choice (or necessity) inhabit a border country between academic and professional practice, that choice may also be influenced by current life events (child or elder care for instance) which change over time. Given all this, it is not feasible for part-timers to be offered the full range of opportunities open to permanent staff. However, there is scope for part-time teachers to develop in relation to their teaching and, in particular, to adopt a scholarly approach to that teaching, both for their own satisfaction and as part of their professional responsibility to their students and their subject. These are aspects which have been amplified in, for example, Chapter 4 and Chapter 6 but form a narrative thread throughout much of this book.

What might this look like?

The scholarly approach to teaching, as exemplified by Glassick's scholarly *standards* to which Hall and Sutherland refer (p. 88), provide an equally valuable basis for current practice as an HE teacher, for someone considering a future as an academic and for someone whose future career may lie in another field where critical reflective thinking is privileged. The six elements

- clear goals;
- adequate preparation;
- appropriate methods;
- effective presentation;

- significant results;
- reflective critique

all inform central aspects of teacher education and enable the new teacher to see their work as being a reflective process. As educators ourselves we can model this both through example in relation to our own teaching and by making explicit the process of reflecting on our practice, articulating why we do what we do and the thinking behind changes made over time. We can also cultivate an atmosphere of trust and mutual respect so that all teachers can develop the confidence and curiosity to explore and articulate their approach, raise questions and seek feedback in a constructive and supportive environment. Above all, it is important that the nature of reflection is made explicit, namely that it is a constructive iterative attempt to review assumptions about our practice with the intention of becoming more skilled at what we do and how we do it. Mirroring the principles of student-centred learning for staff, including part-time staff, in relation to their own professional learning, simultaneously models and provokes discussion about the value of such an approach. We can also consider practical strategies to enable part-timers to participate in the wider subject community, for example through financial support to attend – and subsequently cascade back to peers – conferences and other relevant events. This leads to the final aspect of this section, namely the overlap between professional development for the individual and the benefits for their employing institution.

Professional development: individual development and institutional capacity

Being taught by someone who embodies the qualities listed above, and who in addition is enthusiastic both about their subject and communicating it to others tends to be identified as a highly motivating and rewarding experience. If part-timers are not to remain Tony Brand's 'lost or invisible tribe', it is crucial for there to be a strategic approach to planning professional development for academic teaching staff, and that there are individuals whose roles include taking responsibility for part-time teachers and their professional development. We recognise of course that this is likely to be part of someone's role rather than their entire job description. It is especially important that these roles function at different levels to provide as holistic an experience as possible. Within a department there should be someone who is responsible for briefing and supporting part-timers in the day-to-day business of disciplinary teaching and heads of department play an important role here in encouraging individuals with the interest, experience and qualities to take this role on. Programme leaders and tutors of centrally delivered programmes such as Postgraduate Certificates for early career teachers can combine support and professional development for staff as educators with opportunities for part-time teachers to meet both each other and new full-time staff, giving scope for a wider perspective and opportunities to build up networks. At an institutional level there is a clear need for thoughtful and systematic opportunities to take part in departmental, faculty- and institution-wide events with funding or other incentives which demonstrate institutional recognition of the practical challenges for part-timers. Institutional recognition and reward for staff engaged in teaching or supporting learning can celebrate the work of teaching staff, including part-time teachers, by showcasing teaching projects and initiatives they have undertaken or by supporting the development of that work for wider dissemination, for example through subject networks. The same approach can usefully apply to recognition for staff who champion or mentor part-time teachers.

Taken collectively, this combination of different kinds of support, recognition and community-building enables an institution which is dedicated to learning to demonstrate, through its structures and actions, a commitment to supporting all staff as learners and teachers. This is, perhaps, the greatest single challenge for institutions: embedding practical steps embodying an ethos of building academic communities, which is made manifest in institutional behaviour at all levels. We hope that the strategies and practical examples offered in this book will empower all those with responsibility for this task in twenty-first century universities.

Index